KASHMIR
Towards Demilitarisation

KASHMIR
Towards Demilitarisation

Brig Pramathesh Raina (Retd)

Foreword by

Amitabh Mattoo
D.Phil. (Oxon.)
Advisor to the Chief Minister of Jammu and Kashmir
Professor, School of International Studies, Jawaharlal Nehru University, New Delhi
Honorary Professor of International Relations, University of Melbourne
Honorary Director Australia India Institute Delhi

PENTAGON PRESS

KASHMIR: Towards Demilitarisation
by Brig Pramathesh Raina (Retd)

ISBN 978-81-8274-876-7

First Published in 2016

Published by
PENTAGON PRESS
206, Peacock Lane, Shahpur Jat,
New Delhi-110049
Phones: 011-64706243, 26491568
Telefax: 011-26490600
email: rajan@pentagonpress.in
website: www.pentagonpress.in

Branch
Flat No.213, Athena-2,
Clover Acropolis,
Viman Nagar,
Pune-411014
Email: pentagonpresspune@gmail.com

Printed at Aegean Offset Printers, Greater Noida, U.P.

In memory of the intrepid soldiers of the Indian armed forces who have made the ultimate sacrifice in order to preserve the integrity and safety of their country while combating terrorism in Jammu and Kashmir.

Contents

Foreword

At the outset, I must compliment the author for having ventured into uncharted waters. Much has been written about the "Kashmir Problem" and many solutions have been put forth. The topic of demilitarisation of the state figures in practically every discussion on Kashmir. However, no one has yet got down to mentioning in specific terms as to how this aspect should be approached and what numbers and type of troops would constitute this demilitarisation. To that extent, this endeavor is praiseworthy.

Jammu and Kashmir is an international hotspot. Four wars and a major conflict have been fought in this region since independence. A full scale insurgency arose in the nineties. It took a considerable effort from the security forces to quell the same. Pakistan spares no amount of effort and money to keep stoking the fire and fomenting trouble both in the State and in the rest of India. India has paid, and continues to pay, a heavy price in terms of losses of manpower and finances. There is now little doubt, in international circles, on the legality of the Indian position on Kashmir, a far cry from the past decades when the very presence of India in Jammu and Kashmir was being questioned, particularly by the West. Though India is trying its level best to universally expose and ostracize Pakistan as a global sponsor of terror, it is equally important for us to keep our own house in order. We cannot afford to antagonize any section of society, regardless of religion, to such an extent that it takes to arms against the legitimately elected state. And though the action to take up arms against the state is illegal, it is also a reflection of the failure of the state administration to address the grievances of the public. Tackling such issues requires sagacity, a sensitive approach, tact and a willingness to set aside egos; to be willing to stoop to conquer. Alas, that breed of statesman in today's milieu is rare indeed!

Brigadier Raina has rightly identified the fact that demilitarisation by itself will achieve nothing; it has to go hand in hand with improvements in administration, infrastructure, quality and nature of policing, intelligence gathering capability, opening up of the civilian space and so on. He has attempted to think out of the box, thus a number of his recommendations may raise eyebrows in the corridors of power. He is blunt, within the limits of acceptable language, in his poor opinion of wily politicians and pliable bureaucrats. Many of the measures he has recommended to be adopted are definitely implementable; some are utopian. One cannot expect human nature to change overnight. Politicians will continue to indulge in chicanery; bureaucrats will continue to defer to the will of the politician even against their better judgment; corruption will not be eradicated so easily; the odd police man will continue to oppress the common man and the occasional violation of human rights will occur. However, it is evident that the ray of light has begun to dawn upon all those responsible for the administration. One can see an honesty of purpose in the manner in which the Chief Minister and his team are tackling the governance of the state. Reconciliation and getting the entire population, including the fringe elements represented by Masarat Alam and his ilk, involved in the rebuilding of society appear to be the guiding lights by which the Mufti is approaching his task. That is not to say that his methods are flawless and without controversy, but the overall effort seems sincere.

As the author has iterated, terrorism flourishes in deprived and underdeveloped societies. The best way to eradicate terrorism, and thereby the need for additional security forces, is to develop infrastructure, education and creation of employment opportunities. This has been correctly identified by the previous and present governments at the centre. The financial package recently announced by the Prime Minister should go a long way in achieving these goals. What needs to be ensured is that all the projects are implemented faithfully, within the specified time frame and with the minimum amount of leakage of funds. More importantly, it also needs to be ensured that what today is purely an armed struggle over territory is not allowed to get a religious overtone. The consequences of that happening would be disastrous for the secular fabric of the state and the country.

In effect, the author is proposing to reduce the number and type of troops actually combating terrorism. That makes sense, as there will be greater cohesion in the command and control structure as also lesser uniforms visible on the streets. He also suggests that special commando battalions of the police be utilized as the first response force in the event of a terrorist strike. This also makes sense because the bulk of the action against the militants would then be directly controlled and coordinated by the DG J&K Police. This would also compel the police force to be more intimately involved with the tackling of the insurgency and reduce the temptation to hand over the situation to the central security forces the moment the situation turns messy.

I agree with the author's assertion that collection, collation, dissemination and analysis of intelligence are of primary importance and have not been accorded the importance they merit. He has used the evidence gathered by studies worldwide to show how vitally important it is to have a vibrant and proactive intelligence set up. The current problem has been with us for the past 25 years and by now we should have been able to penetrate most groups and been able to preempt a number of militant actions. Maybe we have already done so; then it is best for the public not to know. However, based on available feedback, it is evident that there are a number of shortcomings in this department. We need to identify these loopholes and plug them soonest. Interdepartmental rivalries should be curbed and information should be released on a strictly need to know basis. It is not necessary that ground level politicians be privy to tactical information. To assuage hurt egos at times it may be necessary to include them in the planning, but they can always be fed a bit of disinformation in terms of the timing and precise location of the planned operation. We could borrow a leaf or two from the book of J. Edgar Hoover in this regard.

The subjects of AFSPA and Human Rights continue to excite heated debate. The author has dwelt on these at length. These touchy issues would also be resolved to an extent by implementation of the recommendations of the author. That, however, does not imply that accusations and complaints would come to an end, because these are the only two sources of propaganda for the separatist organizations against the state. Perusal of the statistics provided by the author show that the situation is not as bad as is being made out in some quarters. In fact, the Indian Army scores much higher than most other armies worldwide. Nonetheless, the security forces should continue to get sensitized in dealing with civilians on a periodic basis. Commanders at all levels need to be especially vigilant, as even one misguided individual can set the peace and reconciliation process back by years.

To conclude, I would like to compliment the author on a well written treatise. He has fashioned his arguments articulately and his detailed knowledge of ground conditions and local aspirations is evident. We do need more such works to give our planners some original thoughts to ponder upon. This book deserves pride of place along with similar works on Jammu and Kashmir; a must buy for all libraries and for inclusion in the personal collection of all serious students of Jammu and Kashmir. I hope the publisher also intends to come out with a paperback edition to make ownership of this book more affordable.

31 December 2015 **Amitabh Mattoo**

Author's Note

My choice of subject raised many an eyebrow within my circle of friends and colleagues some of whom were unable to comprehend my reasons for even thinking in terms of demilitarising a State where the security forces are constantly on call to combat terrorist violence and separatist agitations. In fact a former colleague of mine dismissed the very notion with an oxymoronic "brilliantly stupid". Perhaps the choice of the word 'Demilitarisation' is misleading. 'Reduction, Redeployment and Realignment of the Security Forces in Kashmir' may have been a more accurate, but insipid, title.

The nation got a rude wakeup call in the winter of 1989-90. How magnificently, the Indian armed forces responded and brought Jammu and Kashmir back from the brink is well known. But that was a quarter of a century ago. The world has moved on. Public perception, nationally and internationally, has undergone a sea change. The 'Kashmir Problem' is no longer viewed as a freedom struggle but as an unresolved problem in a region where India has a legitimate and overwhelming presence. It is also acknowledged now that what is generically referred to as "Kashmir" does not represent the whole of the state of Jammu and Kashmir but only a fraction of it, albeit the most populous and noisy fraction. The scurrilous role of Pakistan as fishing in troubled waters has also been exposed. India is no longer seen as an occupying power and 'plebiscite' and 'determining the will of the Kashmiri people' are no longer the *mantra* chanted *ad nauseam* by any and every western "Kashmir expert". The time is now ripe for a permanent solution to the problem, and the Indian security forces have played their part in getting all the stake holders to the negotiating table.

The problem is far from over; however it has ceased to be a military one. The major challenge for the Indian security apparatus is to prevent the *jihadis,* emanating from that perennial spring to the west of the State, from entering the State, while for India the major challenge is to take effective steps to safeguard against the possibility of radicalisation which threatens to engulf the entire society. Threats of terrorist strikes emanating from the ISIS coupled with the exhortation by Ayman al Zawahiri to Indian Muslims to join the Al Qaeda may appeal to some young and misguided youth and they may be tempted to respond positively to the invitation. It is this that we need to be vigilant against. Intelligence agencies need to be at their most alert to monitor the slightest tell-tale signs of the commencement of the process. An effective and proactive intelligence policy is another point repeatedly stressed in the book. It is infinitely more important to develop the capability to preempt a terrorist strike rather than to develop the capability to respond to it.

At state level, the major challenge is for the administrative machinery to develop the capacity to operate on its own in the existing volatile environment. How fragile the State administration and police structures are, was amply demonstrated in their total collapse during the floods in September 2014. As always, it was the Indian army that was at the forefront of the rescue effort; and there lies the argument that I have consistently attempted to make in this book. The state machinery has to develop a spine and strong limbs in order to function on its own. The Indian army cannot perform the dual task of defending the country against external aggression and maintaining law and order in the State indefinitely. The latter is the task for specially raised and trained police forces, which the Jammu and Kashmir Police have not yet been able to put on ground. The maxim that quantity cannot replace quality holds equally true in this case. It is better to have one battalion of well trained and motivated anti-terrorist commandos than five ordinary armed police battalions.

The mandate thrown up by the state elections held in the end of 2014 reflects the mood of the State accurately. There is a clear division in the aspirations of the provinces. Whereas two provinces have supported the concept of growth and progress within a united India, the third is still intoxicated in part by the charm of autonomy and in part by the dream of *Azaadi*. The new Chief Minister, Mufti Mohamed Sayeed has to traverse a tight rope to balance the aspirations of the State as a whole. So far, his attempts have been bold and unconventional. The episodes of the release of Masarat Alam, the proclamation of resettling the Kashmiri Pundits in townships within the valley and the resultant protests and violence could definitely have been handled more deftly. The regular *tamasha*, of waving of Pakistani and ISIS flags and the chanting of anti-India slogans by a handful of ruffians, after the Friday prayers are a deliberate ploy by

Masarat and his ilk to provoke a strong reaction by the security forces. Fortunately, the lessons of the summer of 2010 have not been forgotten. Despite the extreme provocation of the demonstrators, which the government repeatedly points out number just a few hundreds that too in separatist strongholds, the present dispensation believes in giving a long rope rather than cracking down hard. It is a policy fraught with possibilities and the protests may yet escalate forcing a police crackdown. Anyhow it is early days yet and, hopefully, the new Chief Minister has some tricks up his sleeve which may surprise us all.

Brig Pramathesh Raina (Retd)

Post Script

While the book was in the final stage of printing, we received the shocking news of the sudden demise of the Chief Minister, Mufti Mohamed Sayeed. It is indeed a significant loss and a huge setback to the peace and reconciliation process so dear to the heart of the late Chief Minister. He staked his personal reputation and credibility with his untiring efforts to provide a healing touch, assuage the hurt of the people and to bridge the divide between the provinces of the State. In his death the nation has lost a true patriot and a statesman of towering stature. RIP, great soul and worthy son of Kashmir!

Acknowledgements

I would like to place on record my gratitude and thanks to the Army Headquarters and the Savitribai Phule University of Pune for having provided me the opportunity to conduct research on a subject having national relevance. It is that research which has provided the foundation for this book.

My sincere thanks to the faculty and staff of the Department of Defence and Strategic Studies of the University of Pune, for their encouragement and guidance. It was truly a unique experience for me to interact with the professors, resident scholars and students with whom I had the opportunity to interact, teach and work with during my time at the University. I must single out for special mention Nagma Naaz Shaikh who willingly and cheerfully devoted her spare time to edit the manuscript.

I must thank Vitasta for the painting on the cover. This painting is of special significance to me as it depicts the waterfront of the River Jhelum with the Shah-e-Hamdan Mosque in the foreground and the Hari Parbat Fort in the background as seen from Fateh Kadal, barely a stone's throw from my ancestral house in Srinagar. It is a return to this milieu that my heart yearns for. Hopefully in time and with enlightened leadership, this will be a possibility.

I am grateful to Prof Amitabh Mattoo who graciously consented to write the foreword. His words of encouragement truly mean a lot to me. My thanks also to Mr Rajan Arya and his team at the Pentagon Press.

I also wish to convey my grateful thanks to all those, too numerous to mention by name, whom I was fortunate to interact with in Delhi, Pune, Jammu and Srinagar and whose suggestions and comments helped me no end in formulating my recommendations. My thanks also to Jogesh Sabharwal for painstakingly going through the manuscript and for his learned suggestions. And lastly, my gratitude to my dear wife Roma for patiently bearing with me while I was busy pounding away on the keyboard.

Brig Pramathesh Raina (Retd)

1

Introduction

The insurgency movement in the State of Jammu & Kashmir is now in its third decade. The speed and virulence with which the insurgency started and gathered momentum caught even seasoned Kashmir experts by surprise. Kashmiri youth had crossed the LC in droves to receive training in arms at camps in POK and returned from there filled with the fire of *Azaadi* and hatred for all things Indian, with special venom reserved for the Indian Army perceived to be the main obstacle in the path to *Azaadi*. The general propaganda fed to the people in the winter of 1989-90 was that an independent state of Jammu and Kashmir was imminent. People were led to believe that come spring when the passes opened, the Pakistani Army would walk into the Valley riding roughshod over the Indian Army and assist in the formation of "The Islamic Republic of Jammu and Kashmir".

This optimism was not without logic. If one considers what was happening across the world during that period, one would see that this was a period of spectacular liberation movements across Europe and Asia. This period also coincided with the arrival in South Asia of 24x7 television coverage via satellite. The collapse of the USSR and demolition of the Berlin wall was witnessed by billions across the world. So also was the fact that a crowd of 70,000 people demonstrating on the streets of Bucharest could orchestrate the fall of the highly unpopular Ceacescu regime. Closer home, we saw the overthrow of the monarchy in Iran by Ayatollah Khomeini followed some years later by the ouster of the Soviets from Afghanistan ostensibly at the hands of a motley band of Taliban (assisted in no small measure by the US and Pakistan, but the credit mostly, in public perception, went to the Taliban, perpetuating the myth of the Afghan super-guerrilla).

These events, especially in Iran and Afghanistan, had an electrifying effect on the minds of the Muslim world in South Asia. Three points from these developments made an impression on the minds of the anti-India elements in Jammu and Kashmir:

- If you are able to gather in impressive numbers on the streets, your cause gets automatic legitimacy.
- Constant media coverage will deter the government from taking strong measures.
- With adequate support in terms of training, bases, logistics and arms from a willing sponsor, an indigenous force of guerrillas should be able to overthrow the established government.

Pakistan was quick to grab the opportunity and found willing agents in the Valley to further their long standing aim of wresting the State of J&K from India. The separatist Kashmiri leaders were promised the moon and they fell for it. Enough has been written on the events that followed and the depths of despair that the State and its citizens sank to when the terrorists were ruling the roost and enforcing their writ in every walk of life, be it dress code or recruitment to their ranks, during the 1990s till the early years of the new millennium, by when the Indian Security Forces had regained the initiative and the situation was brought back to a state of near-normalcy by 2006.

The situation called for tough measures and the Indian Army responded accordingly. They had to start from scratch, which is surprising since Jammu and Kashmir has always been the arena for power politics between the three countries in the region viz India, Pakistan and China. Four major wars have been fought in the region. The state has been a hotbed of intrigue and conspiracy. Members of the secret services of all three countries are constantly and actively engaged in collection of intelligence and monitoring the movements of each other's armed forces. However, the possibility of an armed insurrection by the locals on the Indian side obviously had not figured prominently on the Indian list of contingencies to be prepared for.[1]

It was a glaring lack of knowledge of what was happening on the ground and inexcusable. To say that the Indian intelligence apparatus was caught flat-footed is an understatement. The only explanation that can be offered in their defence is that they did not think that the Kashmiri peasant (for centuries, contemptuously dismissed as a coward, more on that later) had it in him to challenge the mighty Indian war machinery. Possibly recent history also lulled them into a false sense of complacency since in two previous attempts, i.e. 1948 and 1965, the Kashmiris had refused to collaborate with the tribal intruders and the Pakistani infiltrators and turned them over to the authorities.

During the early years of insurgency, there was a near-total collapse of the state administrative machinery. The state police was demoralized and riddled with informers. Any police officer daring to show spine or refusing to obey the terrorists' diktat was eliminated. The politicians lay low, testing the winds before voicing an opinion. Some simply fled the State to safer locations. The media and judiciary both, bar and bench, were dominated to such an extent that it was impossible for them to declare a fair verdict. To compound matters the minority, but highly vocal and influential, Kashmiri Hindu community was literally hounded out of the Valley fearing for their lives. A state of anarchy had set in and the general opinion was that Kashmir had all but slipped out of Indian hands.

Adding fuel to the fire was the rampant infiltration from across the borders and the LC. Accompanying the youth who had gone across to receive training in arms were foreign terrorists from all over Pakistan and other Islamic nations, including from as far away as Chechnya and Sudan. Huge quantities of arms and ammunition were also smuggled across and stored in caches for future use. Within no time, the armed struggle lost its ethnic Kashmiri nature and acquired a religious hue. The State became a magnet for *jihadis* from all over to participate in a vicious battle against the Indian State. It was a huge challenge for the security apparatus which was caught unprepared for this turn of events.

It was in this milieu that the situation was handed over to the Indian Army. Additional formations from the North East and some reserve formations were rushed in to stabilize the situation. Later an entire force called the Rashtriya Rifles was raised as a specialist counter- terrorist force and located within various parts of the State. It took years of painstaking effort to turn the situation around.

The Security forces have paid a heavy price in terms of casualties suffered. But the call to save the country from disintegration (the secession of Kashmir being seen as the first step in that direction) was strong enough to justify any sacrifice and the troops responded accordingly. The situation has been turned around thanks to a determined effort by the Indian Amy and other central security forces notably the Rashtriya Rifles, CRPF and the BSF. Infiltration from across has reduced to manageable figures and the number of resident terrorists is down to less than 400 (although intelligence reports have confirmed that there are a fair number waiting to be pushed into the State from training camps in POK). Ostensibly the terrorist movement has been crushed. All this has come at a price. The image of the Indian Army and other central security forces has taken a beating and is at an all time low. Allegations of highhanded behavior and human rights violations surface with alarming regularity. It is vital to initiate steps to remove the perception of the Indian Army being an occupation force.

Today a situation of outward normalcy prevails. A number of elections at various levels have been conducted successfully. The state administration is able to function. The state police have regained control over most areas except some pockets which are still under the influence of separatist elements. Tourism is flourishing and the markets function normally. A serious attempt is being made to woo the minority Kashmiri Hindu community to return to the Valley. The media is able to function without the fear of the gun. One can notice an increase in the democratic space available to the common citizen. He is able to express his views or register his protests on the streets without the fear of the security forces or the militants. Outwardly, Jammu and Kashmir is back to being a functional democracy. But it is too early to let one's guard down or rejoice. The gains need to be consolidated and a mechanism put in place to ensure that we do not allow a situation of anarchy to prevail again.

An underlying current of tension lurks beneath the calm exterior. The locals believe that every time there is optimism that the situation is turning towards normalcy, some incident sparks off a fresh wave of violence and we are back to Square One. The stone throwing protests of 2010 are perceived as a new phase in the civil unrest, wherein the separatist leaders call it a spontaneous expression of the desire for freedom and elements within the security establishment view it as dangerous development where the terrorists are using the protestors as human shields.

The Indian government has had this problem on its hands for over sixty years and is still searching for a satisfactory solution. Obviously something has been fundamentally wrong in our approach and it is time to try something new. There is a constant refrain among sections of the political parties and separatists demanding the complete withdrawal of the security forces from Jammu & Kashmir. This is obviously an unreasonable demand given the fact that we have a border dispute with China and Pakistan. But the situation can never be termed normal unless there is a perceptible reduction in force levels. To that extent, there is a definite case for demilitarisation because unless there is a visible reduction in forces, no one will buy the argument that the situation is normal. The concept of demilitarisation is not new. There have been a number of formulae, which have suggested by various personalities from within the

State, India and Pakistan. However, these are mostly political in nature. No one has seriously considered the mechanics of the actual process of demilitarisation.

The Jammu & Kashmir problem has two dimensions - external and internal. The Indian Army has a major stake in both. Maintaining the territorial integrity of the nation is its *raison de etre*. As long as the borders need to be secured against Pakistan and China, there is no question of even considering its withdrawal from the State. Therefore, reduction of troops from the borders is directly linked to the threat perception from across. However, there are definite gains also for the security forces in demilitarisation from the internal areas. Maintenance of law and order in the interiors is primarily the task of the civil administration. The longer the security forces remain bogged down in aid to civil authorities, the greater are the dangers of the forces losing their professionalism in the long run. Thus there is a definite benefit for the security forces in creating conditions for a gradual transfer of power to the civil administration and returning to the barracks.

The average man in the streets of Srinagar is as interested in living a normal life, as anyone else in the country. The realisation has also set in that the terrorists/separatists can never achieve their aim despite the full backing, covert or overt, of Pakistan. It is also understood that there cannot be a military solution to the Jammu & Kashmir problem. The people of Jammu & Kashmir have to resolve their own problems and this cannot be achieved without the backing and consent of India.

Prolonged employment of any Army in counter-insurgency/counter-terrorism operations is undesirable as it has adverse ramifications on stress levels, discipline and morale. The handing over of the situation to the civil police is an issue that has vexed policy makers for over a decade. Demilitarisation is being debated at myriad national and international fora. But the mechanics of how this can be implemented have not yet been properly worked out. The author has attempted to formulate a cogent, workable and time-bound plan without compromising national security and national interests in any way. The aim of this book is to suggest a method of gradual demilitarisation in the state of Jammu & Kashmir over a five to ten-year period and identify the improvements on ground that must take place concurrently before such reduction can be implemented.

Both the external and internal dimensions of the Kashmir problem need to be addressed before a lasting solution can be arrived at. In this book, the author does not presume to find a permanent solution to the problem of Jammu and Kashmir, nor does he seek to moralize or justify the Indian stand. That is left to the politicians and better informed experts. This book is merely a realistic appraisal of the requirement of the quantum of troops over and above those deployed in the State to ensure the sanctity of the borders. It is an attempt to identify the number of troops required to ward off any challenges posed by the terrorists.

Terrorism in Jammu and Kashmir is a reality and cannot be wished away. But combating terrorism is not the basic task of any army. No army is raised purely for a counter-insurgency role. An army is raised and trained for combat against an enemy in uniform. In fact, when the army is requisitioned for counter-insurgency, the troops have to operate in a manner contrary to what they are trained for. A conventional army is trained to use maximum force for maximum effect. They are programmed to fight the enemy - not own citizens, and collateral damage is an accepted fall-out in any army operation. However, this approach is highly counter-productive when fighting terrorists on your own soil. Counter-terrorism operations are specialist tasks best undertaken by specially trained troops. There is, therefore, a requirement of raising a trained police counter-terrorist organization to eradicate all residual terrorists and sleeper cells to ensure that the spectre of terrorism is not allowed to raise its head again. A number of states have raised anti-terrorist police battalions that are conducting counter-terrorism operations on a regular basis. The state of Jammu and Kashmir needs to follow suit. Once this is done, the central security forces can be relieved from this onerous and distasteful task.

It is also in the interests of the Indian Army to demilitarise. Some elements within the establishment may consider it as a kind of defeat or loss of empire. Some believe that Kashmir cannot survive without the Army and that the State will revert to anarchy if the Army is withdrawn from the State. However, they must consider that the Army has its own role in Jammu & Kashmir. The basic role of any Army is to defend the territorial integrity of the country. The counter-insurgency and counter-terrorism role entrusted to it is over and above its primary role. The longer it stays involved in roles other than its primary role, the greater are the dangers of diminishing professionalism. Prolonged involvement in counter-insurgency and counter-terrorism invariably goes against the security forces and is the surest way to ensure that the security forces increasingly get embroiled, rightly or wrongly, in allegations of human rights violations and become the whipping boy for everything that goes wrong. As former Chief of Army Staff, Gen VP Malik said, "the Kashmir problem is political not military and the solution can only be political not military". Hence, there must come a time when the security forces take a back seat and let politics play its part. And that time has arrived.

The subject assumes importance because the state of Jammu & Kashmir is regarded as an international hotspot and a potential flash point in South Asia. The issue of human rights violations is regularly raised within the country and internationally. India does not like to be reminded that the Kashmir issue needs to be resolved. It is in the interest of the nation that the situation reverts to normal as early as possible. Reduction in troop levels and the absence, or minimal presence, of uniformed personnel on the streets is the best indicator that the situation is normal.

The main arguments that have been made in the book can be listed as under:

- **Total Demilitarisation Linked With Peaceful Borders**. Total demilitarisation is directly linked with peace on the borders. Only once we have resolved our differences with our neighbours, can a substantial troop pullout from the border areas be considered.
- **Need to Raise a Counter-terrorist Force**. Until we have a credible alternative in place, which is a well-trained and well-armed and motivated local police force to combat the terrorists, demilitarisation will remain a mere slogan.
- **The Problem is Political**. At no time can we overlook the fact that the Jammu & Kashmir problem is a political one. Expert after expert has stressed that Kashmir is essentially a political problem and not a military one. So there has to be a political solution to the problem. The politician and the civil administration have to address the root cause of the problem. The armed forces are there only to enable and empower the civil administration to perform its functions and not to replace them. It is, therefore, axiomatic that demilitarisation cannot take place in isolation. It has to be accompanied by civil reforms.
- **Demilitarisation is also in the Interests of the Security Forces**. It is equally in the interests of the central security forces including the Indian Army to demilitarise to the extent possible. There are major pitfalls in prolonged involvement in counter insurgency/ counter terrorism and that invariably works against the security forces in the long run. Human rights violations are bound to occur. This is the surest way to become the whipping boy of populist movements and target of local ire and frustrations
- **Demilitarisation - a Long Drawn Process**. Demilitarisation necessarily is going to be a gradual, prolonged and long drawn-out process. Conditions have to be created for a gradual pull out so that there is no trauma or power vacuum once the forces pull out. In the absence of the central security forces, the local police

will be totally hamstrung to provide security to the citizens. A special task force will need to be raised for this purpose. Adequate time has to be given for the police to raise, equip and train a counter insurgency/counter terrorism force.

- **No Space for Political Pressures and One-up-man-ship**. There is no space for political pressures and political immaturity. There is bound to be tremendous pressure to speed up the process of demilitarisation with politicians of various hues vying to claim credit for the process while at the same time pulling the rug under each other's feet in a game of one-up-man-ship. While the importance of regional politicians cannot be undermined, they should not be allowed to dictate the agenda or time frame. A smooth transfer of control to the civil administration should be the sole guiding principle. Re-location and re-deployment has to be worked out and this has to be linked to the attainment of a safe, secure and politically stable environment.

Experience in counter-insurgency operations reveals that it always pays greater dividends to develop the affected state's capabilities in combating terror and maintaining law and order, rather than depending upon central police forces for an extended period of time. Central forces will always be seen as outsiders and resented, no matter how noble the intentions. The process of strengthening the fibre and improving the capabilities of the state police force has already commenced. A parallel may be drawn with the State of Tripura which was an extremely disturbed state for over twenty years. Resisting constant demands for deployment of the Army, the State machinery was held together by the Assam Rifles while the State Police force was re-organized and developed to take over the situation. Today the State of Tripura ranks amongst the better policed states of the Indian Union.

Role of the Army in helping resolve the crisis and ensuring a climate that allows the civil administration to operate un-hampered has to be acknowledged. But for the timely assistance provided by the Security Forces, the situation could not have been brought under control in such a quick time frame. The Indian Army has more or less achieved its objectives as far as counter-insurgency operations are concerned. As per current estimates, between 350 to 400 active terrorists remain in the Valley. Formations have been disengaged from active operations and have been mostly been de-inducted or redeployed. Some continue to remain in the Valley as a threat-in-being for the terrorists.

Demilitarisation has to be a gradual process. It is bound to be prolonged and long drawn. The experience gained by the Army in combating terrorism must be passed on to the police force so that the transfer of control is as seamless as possible. There is no space for political pressures and political immaturity. A plan for re-location and re-deployment has to be worked out and this has to be linked to the attainment of a safe, secure and politically stable environment. Responsibility for law and order once the central forces are withdrawn has to be clearly stipulated. The pull out of troops must be gradual and phased out to ensure that there is no trauma caused by the vacuum consequent to pull out. The police have to learn to operate without the crutch of the central security forces. Training of the police in counter terrorism tasks must commence immediately and should continue till they reach a standard when they are confident of taking care of the situation on their own. Initially they can be handed over the areas where relative stability has been achieved.

The time is ripe for a series of serious negotiations to commence between the Indian government and all stakeholders including the separatists and those terrorists who have laid down arms and are willing to come to the table. **We must consider that the latter have fought an insurgency for over 15 years and are an ageing lot. It is too late for them to go back to the gun, and this is the reason why they would be willing to negotiate an "honourable" settlement.** If we let go this opportunity and allow the cycle of violence to commence again, the leadership of the armed struggle would fall into the hands of the next generation which is more indoctrinated, more hard line in their observance of radical Islam and less enamoured by the concept of *Kashmiriyat*. We can then expect the insurgency to continue with renewed vigour for another 10 to 15 years with the attendant loss in terms of popular support, casualties and development.

Hence, negotiations must commence in earnest so that the military gains are capitalized upon and not frittered away. The interlocutors' report can be the starting point. It is very important that the right type of negotiators are selected by the government. They should be persons of integrity and trusted by the opposing side. They should be given a clear mandate of the negotiables and the non-negotiables and should know exactly what they are bringing to the table. It is also extremely important to ensure that those who represent the majority segment of the population are included in the negotiations, otherwise the dialogue will be a non-starter.

NOTES

1. How unprepared the average Indian was for the events that were to unfold is best illustrated by a conversation that took place in the headquarters of a brigade in the Valley in September 1989. An officer remarked that it was surprising to see how bold the locals had become of late and how they were prepared to talk back and stare you down. A relatively junior officer agreed that the situation was quite serious and added that he foresaw an insurgency within two years. Every one present in the room laughed at the idea that the Kashmiris might commence an insurrection. The Kashmiri does not have it in him to take to arms, was the general refrain.

   Some months later the same officers were attending a conference in the office of the Sub Area Commander in Srinagar to discuss the situation in the aftermath of the initial few serious incidents. "Brother, you said two years. It has happened in less than four months. How did you know?" The reply: "Because I am a local and am aware of what was happening in my neighborhood. It is common knowledge that the AK 47 is a terrorist's weapon and a number of these have been in the possession of the lumpen elements in the Valley for a number of years now. Certainly you don't need an AK for crimes of routine nature. And if I was aware of this fact, I assumed that those whose business it is to know were also aware".

2

Geography, History, Religion and Civil Society

GEOGRAPHY

The State of Jammu and Kashmir lies at the northern tip of the Indian subcontinent. Located just south of the Pamir Knot, it occupies one of the most strategic locations in the World. The State shares common borders with China and the narrow Wakhan Corridor of Afghanistan (beyond which lies Tajikistan) to the north, Tibet to the east, Pakistan to the west, and the Indian states of Punjab and Himachal Pradesh to the south. The fabled Silk Route passed through the State and the region was well known to travelers since ancient times. During the Cold War of the 20th Century, the State's strategic location attracted the attention of the superpowers as it exposed the vulnerable soft underbelly of the USSR. Even after the dismemberment of the USSR, the strategic importance of the State has not diminished as it provides an access to the Arabian Sea for China via the Karakoram Highway.

In the Mesozoic age, this part of Asia was under the sea of Tethys.[1] With the continental shift and the formation of the Himalayas, the waters of the Sea drained out leaving behind a huge mountain lake in the present-day Kashmir Valley. This lake was known to the early Hindus as Satisar[2]. Physical evidence of the lacustrine origin of the Valley can be found all over including on mountain slopes at surprising altitudes. The extent of the lake can easily be visualized when one approaches Srinagar Airport by air on an overcast day. One can also see where the mountains split apart downstream of Baramulla draining out the lake creating the beautiful valley of Kashmir as it is today with the River Jhelum flowing through it. The enormous lake fringed by towering mountains must have been a majestic sight, with all the major landmarks of today, including Srinagar, under water.

The State is one of the world's most mountainous regions, with 5 of the 14 giants (mountains over 8000 metres in altitude) of the mountain world located within its territory.[3] The continuous chain of mountain ranges have long served as effectual barriers against foreign invasion, and as a sure means of preservation of indigenous cultures. The mountains have largely determined the political fortunes of the territory they encircle. It is the inaccessibility and practical impregnability of these natural defences and not just the valour of Kashmiri troops that has often turned the tide of invasion from the Valley. This inaccessibility, again, enabled Kashmir to preserve and consolidate its peculiar social and economic conditions up to very recent times.[4]

Since the earliest days Kashmir has been known both in Greece and China as recorded by their travelers and envoys to India. The earliest mention of the Valley and its adjacent territories is found in Ptolemy's *Geography*.[5] The Chinese pilgrim, Huien Tsang who visited the Valley in 631 AD has described the Valley in great detail. A Tang dynasty record from the fifth century AD based on the account of an Indian envoy describes Kashmir as belonging to the northern portion of India and "enveloped on all sides like a precious jewel by the snowy mountains with a valley in the south which leads to it and serves as the gate of the kingdom".[6] From these accounts it is abundantly clear that in ancient and medieval history, that Kashmir as a country referred to present day Kashmir Province and the Jhelum Valley in particular. As a result the word Kashmiri, which in its original term described the denizen of the Valley, today is loosely used to describe the denizen of the State of Jammu and Kashmir whereas in fact there is very little in common between the denizens of the three provinces. The characteristics, language, culture, dress, physical features and cuisine are distinctly different.

The state of Jammu and Kashmir came into being in its present territorial configuration after the 1846 Treaty of Amritsar, when the Raja of Jammu was awarded all the territories of the Sikh Kingdom to the north of his realm, in recognition of his support to the British in the Anglo-Sikh War. Prior to that, the provinces of Kashmir and Ladakh had been independent countries or parts of different empires. It is only after the Treaty that the three provinces began to share a common destiny.

Map of Jammu & Kashmir

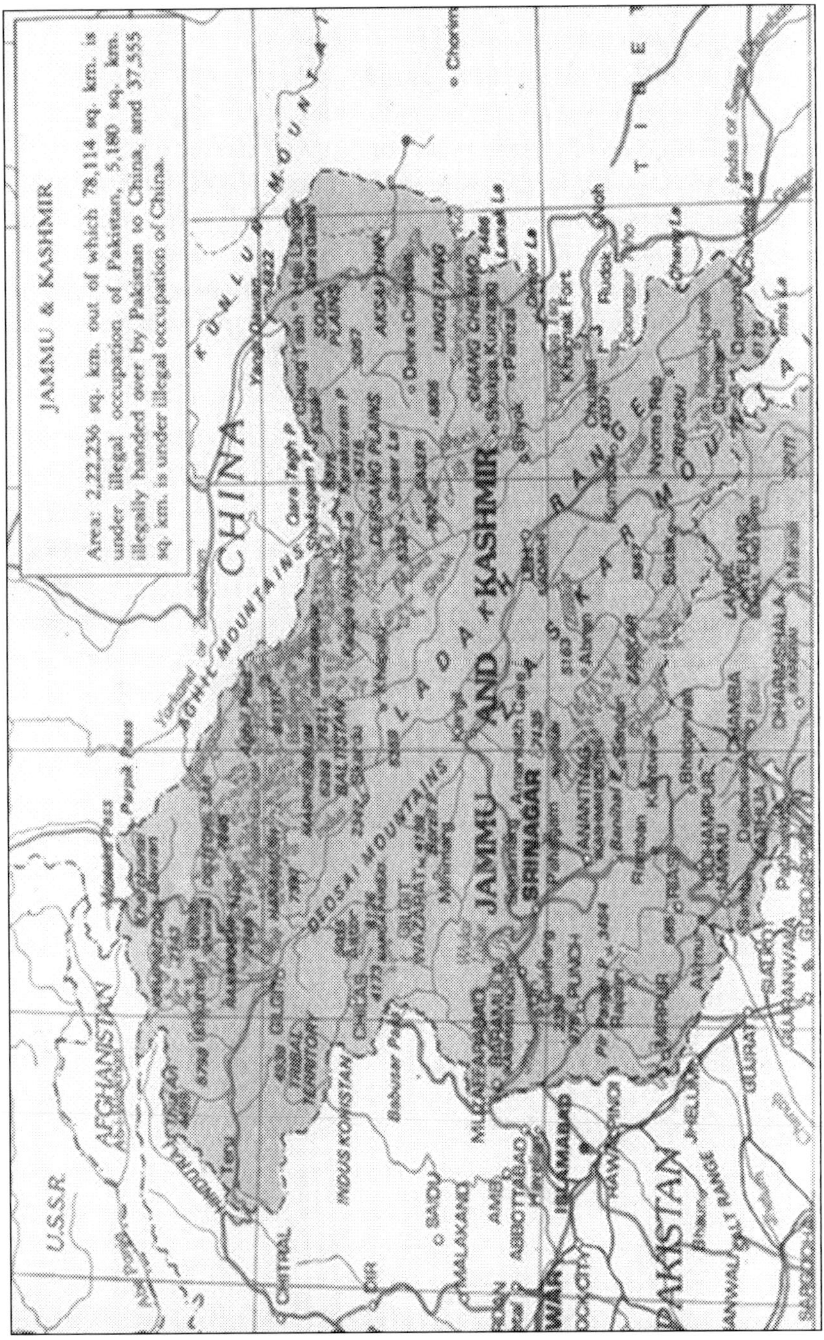

Source : Official Website of the Government of J&K

GEOGRAPHICAL DIVISIONS

The State of Jammu and Kashmir is one of the largest states of the Indian Union. It lies between Latitudes 32° 17′ to 36° 58′ North and Longitudes 73° 26′ to 80° 30′ East. It consists of a number of distinct areas (with different histories and ethnicities) and is currently in the physical occupation of three countries. Geographically, the State consists of the provinces of Kashmir, Jammu, Ladakh, Gilgit and Baltistan. Indian Kashmir consists of the provinces of the Kashmir Valley, Jammu and Ladakh. The area under the control of Pakistan (known as Pakistan Occupied Kashmir or POK in India) consists of a strip of land which it calls "*Azad* Jammu and Kashmir" or AJK and the Northern Areas which consist of Gilgit and Baltistan. China controls the northeastern part of Ladakh (called Aksai Chin) which it wrested by force in the 1962 Indo-Chinese War and some territory of Shaksgam in Hunza/Baltistan that Pakistan ceded to it in 1963 over the objections of India. The various areas of the State under occupation of the three countries are depicted in the map overleaf.

Map Depicting Areas Under Illegal Occupation of Pakistan and China

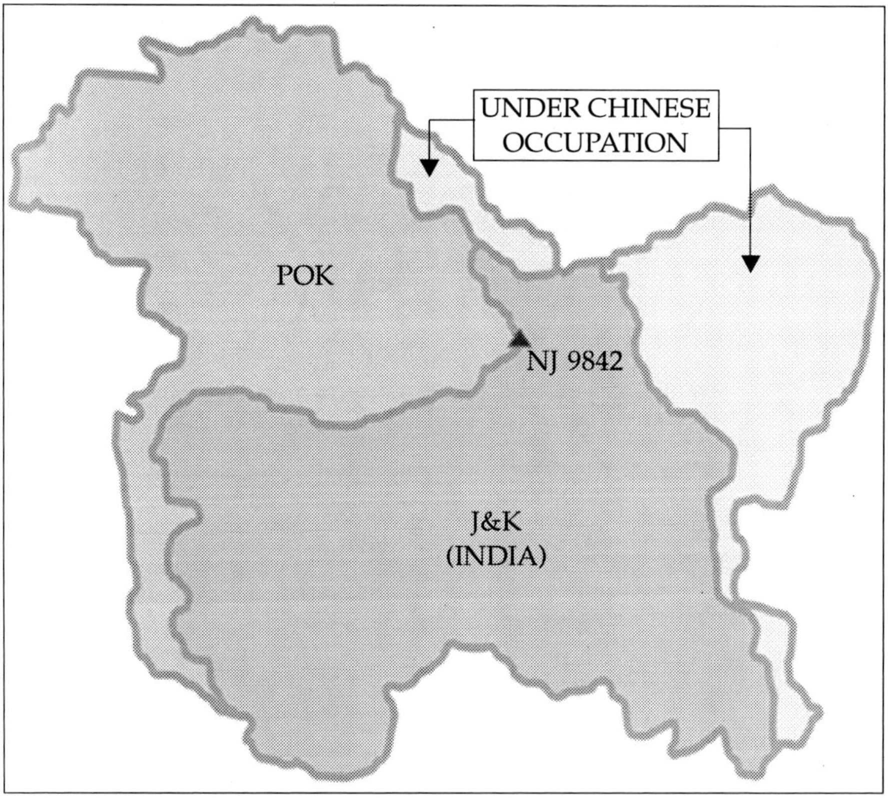

Statistics

Area

The area of the land mass is given below:

Total area of undivided Jammu and Kashmir : 2,22,236 sq km

- Indian Kashmir : 1,01,387 sq km
- POK : 78,114 sq km
- Under Chinese Occupation : 37,555 sq km
- Ceded by Pakistan to China : 5,180 sq km

Source: Official Website of the Government of Jammu and Kashmir

As mentioned, the terrain of Jammu and Kashmir is highly mountainous with only a small portion of its total area suitable for human settlement. The majority of the population of the State (almost 55 per cent) is concentrated in the Valley of Kashmir, a stretch of land roughly 130 km in length and up to 55 km wide astride the Jhelum River (barely 15% of the total landmass of the Indian State of Jammu and Kashmir). The other areas of dense population are along the foothills of the Himalayas and the Shivaliks, on either side of the Line of Control. Astride the Pir Panjal range is a moderately dense and partially migratory population largely dependent on terraced agriculture, pastoralism, and forestry.

Population

The state of Jammu and Kashmir is the only Muslim majority state in the Indian union. Like the rest of India it is highly multi-religious, multi-ethnic, and multi-cultural. The density of population is sparse at just 256 persons per square mile.

Population Figures are tabulated below

Province	*Population*	*% Muslim*	*% Hindu*	*% Sikh*	*% Buddhist and others*
Kashmir (53.9%)	6907623	97.16%	1.84%	0.88%	0.11%
Jammu (43.7%)	5350811	30.69%	65.23%	3.57%	0.51%
Ladakh (2.3%)	290492	47.40%	6.22%	–	45.87%
Jammu and Kashmir	1,25,48,926	66.97%	29.63%	2.03%	1.36%

Source: 2011 Census India District Profiles.

The 2011 Census reveals a skewed sex ratio in favour of males as under:

- Total Population : 1,25,48,926
- Male : 66,65,561
- Female : 58,83,365

Statistical data pertaining to Pakistan Occupied Kashmir is covered in detail later in this section. The Chinese-controlled portion does not have any significant permanent habitation.

Ethnicity

The State of Jammu and Kashmir may have a Muslim majority but it does not have a homogenous religious or ethnic entity, as the constituent units of the State still retain many of their distinctive religious, ethnic and linguistic features. Like the rest of India, it represents a mosaic of different religions, different ethnic groups and cultures. All three divisions are distinguished by their diversity. An account of the ethnic groups residing in the State is given by *Majid Hussain* in his work Geography of Jammu & Kashmir. According to him, "The various ethnic groups of Jammu and Kashmir state, though intermingled, have their areas of high concentration. For example, Kashmiris are mainly concentrated in the bottom of the Valley; Dards occupy the Valley of Gurez, Hanjis are confined to water bodies of Kashmir; Gujjars and Bakarwals are living and oscillating in the Kandi areas; Dogras occupy the outskirts of the Punjab plain, while Chibhalis and Paharis live between Chenab and Jhelum rivers. Moreover, there are numerous small ethnic groups like Rhotas, Gaddis and Sikhs which have significant concentration in isolated pockets of the State".[7]

The ethnicity of the three provinces of the State is as follows:

Jammu. It has a majority Hindu population (65%), but with substantial Muslim and Sikh minorities. Three of its six districts (Poonch, Rajouri and Doda), have Muslim majorities. Dogri and Pahari which are classified as dialects of Punjabi are the languages most widely spoken, with a smattering of people in the Doda district claiming Kashmiri as their mother tongue.

Ladakh. It has only two districts; Leh which is overwhelmingly Buddhist and Kargil which is overwhelmingly (73%) Shia Muslim. The denizens of this division are distinct from the rest of the State due to their predominantly Mongoloid features. The main languages are Ladakhi and Balti.

Kashmir. The Kashmir Valley itself is predominantly Muslim, with a numerically small but politically significant population of Hindus and Sikhs. Kashmiri is the predominant language, but with the entire mountain region speaking Shina and Pahari or Gojri. According to political scientist Alexander Evans, over 300,000 Kashmiri Hindus (approximately 95% of the total population) have been internally displaced.[8] Local estimates place the figures at least 50,000 persons more.

Languages

The major linguistic population groups of Jammu and Kashmir are tabulated below:

Language	*J&K State*	*Kashmir Division*	*Jammu Division*	*Ladakh Division*
Kashmiri	52.33%	46.87%	5.48% (Mainly in Doda district)	0.025%
Dogri	24.295%	0.049%	24.24%	0.003%
Hindi/Urdu* Pahari/Gojari	17.03%	4.33% (Mainly in Baramulla and Kupwara Districts)	12.87% (Mainly in Doda, Punch and Rajouri Districts)	0.003%
Ladakhi	1.2%	0.008%	0.20%	1.17%
Punjabi	2.72%	0.69%	2.03%	0.003%
Lahanda (Pothwari)	0.22%	Negligible	0.22%	Nil
Balti	0.80%	0.02%	Nil	0.78% (Mainly in Kargil)
Shina (Dardi)	0.25%	0.20% (Mainly in area of Gurez)	Nil	0.05% (Mainly in Dah Hanu)
Tibetan	0.07%	0.013% (Mainly in Srinagar)	Nil	0.057% (Mainly in Leh Tehsil)

*Gojari, the language of the Gujars has been clubbed along with Hindi/Urdu.
Source: Kashmir Information Network 2001.

As can be seen from the above table, each region is dominated by a particular language group. Though the dominant language, Kashmiri is not indigenous to the two geographically largest constituents of the State. It is spoken mainly in the Kashmir Valley and parts of the hill district of Doda in Jammu division, which in terms of real estate account for less than 20% of the total landmass of the State. "The transitions from one language area to another do not normally follow administrative boundaries. For example, in Kashmir, the lowlands of all districts are overwhelmingly Kashmiri-speaking while the numerically dominant population in the adjoining hills speaks Gojri. Similar situations apply in respect to speakers of Dogri and Pahari in Jammu." [9]

Climate, Physiography and Topography

Climatically, the State of Jammu and Kashmir comprises three distinct regions: the cold arid desert areas of Ladakh, the temperate Kashmir Valley, and the humid sub-tropical region of Jammu. In this context, Lawrence's quotation is relevant, "Every hundred feet of elevation brings some new phase of climate and the vegetation, and in a short ride of thirty miles one can pass from overpowering heat to a climate delightfully cool".[10]

The territory of the State is divided into seven physiographic zones closely associated with the structural components of the western Himalayas. These include:

- **The Plains**. The plains of the Jammu region are characterized by interlocking sandy alluvial fans that have been deposited during the Pleistocene age by the streams flowing from the foothills and by a much-dissected pediment (eroded bedrock surface) covered by loams and loess (fine deposits of silt).
- **The Foothills**. Rising from 2000 to 7000 feet, the foothills form the outer and inner zones.
- **The Lesser Himalayas.** Composed of volcanic rocks of granite, gneisses, quartz and slate, the Pir Panjal constitutes the first mountain rampart comprising the western-most part of the Lesser Himalayas.
- **The Greater Himalayas.** This contains ranges reaching more than 20,013 feet (6100 metres) in altitude. These ranges act as a climatic barrier and prevent the cold winds from Central Asia from reaching further south into the State.
- **Valley of Kashmir**. Between the Pir Panjal and the western end of the Great Himalayan ranges lies a deep asymmetrical basin called the Vale of Kashmir. The Valley is an ancient lake basin with an area of 15,220 sq kms. The average elevation of the valley is 5000 feet above sea level. It is enclosed on all sides by ranges of snow-capped mountains, which vary from 12,000 to 18,000 feet in height. The most striking features of the Kashmir landscape are its mighty mountain ramparts, its beautiful lakes and rivers, and its numerous dry brown plateaus known as *karewas*. Lawrence described it thus: "If one looks at the map of the territories of His Highness the Maharaja of Jammu and Kashmir, one sees a white foot-print set in a mass of black mountains. This is the Valley of Kashmir, known to its inhabitants as Kashmir".[11] The great Sanskrit poet Kalidasa writes about the Valley: "The place is more beautiful than Heaven and is the benefactor of supreme bliss and happiness. It seems to me that I am taking a bath in the lake of nectar here."[12] The Moghul emperor Jahangir wrote in his memoirs: "Kashmir is a garden of eternal spring or an iron fort to a palace of kings—a delightful flower bed, and a heart-expanding heritage for dervishes. Perhaps nature had to place a purdah around something so beautiful." [13]
- **The Upper Indus Valley.** The Valley of the upper Indus river follows the geological strike (structural trend) westwards from the Tibetan border to the point in the Pakistani sector where it rounds

the great mountainous mass of Nanga Parbat to run southwards in deep gorges cut across the strike. In its upper reaches, gravel terraces flank the river; each tributary builds an alluvial fan out into the main valley. The town of Leh, 11,483 feet (3500 meters) above sea level, stands on such a fan.

- **The Karakoram Range**. The Karakoram region contains some of the world's highest peaks. K2, the second highest peak in the world (8,615 metres) lies within this range.

Administrative Divisions

Jammu Division. This region comprises the plains, foothills and mountains south and west of the Pir Panjal Ranges that separate Kashmir Valley from the plains of the subcontinent. The Jammu region comprises the districts of Kathua, Jammu, Udhampur, Doda, Rajouri and Poonch.

Kashmir Division. The Kashmir region or the Jhelum Valley is the most significant part of the State. The traditional entry into the Valley prior to the partition of India was along the Jhelum River from Rawalpindi via Muzzafarabad to Srinagar. The other metalled roads are the Jammu-Srinagar Highway No 1A across the Banihal Pass and the Srinagar-Leh Highway across the Zojila pass. The other major passes into the Valley are the Pir Panjal, Sadhana, Tosamaidan and Burzil. The division comprises six districts, viz. Anantnag, Baramulla, Budgam, Kupwara, Pulwama and Srinagar.

Ladakh Division. Ladakh constitutes the eastern-most part of the State of Jammu and Kashmir. It comprises the districts of Leh and Kargil. This is one of the most breathtakingly beautiful parts of the state and its surreal landscape has often been termed as 'moonscape'. Ladakh covers about 1,17,000 sq km and includes the Karakoram Range and the upper Indus River valley. Situated on the leeward side of the mountain range, Leh hardly gets any rain, though the surrounding mountains receive heavy rain and snowfall and passes remained closed for 5 to 6 months in a year. Winters are bitterly cold. People live a very traditional life, herding sheep and yak, and growing barley near the riverbeds in summer.[14]

Pakistan Occupied Kashmir (POK)
Brief Description

Pakistan Occupied Kashmir is spread over an area of 78,114 sq km. It comprises what Pakistan calls 'Azad Jammu and Kashmir' (AJK) and the Northern Areas of Gilgit-Baltistan. For the purpose of this study, the term 'POK' shall apply only to the province termed by Pakistan as AJK. The rest of the territory under Pakistani occupation will be termed as the Northern Areas or Gilgit-Baltistan.

The topography of the area is mainly hilly and mountainous with valleys and stretches of plains. The area is full of forests, fast flowing rivers and winding streams. The main rivers are the Jhelum, Neelum and Poonch Rivers. The climate is sub-tropical highland with an average yearly rainfall of 1300 mm. The elevation ranges from 360 meters in the South to 6325 meters in the North.

POK has a majority Sunni Muslim population. Many merchants in Poonch are Pashtuns, however, these individuals are not legally considered to be Kashmiris.

Statistics

Area	-	13,297 sq km
Population	-	2,973,000 (1998 population census figures, estimated to have grown to 3,868,000 in 2009)
Religion	-	Practically 100% Muslim. (Predominantly Sunnis)
Population density	-	258 persons per sq km
Districts	-	10 (Muzaffarabad, Hattian, Neelum, Mirpur, Bhimber, Kotli, Poonch, Bagh, Haveli and Sudhnoti)

Sources: 1. Official Website of the Government of POK
2. Population Census Organization Islamabad, Pakistan

Northern Areas (Gilgit-Baltistan)[15]

Number of districts	-	5 (Gilgit, Skardu, Diamir, Ghizer and Ghanche.)
Population	-	Approx 1.8 million as per 2008 estimates
Area	-	72,495 sq km
Religion	-	Almost 100% Muslim (Baltistan is mainly Shia, with a few Buddhist households, while Gilgit is Ismaili)
Ethnic groups	-	Baltis, Shinas, Vashkuns, Mughals, Punjabis, Pathans, Ladakhis and Turks. A large number of Sunnis from Punjab and NWFP have been resettled in Gilgit, radically altering the demographic profile.
Languages	-	Balti, Shina, Brushaski, Khawer, Wakhi, Turki, Tibeti, Pushto and Urdu.

The Northern Areas are the only region in Pakistan whose status is not specified in the Constitution. While Kashmir is mentioned as a disputed territory, the Northern Areas find no mention in the relevant schedule, nor do they have an autonomous or constitutional status of their own.

The people of the Northern Areas are, consequently, not citizens of Pakistan within the meaning of the Constitution and do not enjoy any fundamental, legal, political or civil rights guaranteed by the Constitution. The region is also out of bounds to foreigners and journalists, except for occasional tightly controlled guided tours selectively organised by the Army or the intelligence agencies. The Northern Areas have been under virtual Martial Law for over five decades.

They are governed directly from Islamabad through a Northern Areas Council which is headed by Pakistan's Minister for Kashmir Affairs. Until 1994, the people of the Northern Areas had no elected assembly, or even a municipal council, and no representation in the Federal National Assembly. In October 1994, the Federal Government allowed the political parties of Pakistan, but not of 'AJK', to extend their activities to the Northern Areas.

The Pakistani administration has also been involved in efforts to alter the demographic profile of the region, reducing the indigenous people to a minority. In the Gilgit and Skardu areas, large tracts of land have been allotted to non-locals, violating the United Nations Commission for India and Pakistan (UNCIP) resolutions and the J&K State Subject Rule. Outsiders have purchased substantial stretches of land since they are, by and large, economically better off than the locals. In January 2001, the old population ratio of 1 : 4 (non-locals to locals) in these areas had been transformed to 3 : 4. The rapid induction of Punjabi and Pakhtoon outsiders has created a sense of acute insecurity among the locals.

The Northern Areas remain the most neglected and poorest part of Pakistani-administered Kashmir. In 1981, the female literacy rate in the region was just three percent and the male literacy rate was 14.7% (well below the then national average of 26%). In the 1995 national achievement surveys, children and teachers in the Northern Areas scored the lowest in the country. There is no industry to speak of except a few brick kilns. According to an article on the World Bank website, "Over 90% of the region's people live in small villages scattered along valleys carved by glacial streams and rivers. Subsistence agriculture is the norm and access to basic social services is often limited or unavailable. Roads are few, with one highway as virtually the only link to the rest of Pakistan."

There are only 12 high schools and two regional colleges in the Northern Areas, with no post graduate facilities. Very few locals are able to secure government jobs, and when they do, they are paid 25% less than non-native entrants from Pakistan's Punjab province. There are no local dailies, or local radio or television stations. According to the most recently available data, there is just one doctor for 6,000 people. Piped water supply is virtually non-existent and two thirds of the population must do without electricity in an area where winters are extremely harsh.

Strategic Importance

Quoting Amir Rana in 'The Other Kashmir', Wilson John[16] states that, "POK has long been a gateway of *jihad* with the Pakistani State setting up a vast network of terrorist training camps, religious schools and centers and weapons stores. As a result, all terrorist groups based in Pakistan, some 104 of them on the last count,[17] have maintained a training base in towns and villages in POK like Muzaffarabad, Kotli and Balakote. So long as these terrorist groups remained focused on carrying out violence against India, particularly in Kashmir, the world, by and large, chose to ignore this terrorist sanctuary. Till today, the war on terror, progressing in fits and starts, has not reached this mountainous area straddling between the lawless western frontiers of Pakistan and the seething eastern-most tip of China'. John goes on to argue that Pakistan occupied Kashmir will emerge from being merely an isolated jihadi outpost to become the epicenter of Global Jihad in the days to come.

NOTES

1. www.britannica.com/EBchecked/topic/588887/Tethys-Sea.
2. *Nilmat Purana* Vol I, translated by Dr Ved Kumari, 1973, J&K Academy of Art, Culture and Languages.
3. http://en.wikipedia.org/wiki/List_of_highest_mountains
4. Bamzai, Prithivi Nath Kaul. *A History of Kashmir: Political, Social, Cultural, from the Earliest Times to the Present Day*. Delhi: Metropolitan Book Co, 1962.
5. Ptolemy's *Geographia* [Electronic resource] : Books I & II
6. Bamzai, Prithivi Nath Kaul. *A History of Kashmir: Political, Social, Cultural, from the Earliest Times to the Present Day*. Delhi: Metropolitan Book Co, 1962.
7. Hussain Majid, *Geography of Jammu & Kashmir*, Rajesh Publications, New Delhi
8. http://en.wikipedia.org/wiki/Panun_Kashmir https://www.cia.gov/library/publications/the-world-factbook/print/in.html
9. Raina. A.N.: *Geography of Jammu and Kashmir*, National Book Trust, 1981, p.50
10. Lawrence, Walter, *Valley of Kashmir*, London 1895, p.12
11. Ibid
12. Bamzai, Prithivi Nath Kaul. *A History of Kashmir: Political, Social, Cultural, from the Earliest Times to the Present Day*. Delhi: Metropolitan Book Co, 1962.
13. Ibid
14. Indicators of Economic Development, Jammu & Kashmir-1999-2000, Directorate of Economics and Statistics, Planning and Development Department, J&K, Srinagar
15. http://www.ajk.gov.pk/

16. Warikoo K, *The Other Kashmir, Society, Culture and Politics in the Karakoram Himalayas*, Pentagon Press, New Delhi, 2014, p. 307
17. Rana Amir, *The Seeds of Extremism*, New Millennium Publications, London 2005, p. 99 (quoted in 16 above)

HISTORY

There are various versions available for the History of the State of Jammu and Kashmir in general and for the Valley of Kashmir in particular. Since the intention here is not to write history but only to provide a historical perspective for the study, extracts from various versions was considered a suitable option. The authoritative and exhaustive 'History of Kashmir', by PNK Bamzai[1], the Wikipedia History of Kashmir, the chapter on the State's history given in the Planning Commission Report on Jammu and Kashmir[2] and RS Pandit's translation of the *Rajatarangini*[3] have been the main sources. As with the section on Geography, most of the emphasis in this section is laid on the history of the Kashmir Valley, because ultimately, that is the area of the main dispute and needs to be understood better than the other provinces of the state.

Ancient History

Ancient Kashmir is steeped in legend. As per the oldest existing text, the *Nilmat Purana*[4], the Kashmir Valley was once the great lake Satisar, home to a ferocious demon. Responding to the penance of *Rishi* Kashyap, the gods destroyed the demon of the lake. Thereafter, the *Rishi* drained the waters of Satisar through a breach in the mountains at what is now the mouth of the Valley, beyond the northern town of Baramulla. From then on the Kashmir Valley has carried the name of its founder (*Rishi* Kashyap). Whether man actually existed at the time of the draining of the great lake is questionable, however, geological evidence confirms the lacustrine origin of present day Kashmir and to that limited extent also confirms the legend of *Satisar*. Unlike the rest of India, the ancient history of the State is documented in detail in the *Rajatarangini* (The River of Kings) by Kalhan.

The Kashmir Valley has been inhabited continuously for over 5000 years. Sectional diggings at the ancient site of Burzahoma have revealed the existence of neolithic pit dwellings dating back to well before 3000 BCE. The Nilmat Purana mentions that *Rishi* Kashyap had settled people from the South in the Valley. The earliest settlers were thus both from the northern regions of Ladakh and Dardistan and from the plains of India from the South. From the evidence of their appearance and language, it is established that the Kashmiris form a branch of the Aryan race which brought the language of the Indo-Aryan type into India. Dr Grieson, in his *Linguistic Survey of India*[5] has claimed that Kashmiri language has a Dardic base. According to him, speakers of this language belong to the branch of Indo-Aryans who settled in what is called Dardistan (the mountainous tract between the Hindukush Mountains and the frontiers of India proper). The Aryan languages spoken in this region are, therefore, called Dardic. The main languages of the Dardic Group are Kafir, Chitrali, Shina, Kashmiri and Kohistani.

In the *Rajtarangini*, Kalhan begins his narrative with the reign of King Gonanda III, whose reign he definitively dates as 1184 BCE. He also refers to an earlier period spanning 1266 years of which he does not have specific details but mentions the earliest King Gonanda I as being a contemporary of the Pandavas. That would date the reign of the earliest king of Kashmir at around 2450 BCE. These dates may be debatable as it is difficult to separate fact from myth in the absence of corroborating data. However, there is no questioning the fact that the early history of Kashmir dates back to the pre-Aryan era. Kashmir was already well known in the time of the Greeks and also finds mention in Ptolemy's Geography.

In the 3rd Century BCE, the state was incorporated into the Mauryan Empire under Asoka, founder of the city of Srinagar. Buddhism became the principal religion which continued into the times of the Kushanas (1st and 2nd centuries AD). The names of many towns in the Valley were named after several rulers of this dynasty, such as Kanispora after Kanishka, and Hushkora after Huvishka. It was in Kanishka's time that the 3rd Great Buddhist Council was held in Srinagar, formalising the split between the *Hinayana* and *Mahayana* schools of Buddhism. Thereafter Buddhism declined in the Valley though it retained its vibrancy and continues to thrive in Ladakh.

In the 8th century, Kashmir rose to become the centre of a great kingdom, spanning much of North India and parts of Central Asia under Lalitaditya Muktapida, builder of the exquisite Sun Temple at Martand, and founder of the Valley's canal irrigation system which has survived for centuries, helping water rich harvests of the finest rice, a variety of temperate fruit and exotic crops such as saffron.

Gilgit, Ladakh, Kashmir and Jammu have seen rise and fall of several kingdoms. For much of their history these areas existed as principalities.

Medieval History

Though Islam came to India from the 8th Century onwards, the faith came to Kashmir much later through the Sufi saint Bulbul Shah in the early 14th Century. The ruling monarch Rinchen Shah converted to Islam and assumed the name of Sadruddin in 1327 AD. Thereafter, beginning with his former general Shahmir, a series of Muslim dynasties ruled the State. The most notable Kashmiri Muslim ruler of this period was Sultan Zain-ul-Abedin, whose reign is referred to as the Golden era of Kashmiri and who was affectionately known as *Badshah* (or Great King) by his subjects. The other ruler of note of this period was the Last Kashmiri king Yusuf Shah Chak who led the valiant campaign against the Mughal Emperor Akbar and inflicted a couple of humiliating defeats on the invading armies until he was vanquished by the numerically superior Mughal forces.

Kashmir became a part of the Mughal Empire in 1587. The State was fully incorporated into the systems of administration and land settlement which long remained a legacy of that Empire in India, well after its own disintegration. The rule of the Mughals is characterized by masterful architecture, the remnants of which still exist and the world famous gardens of Shalimar, Nishat and Chashm-e-Shahi. A graphic account of the pomp and panoply of the Emperor's cavalcade to Kashmir has been left to us by the French physician Francois Bernier who was in the court of the Emperor Aurangzeb.

The defeat of the Mughal Empire at the hands of the Afghan ruler, Ahmed Shah Abdali, led to the ceding of Kashmir to the Afghan Durranis in 1752 AD. This was a period of unmitigated brutality and widespread distress, which remains cruelly etched in public memory as one of the most terrible in entire history of Kashmir.

In 1780, the kingdom of Jammu was captured by the Sikhs. By 1819 the Kashmir Valley also fell to the conquering Sikh armies of Maharaja Ranjit Singh, bringing to an end four centuries of Muslim rule under the Mughals and the Afghans. Gulab Singh, who distinguished himself in various campaigns, especially the annexation of the Kashmir valley, was crowned Raja of Jammu in 1820 in recognition of his services. With the help of his legendary General, Zorawar Singh, Gulab Singh soon annexed the regions of Ladakh and Baltistan. The Sikhs ruled Kashmir for barely 26 years till their defeat by the British.

In 1845, the First Anglo-Sikh War broke out, and Gulab Singh contrived to hold himself aloof till the battle of Sobraon in 1846, when he appeared as a useful mediator and the trusted advisor of Sir Henry Lawrence. He was rewarded in the Treaty of Kashmir by which the British made over to Gulab Singh for Rupees 75 lakhs all the hilly or mountainous country situated to the east of Indus and west of Ravi, which included the Kashmir Valley. As a result of the treaty, Jammu and Kashmir was founded and unified as a single entity by Maharaja Gulab Singh on 16 March 1846. Soon after Gulab Singh's death in 1857, his son, Ranbir Singh, added Hunza, Gilgit and Nagar to the kingdom.

The Princely State of Jammu and Kashmir was "somewhat artificial in composition and it did not develop a fully coherent identity, partly as a result of its disparate origins and partly as a result of the autocratic rule which it experienced on the fringes of Empire." It combined disparate regions, religions, and ethnicities. The State sided with the British in the war of independence 1857, and with the subsequent assumption of direct rule by Great Britain, the princely state of Kashmir came under the suzerainty of the British Crown. The Dogra dynasty ruled the State under British tutelage till 1947. When the British left India the Maharaja of J&K resisted overtures by Pakistan to accede to them and chose to exist as an independent country.

Modern History

The modern history of Kashmir begins with the reign of Maharaja Hari Singh who was the monarch at a crucial time in Indian history when the freedom struggle had gripped the entire subcontinent. The non-cooperation and salt movements launched by the Congress under leadership of Mahatma Gandhi had its repercussions in the State too. A number of demonstrations took place on a regular basis. Ostensibly, anti-British, these were actually expressions of the people's voice of popular discontent with the rule of the Maharaja and the urge for freedom. Meanwhile, several Muslim young men, fresh from the universities in India, particularly Aligarh, where they had come in contact with Muslim leaders and propagators of pan-Islamism, organized themselves in Srinagar.

1931 was a watershed year in the modern history of Kashmir. Kashmiri nationalism emerged in full force as an expression directed against the Dogra rule. There were two main expressions of the Muslim sentiment; first, the conservative Muslim League led by Mirwaiz Ahmedullah, the chief preacher of Srinagar, succeeded on his death in 1931 by his son Mirwaiz Yusuf Shah and second, the liberals, a bunch of educated and disaffected young Muslims who had organised themselves into the Reading Room Party. The most conspicuous leader of the latter was Sheikh Mohammed Abdullah who was to later gain iconic status as the "Lion of Kashmir".

On 13th July 1931 massive demonstrations erupted all across the valley, especially in Srinagar. 21 people died and many more were injured. The dead bodies were carried in procession all across the city and mayhem ensued. The authorities lost total control over the situation as the mobs went berserk and, in a spontaneous outburst of hatred against the Dogra rule, went on a rampage destroying shops and businesses belonging to Hindus. Three Hindus were killed in the communal violence.

The political developments of 1931 provided an excuse to the British

Indian government to take an active and interfering role in the governance of Jammu and Kashmir. There was a demand for instituting an impartial commission of inquiry which was supported by the British. They now assumed a commanding role and the control of the Administration passed into the hands of the British Indian government. The British were keen to retain active control over Gilgit due to its strategic location, so they exerted pressure on the Maharaja to cede control of that territory. In March 1935, administration and control of the Gilgit *Wazarat* was handed over to the British on a 60 years lease (which explains why the Northern Areas are governed directly from Islamabad and not clubbed with the rest of POK). Having attained that objective, the British relaxed pressure on the Maharaja, giving him complete freedom to deal with the agitation in any way he liked.

The communal discord, which was contrary to the traditions of Kashmir, subsided considerably by the middle of 1932. When, therefore, the Jammu and Kashmir Muslim Conference came into existence in October that year, Sheikh Mohammed Abdullah, its first president, actually voiced the sincere feeling of the masses when in his address he declared that "our country's progress is impossible so long as we do not establish amicable relations between the different communities". Though communal in name, the policy of the Conference from its very inception remained national in essence. But communalism in politics did not vanish overnight. It lingered long enough to give birth to a party of communalists both in Jammu and to a lesser extent in the Kashmir Valley. The Jammu leaders of the Muslim agitation did not bring themselves around to accepting the secular and nationalist leanings of leaders from Kashmir. In Kashmir also the Mirwaiz and his followers openly severed their connection with Sheikh Abdullah and his colleagues. This split was to have wide repercussions on the political field at a subsequent stage.

In 1938-39 the political atmosphere in Kashmir was changing rapidly. In an epoch making development, the working committee of the Muslim Conference met at Srinagar and passed a resolution recommending to the general counsel to allow all people to become its members, "irrespective of their caste to creed or religion". In 1939 the recommendations of the working committee and were accepted by the general counsel and thus the Muslim Conference was converted into the National Conference.

In 1944 the National Conference adopted a program of socialistic pattern of society as its goal. It laid down a plan for "an all sided advance along all avenues of human activity regulated in a democratic manner on a countrywide scale". The plan covered agriculture, industry, transport distribution, utility services, currency and finance. The scheme was based on the "democratic principles of responsible government" and came to be known as the "New Kashmir Plan". During this period the political atmosphere in the rest of India was highly polarized on the issue of the creation of Pakistan. The Muslim League, under the leadership of Mohamed Ali Jinnah, made a number of overtures to the National Conference to support the two nation theory. In a visit to Kashmir he made a statement, "I will request the Muslims to come under the banner of the Muslim conference and fight for their rights". This brought a sharp rejoinder from the National Conference who said that, "The ills of this land can only be remedied by carrying Hindus, Muslims and Sikhs together." Jinnah had to leave Kashmir disappointed that he could not garner the support of the Kashmiri Muslims for the cause of Pakistan.

1947 saw the end of British rule of the subcontinent and the subsequent partition of the British Indian Empire into the newly independent countries of India and Pakistan. Rulers of princely states were encouraged to accede their States to either dominion - India or Pakistan, taking into account factors such as geographical contiguity and the wishes of their people. The Maharaja of Jammu and Kashmir wished to retain his independent status and was not inclined to accede to either country. To postpone making a hurried decision, the Maharaja signed a "Stand Still" agreement with Pakistan, which ensured continuity of trade, travel, communication, and similar services between the two. Such an agreement was pending with India.

In October 1947 Pakistan decided to force the issue and invaded Kashmir by sending regular soldiers supported by Pashtuns recruited from the various tribes of its North-West Frontier Province (known locally as *Kabailis* or tribesmen) with the ostensible aim to coerce the Maharaja into merger with Pakistan. The tribesmen engaged in looting and killing along the way. The Maharaja appealed to the Indian government for assistance, and the Indians agreed to intervene on the condition that the ruler accedes to India. Once the Maharaja signed the Instrument of Accession, the Indian Army entered Kashmir on 27 October 1947 and after a grueling campaign lasting almost 15 months, succeeded in driving out the invaders from all but most of the state. The ceasefire came into effect from 1 January 1949 with Pakistan still in possession of more than a third of the state which, though Muslim in character, was thinly populated, relatively inaccessible, and economically underdeveloped.

India accepted the accession as provisional until such time the will of the people could be ascertained by means of a plebiscite. India invited the

UN to mediate but insisted that no referendum could occur until all of the state had been cleared of all Pakistani troops and irregulars as per the terms of the 1948 UNCIP Resolution.

When the Maharaja and his entire council of ministers left Srinagar on the night of 26 October 1947 in the face of the *Kabaili* invasion, the valley was left without a government and there was an apprehension of widespread disorder and chaos seizing the land. It was at this moment of great crisis that the National Conference stepped in to fill the vacuum. The district and *Mohalla* committees of the conference took over the functions of local administration and organized companies of volunteers to keep the peace and restore confidence among the people. This Emergency Administration rendered all out assistance to the army in its operations. On 5th March 1948 the Emergency Administration was converted into a regular council of ministers with Sheikh Abdullah as the Prime Minister.

Robert Wirsing states: "In an interview with the author in June 1986 in Rawalpindi, a retired Pakistan army officer and then known figure in the politics of Pakistan Occupied Kashmir told the author flatly and with apparent sincerity a few years ago that the Kashmir problem had been precipitated in the first place by the foolishness of Pakistan's leaders, not by the Maharaja and not by India. Claiming to have been posted to Srinagar by Pakistani Military Intelligence in the months immediately following partition, he says that the government of Pakistan authorized a whole string of self defeating activities in Kashmir, including clandestine operations in the valley, the interdiction of crucial supplies, and the deliberate expulsion of Hindu and Sikh refugees from Pakistan across the border into Kashmir, that had "prematurely forced the issue of Kashmir" and led directly to India's successful military intervention. My informant who was a participant in Pakistan's ill fated 1965 efforts to infiltrate a guerilla force into the Kashmir Valley and who says that he remains today a stout supporter of continuing military confrontation with India over Kashmir, argued nevertheless that the government of India would not have interfered militarily in Kashmir had Pakistan not provoked it."[6]

Once the popular government was in place, Sheikh Abdullah commenced to implement the program of social and agrarian reform as envisaged in the 'New Kashmir' Plan. The salient aspects of the plan were as under:

- **Formation of Debt Reconciliation Boards**. The Government declared a moratorium on debts incurred by peasants to relieve them of the crushing burden of debts and constituted Debt

Conciliation Boards for the purpose. It was a radical measure beyond any shadow of doubt, hailed by all sections of the Kashmiri populace. The old accumulated debts, scaled down from 11.1 million to 2.4 million rupees, provided sufficient relief to the peasantry.

- **Land Reforms**. Land reforms were a significant component of a wider socio-economic programme of reconstruction and regeneration. In the blue-print of 'New Kashmir', the land reforms were envisaged as a key to freeing the peasantry from feudalism which was seen as the major obstacle in the march to freedom from exploitation and abject poverty.

The Sheikh's secular credentials were further reinforced when in the aftermath of the murder of six National Conference workers in Jammu he made a stirring appeal to the crowds to maintain communal harmony. On 6th November 1947, in an address to a mob intent on taking revenge for the murder, he convinced them all that violence in Srinagar served no purpose when the crime had been committed in Jammu. This greatly restored the confidence of the minorities and ensured that the Kashmir Valley remained an oasis of peace in the midst of mayhem and the turmoil in rest of the subcontinent.

The reforms initiated by the government raised Sheikh Abdullah to iconic status in Kashmir Province. He came to be known as the undisputed leader of Kashmir with the epithet *Sher-e-Kashmir* or the Lion of Kashmir. The Sheikh had a free hand to conduct the internal administration of the state. But with the loss of revenue due to the invasion and a rapid increase in expenditure to finance the numerous development projects, he was dependent upon grants and subsidies from the Centre. At the same time he had severe differences with the Council of Ministers in New Delhi. As Prime Minister of the State, he considered himself the equal of Prime Minister Nehru and refused to engage with anyone else. He started drifting away from the rest of India. This attitude was responsible for creating a strong opposition to his policies in Jammu and Ladakh, especially in the former where his land reforms were not well received by the ruling class. These developments created a psychological crisis in the mind of Sheikh Abdullah. He had already given out his idea of the Valley of Kashmir remaining an independent and neutral state. In formulating this idea he was encouraged by several foreign individuals. "On top of these reports," writes Korbel,[7] "came the highly inflammatory rumors that the United States was backing the idea of Kashmiri independence and that Sheikh Abdullah had been encouraged in it when Adlai Stevenson visited Srinagar in May 1953".

People in general and the National Conference in particular were astounded at the change in attitude of Sheikh Abdullah towards the position of the State in the Indian Union. The majority of the working committee members headed by Bakshi Ghulam Mohammed were opposed to the attitude adopted by the Sheikh. This question was discussed in a marathon session of the working committee extending to three weeks in May 1953. Sheikh Abdullah failed to convert the members to his point of view and a resolution endorsing the accession to India and supporting the Delhi Agreement (which accorded a special status to the state of Jammu and Kashmir in the Indian constitution) was passed by a majority of 15 against four votes. Matters came to such a pass that the Governor was left with no choice other than to recommend the dismissal of the Prime Minister. Sheikh Abdullah was arrested on 9 August 1953 and Bakshi Ghulam Mohammed succeeded him as the second Prime Minister of the state.

By 1960 the Indian position had undergone a distinct change in that it held that a solution to the problem was not feasible by holding a plebiscite. Mr. Krishna Menon argued in the United Nations that, "Conditions in Kashmir have materially altered since the time when the Security Council was seized of the question. During these 15 years, Kashmir, the part of a state that is free, has made all round progress politically, economically and socially. Land reforms have been implemented, canals dug and a network of roads built.... Refugees have been rehabilitated and development plans are being implemented courageously and with enthusiasm..... The Constituent Assembly of the state based on universal adult suffrage has confirmed the accession of the State to India. To have a plebiscite now would amount to throwing all this progress to the winds by creating uncertainty and chaos which might throw open the floodgates of communal disorder not only in Kashmir but in India and Pakistan.... What the people of the State and the people of the rest of India now demand is the removal of aggression by Pakistan from Indian territory in Kashmir. That the entire state of Jammu and Kashmir was legally and constitutionally a part of India has never been in dispute. But as far as India is concerned, even in order to redress her wrongs, even in order to restore her territories to assert the sovereignty which the Security Council had at no time challenged, and what is more repeated time after time, she will in no case resort to force. But at the same time, if her territory is violated she will use the provisions of the charter to defend what is hers under the law and in terms of the possession."[8]

Meanwhile the eastern region had also been beset with a boundary dispute with China. In the late 19th- and early 20th centuries, although some boundary agreements were signed between Great Britain, Afghanistan and Russia over the northern borders of Kashmir, China never accepted these agreements, and the official Chinese position did not change with the communist revolution in 1949. By the mid-1950s the Chinese army had entered the north-east portion of Ladakh. By 1956–57 they had completed a military road through the Aksai Chin area to provide better communication between Xinjiang and western Tibet. India's belated discovery of this road led to border clashes between the two countries that culminated in the Sino-Indian war of October 1962. China has occupied Aksai Chin since 1962 and, in addition, an adjoining region, the Trans-Karakoram Tract (Shaksgam Sector) measuring 5180 sq km was illegally ceded by Pakistan to China in 1963.

India and Pakistan went to war again in 1965 consequent to Pakistan's two-pronged strategy of launching attacks all along the LOC and to insert infiltrators comprising regular soldiers disguised as civilians with the aim of instigating a mass uprising against "Indian rule". The attempt to incite an insurrection was a failure as the presence of foreign infiltrators was reported by the locals at once and the Indian Army swiftly swung into action. The offensive was blunted by the Indian Army and a cease-fire was agreed upon. The two countries signed an agreement at Tashkent (Uzbekistan) in 1966, pledging to end the dispute by peaceful means.

In 1971, the two nations again went to war that resulted in the creation of Bangladesh. The Simla accord was signed in 1972 between the two Prime Ministers - Indira Gandhi and Zulfiqar Ali Bhutto. A decade of peace followed. However, neither the Government of India nor the State government could convert this advantage into visible progress on ground. Successive state governments failed to live up to their election promises. Rampart corruption and nepotism was the order of the day. While the ruling class grew visibly prosperous, the same prosperity was not transferred to the common man. The blame for the dissatisfaction with the ruling elite was conveniently laid upon the doors of New Delhi, as usual.

Fed up with the shenanigans of the ruling class, whose popularity was at an all time low, the people began to look for alternatives. At this time considerable funds were being pumped into the valley from prosperous Middle Eastern countries. These funds were meant for promotion of Islamic studies and charity. A portion of these funds was diverted to finance an insurgency by those who saw an opportunity to establish an 'Independent Islamic Republic of Jammu and Kashmir' by force of arms. Following the disputed elections in 1987, young disaffected Kashmiris in the Valley were recruited for the 'cause' and sent across the LC for training in camps established in POK. The insurgency in the Kashmir Valley increased in momentum from this point on. The year 1989 saw the intensification of conflict in Jammu and Kashmir as *Mujahedeen* from Afghanistan and other Islamic countries infiltrated the region following the end of the Soviet-Afghan War the same year. Pakistan provided arms and training to both indigenous and foreign militants in Kashmir, thus adding fuel to the smoldering fire of discontent in the valley.

India responded strongly to the challenge to its integrity and has since then maintained a sizeable military presence in Jammu & Kashmir to combat the insurgency and to prevent trans-LC movement. Pakistan has always denied the charge of aiding and abetting the terrorists, calling it an indigenous "freedom struggle."

In 1999, Pakistan attempted a 'Siachen' on India. Soldiers of the Pakistani Northern Light Infantry along with some irregulars occupied the hitherto un-held Kargil Heights which overlook the Srinagar-Leh highway. India responded strongly and intense fighting ensued. The fighting lasted for more than two months. The battle ended with India reclaiming all the area that had been occupied by the infiltrators.

In 2001, Pakistan-backed terrorists launched violent attacks on the Kashmir Assembly and the Indian Parliament in New Delhi culminating in Op Parakram when India and Pakistan almost went to war again. By mid of the first decade of the new millennium, the insurgency was brought down to manageable levels and free and fair elections were conducted and local administration restored. The period of violence is over and the period of peace and reconciliation has begun. That is not to say that there is no violence or that the insurgency has been completely extinguished. The key words here are 'manageable levels'. If the state administration and police function efficiently, peace and stability can easily be maintained and the confidence of the public restored. Sporadic incidents of violence will continue and occasional serious confrontations with law and order such as the stone throwing incidents of 2010 will pose challenges to the Administration. What will really determine the destiny of the State, will be the manner in which the political and administrative class functions in the days to come. If the former continues with its short sighted and destructive policies and the latter with its corrupt and dyslectic manner of functioning, then another cycle of violence is bound to ensue.

NOTES

1. Bamzai, Prithivi Nath Kaul. *A History of Kashmir: Political, Social, Cultural, from the Earliest Times to the Present Day*. Delhi: Metropolitan Book Co, 1962.
2. Planning Commission Report on Jammu and Kashmir.
3. RS Pandit's translation of Kalhana's *Rajatarangini* published by Sahitya Akademi, New Delhi.
4. *Nilmat Purana* Vol I, translated by Dr Ved Kumari, 1973, J&K Academy of Art, Culture and Languages.
5. George A. Grierson, "*Linguistic Survey of India*".
6. Wirsing, Robert G, "*India, Pakistan, and the Kashmir Dispute: On Regional Conflict and its Resolution*", MacMillan, 1996
7. Korbel Joseph, "*Danger In Kashmir*", Princeton, 1954
8. Text of Krishna Menon's speech at the United Nations Security Council (www.jammukashmirnow.com/.../VK-Menon-Speech-in-Security-Council)

RELIGION AND CIVIL SOCIETY IN THE KASHMIR VALLEY

"Kashmiris are, by nature, a peace loving people. They can be an example for Muslims all over the world."

—Senior Professor, Kashmir University

Religion

Kashmir did not remain an isolated island insofar as philosophy and spirituality are concerned. India as a whole from the early Vedic time onwards has had a galaxy of philosophers, sages, poets and thinkers who contributed to the country's distinction as a leader in world thought. Kashmiris as part of the Indian subcontinent have made notable contribution to the uniqueness of its cultural heritage. Like the rest of India, the state of Jammu and Kashmir is a cauldron of many religions and sects though the Kashmir Province is overwhelmingly Muslim. But the form of Islam practiced in the Valley differs from the rest of the subcontinent.

Walter Lawrence's magnum opus, The Valley of Kashmir gives the reader a fair idea of how the religion was practiced more than a century ago as seen through the eyes of a neutral observer. In 1889, Walter Roger Lawrence came to Kashmir as the British Settlement Commissioner for land and apparently did a commendable job as per PNK Bamzai.[1] He toured the length and breadth of the province extensively for over six years and recorded his impressions of life and the people so accurately that even after a span of over 120 years no one has ever accused him of bias or untruth. In his narrative, Lawrence acknowledges the centrality that religion occupies in the life of the ordinary Kashmiri Muslim. Every faith had a place under the canopy. From his observations, it can be surmised that at the turn of the last century the typical Kashmiri was a mystic at heart[2]. It is obvious from the description that the nature of the Islamic religion as practiced in those days has not varied much till the present day, though there is a concerted effort by some members of the clergy to give up some supposedly un-Islamic practices like the worship of relics. This is being equally stoutly resisted by the traditionalists who do not want to lose the uniqueness of their Kashmiri culture.

The *Sufi* Tradition

All Muslims have not felt obliged to distance themselves totally from their previous beliefs and practices even after conversion to Islam; at least to the extent they did not contravene their new Islamic beliefs. Indian Islam, therefore, naturally has its own indigenous flavor. And this finds its best expression in the *Sufi* way of life in the Kashmir valley.[3]

Kashmiri Islam is renowned for its broadmindedness and its deep commitment to tolerance of all streams of thought. The selective killing of Hindus and Sikhs in the state is a new phenomenon, utterly repugnant to this ethos. Kashmir's Muslims had faced the gravest challenge to their secular ethos following Partition. It was no mean thing for them to hear horrendous stories of Hindu-Muslim communal carnage and yet, unlike even their brethren in Mirpur and Poonch not to speak of other parts of the sub-continent, remain utterly unaffected. Instead of giving in to the communal virus, they had welcomed Indian troops to help them in their fight against Pakistani tribal raiders.

Where from does this deep commitment to secularism, to a composite Hindu-Muslim culture emanate? What is the source of this deep connection with India despite the militant separatism of the past decade? Why is *Kashmiriyat* so important to the Kashmiri Muslim? I think the answer lies in the eclectic and syncretic nature of their spiritual beliefs. It is the impact of *Sufi* and *Rishi* visions of Islam that have helped him synthesise the message of Prophet Mohammad with the teachings of earlier prophets of Islam that constitute the core beliefs of Hinduism, Buddhism and Jainism. The most important influence on the Kashmiri Muslims, in terms of their *Kashmiriyat*, is that of the *Rishi* order of *Sufis*. While the *Sufi* orders like the Suhrawardi, Kubravi, Naqshbandi and Qadri, arrived in Kashmir from Persia, Central Asia, and Central and North India, the *Rishi* order evolved in the Valley itself in the beginning of the 15th century.

The Kashmir valley was already permeated with the traditions of Hindu asceticism and Buddhist renunciation. As Prof. Abdul Qaiyum Rafiqi explains in his book Sufism in Kashmir, the term *Rishi* itself is clearly a derivation from Sanskrit traditions. Important chroniclers of this period, Abul Fazal, for instance, or Emperor Jahangir, reveal a close resemblance between the life-styles of the Sufis and the Hindu *Rishi*s as well as Buddhist and Jain monks. Jahangir writes: "... They neither eat meat nor marry. They always plant fruit-bearing trees in uninhabited parts, so that they may benefit people. But they themselves do not hope to reap any advantages from these trees." Baba Dawood Khaki and Baba Naseeb, too give a similar account. With such deep commitment to spiritual growth and the Islamic philosophy of Divine Unity as expressed in both streams of *Wahdat-ul-Wojood* and *Wahdat-ul-Shohood*, which is uniquely similar to the Hindu philosophy of non-duality (*Advaita*), it is not at all surprising that the *Rishis* consistently preached complete harmony among different religions and peace and understanding among their followers. This was not always easy. One of the foremost *Rishis*, Sheikh Nooruddin, also known as Nund *Rishi*, faced restrictions during the reign of Suha Bhatt who had started persecuting non-Muslims in his new-found Islamic zeal after conversion to the new faith. Aware of the tension created between Hindus and Muslims during the reign of Sultan Sikandar, Sheikh Nooruddin wrote: "We belong to the same parents. Then why this difference? Let Hindus and Muslims (together) worship God alone. We came to this world like partners. We should have shared our joys and sorrows together".

All through this period the religious activity of the Shaivites and Sufis continued to flourish, and fed the vibrant stream of Kashmiri culture. Lal Ded, Kashmir's great poetesses was also among her foremost Shaivite ascetics and mentor to one of Kashmir's greatest *Sufi* saints, Sheikh Nooruddin, whose school of Sufism is called 'Rishi' and who is revered by Hindus as Nand Rishi.

Sufi thought has also been an essential ingredient of *"Kashmiriyat"*, which is a concept or a tradition that has been put forward to form the basis for a distinct Kashmiri identity – cultural and national[16]. How far people outside the Valley (Jammu and Ladakh) relate to *Kashmiriyat* in order to acquire their sense of identity is overlooked in the discourse on Kashmiri identity.

The Evolution of the Kashmiri Psyche

In this section we shall examine the impact that the geography of the state of Jammu and Kashmir has had on the psychology of its denizens. It is commonly said that man is a product of his environment. The characteristics of a people are largely shaped by its history. In the case of Jammu and Kashmir the geography of the state has had an equally important role in shaping its history.

For the purpose of this treatise, we shall restrict ourselves to the Kashmiri people who are at the heart of the present problem facing the State, in particular, the Kashmiri who is the denizen of the valley of Kashmir, speaks the Kashmiri language and professes the Sunni Muslim faith. There are also other residents in Kashmir Province, but they are numerically insignificant and by themselves not directly capable of influencing the Kashmir problem or its outcome. In the next few paragraphs, we shall attempt to trace the historical reasons how the simple, god fearing and gentle Kashmiri Muslim transformed into a vengeful and bloodthirsty terrorist.

Since the earliest recorded times the Kashmiri army was renowned for its fighting qualities. Attack after attack over centuries was repulsed by a combination of hostile terrain and an equally hostile and determined defender. Kalhana, the first great historian of Kashmir, adds another dimension to the concept: The country may be conquered by the force of spiritual merit, but not by the force of soldiers. The inhabitants are afraid only of the world beyond.[4]

That is not to say that the Valley had never been overrun by outsiders. But that was invariably as a result of internecine strife and not a military defeat. Kings like Rinchen in the 13th century literally walked into Srinagar and collected the crown like a cherry ripe for the picking, because the nobles were busy fighting each other. Till the end of the 16th Century the Kashmiris were a proud warlike nation always ready to defend the nation against external aggression. Whether Hindu or Muslim, the army was Kashmiri in composition and always gave a good account of its fighting prowess. This was to change after the Mughals under Emperor Akbar overran Kashmir. The Kashmiri army under King Yousuf Shah Chak repulsed a vastly numerically superior Mughal army a number of times. Ultimately the Mughals succeeded in defeating Yousuf Chak, who was taken prisoner and imprisoned in Patna where he breathed his last in 1592. In 1589, Kashmir became a province of the Mughal empire.[5]

The Chak dynasty was the last of the Kashmiri rulers who were the sons of the soil. With their downfall, Kashmir was ruled in succession by the Mughals, the Afghans, the Sikhs and the Dogras. During this period the Kashmiri Muslim was steadily reduced to a state of insignificance both in terms of wealth and status. He was discouraged from bearing arms or holding high office despite the majority community in overwhelming numbers. In a very uncharitable description of the Kashmiris, Edward Frederick Knight has mentioned in his narrative, *Where 3 Empires Meet* that it was an edict of Emperor Akbar that "compelled men of this race to wear a *pheran* with the avowed intention of destroying whatever manliness they may have had and turning them into women."[6] This may or may not be true, but the fact is that the stock of the Kashmiri touched rock bottom during this period as did his self confidence and self esteem. He was exploited and abused. He was given the tag of a coward and over the centuries he also began to believe it. Contrast the difference in perception of the same stock of people in the earliest description of the all-conquering Kashmiri soldier of the army of Lalitaditya or the proud soldier who repulsed Mahmud of Ghazni (in the words of Nehru: this mountain country succeeded in checking and repulsing him[7]) with Sir Walter

Lawrence's description of the same person as timid and effeminate, "The Kashmiri is made up of contradictions. He is timid yet persistent, degraded yet intellectual....Pages might be written by me on facts which have come under my personal observation, but it will suffice to say that the system of administration has degraded the people and taken all heart out of them".[8] What an anticlimax; the ego of a once proud community ground into the dust by a succession of outside rule! (A parallel can be drawn from the Indian subcontinent. The present day resident of Patna must be a far cry from the citizen of Pataliputra at the height of Chandragupt Maurya's reign.) It was not until the middle of the 20th century, when India gained independence and a popular government under Sheikh Abdullah was voted to power, that the Kashmiri Muslim was master of his destiny once again

The modern history of Kashmir is very well documented and the events of 1953 are too well known to bear repetition. Sheikh Abdullah's insistence on autonomy and a special status for the state and his subsequent arrest reaffirmed the fear in the minds of the people that they had just replaced one ruler for another. This led to a resurgence of Kashmiri nationalism. However, to be fair to the Sheikh and his followers, theirs was never intended to be a violent protest, and though it may have harped on anti-India rhetoric, it was most definitely not a religion-centric movement. The main plank was self-determination and was equidistant from India and Pakistan. The armed insurrection was a much later development. It was planned, abetted, financed, given a communal colour and controlled from across the border, when the Pakistani military establishment realized that the situation on the Indian side of Jammu and Kashmir had deteriorated, due to decades of neglect and poor governance, to such an extent that they felt confident of sponsoring what they thought would be a successful insurgency aimed at separating Kashmir from India.

The initial years of insurgency witnessed a kind of euphoria in the minds of the common man. Pacifist by nature and unfamiliar with the use of weapons of any kind, he was amazed and elated to see his compatriots take to arms and challenge the might of the Indian war machinery. Just the thought that he could face the Indian Army on equal terms gave him a sense of pride and washed away the humiliation of centuries of subjugation.

This euphoria, however, did not last beyond a couple of years. The common citizen was not prepared for the violence, bloodshed, cruelty, reprisals and injustice that invariably accompany an insurgency. So far he had been content to lay the blame at the door of the Indian establishment and their so-called puppets in power in Srinagar, who he felt were responsible for all his problems. He had expected, as did the leaders of the movement, a change in government and possibly independence by the end of that year. He was dismayed by the prolonged struggle and the unending misery of curfew, restriction of civil liberties, constant disruption of his daily life, the humiliation and helplessness that he underwent when his house was subjected to search by the security forces or when he was forced at gunpoint to host a bunch of terrorists in hiding, succumb to their will by contributing a son to the "cause" or a daughter for the physical comforts and pleasure of the terrorists. He was especially aghast at the presence of a large number of marauding foreigners who were obviously calling the shots in the insurgency while the local terrorist was reduced to the status of guide, translator and sidekick.

From that point on, all the common Kashmiri yearns for is peace, tranquility, an environment conducive for the conduct of business and above all a chance to live his normal life without the lurking shadow of the terrorist and the oppressive presence of men in uniform. He is definitely not enamored by the idea of an Islamic Republic where strict implementation of Wahabi Islam would be the norm. He is also keeping a close watch on the happenings in Pakistan and is neither impressed nor amused by the antics of the ruling class and the clerics over there. Pakistan, for him, is no more the model of the modern Islamic State.

Kashmiriyat

The medieval concept of nationality based on religious belief has always been foreign to the Kashmiri. The long tradition of religious tolerance has created in him a secular outlook on human relations, which has time and again asserted itself during the course of his long history.

True, there were moments when attempts were made by interested parties to arouse communal passions-in 1923 for example when there were a few skirmishes in some parts of the state and in 1931 when the freedom struggle against the Dogra rule started – but soon the people regained their balance and kept to the path of communal amity and religious tolerance. By 1947 the politically conscious people of Kashmir had gained enough maturity to resist the snares of communal hatred as preached by the leaders of the Muslim league. The partition gave them a severe shock, but they were not directly affected by it.[9]

Nyla Ali Khan has mentioned that the Kashmiri Muslim occupies the space between Vedic Hinduism and *Sufi* Islam.[10] *Sufi* thought has been an essential ingredient of "*Kashmiriyat*", which is a concept or a tradition that has been put forward to form the basis for a distinct Kashmiri identity – cultural and national. How far people outside the Valley (Jammu and Ladakh) relate to *Kashmiriyat* in order to acquire their sense of identity is overlooked in the discourse on Kashmiri identity.[11]

The Erosion of *Kashmiriyat*

If, on the one hand, violence becomes a means to a political end and a religious calling, it also hits back and erodes what it is trying to save. Violence has never been a part of *Kashmiriyat*. Yet, it becomes a means to define it, and in the process negates the very idea of *Kashmiriyat*. It affects the people it intends to save from the outsider.... "But Kashmiris by nature are not violent", is asserted by every Kashmiri, be it a politician, an intellectual or a Kashmiri on the street....Yasin Malik maintains that *Kashmiriyat* is a spiritual institution but politics has ruined it. And political violence is steadily decreasing any chance of its resurrection.[12]

The Pandits were neither Kashmiri in Kashmir nor Indians in Jammu as far as the national identity was concerned. Secularism, a feature of both Indian nationalism and *Kashmiriyat*, was wind-swept. According to the Jamaat's ideology, the concept of nation or nationalism is antithetical to Islam. The contours had changed. "With nightfall, the minarets resounded with new slogans. 'Pandits must leave. Freedom is ours! The land must be purified!'"[13]

Regaining *Kashmiriyat*

In January 2003, a group of Muslim women from Kashmir visited Jammu and interacted with the Kashmiri Hindu women residents of refugee camps. Syeda Saiyidain Hameed has narrated the account of an exchange which took place between the ladies as they narrated their respective tales of misery and hardships:

> "Naturally, the Hindu women blamed the Muslims for their plight as they could have prevented the exodus of the Hindus if they had chosen to. A lady who was a distinguished educator and the principal of a women's college had this to say, *"Ham dekhte hi rah gaye aur aap yahan aa gaye* (We just watched helplessly as you moved here)," I told the Pandit women. "Do you know what you have done to us? You have taken away the season of spring from Kashmir. Our flowers and trees are desolate; our lakes have lost their luster. We miss you everywhere. Our festivals are incomplete; our songs have lost their lilt. My Pandit teacher - who was closer to me than my own father - could I ever imagine a life without him? We are nothing

without you - you complete our existence; and without us, your existence is incomplete." There were not too many dry eyes in the room. Today, as I write these lines, my eyes too are tear-soaked. What I saw in Jammu last month was a self-healing process. I saw the birth of hope. These women - with or without us - may be able to build the bridges and regain their lost *Kashmiriyat*. Perhaps, once again, Kashmir will show the way to the rest of us who are floundering in this miasma - just as it showed the way to Mahatma Gandhi 55 years ago".[15]

Change in the Muslim Thought Process

In the last few years there has been a gradual but perceptible change in the way the average Kashmiri Muslim has started perceiving the Kashmir problem and its possible resolution.

Hurriyat leader Prof Abdul Gani Bhat caused a major controversy in May 2012 by his statements that UN resolutions on Kashmir were "impracticable" and that separatists should "join hands with mainstream political parties on a common minimum political agenda". Bhat angered the separatist groups including leaders from his own faction of *Hurriyat* as he said that UN resolutions on Kashmir were not practically implementable in the present geo-political scenario.

In an article titled *Three Congenital Ailments of Hurriyat*, Niloofar Qureshi questions why separatists are adamant in clinging on to UN resolutions that have failed to deliver even after more than six decades? She says, "United Nations Security Council Resolution 47, calling for a plebiscite in J&K was passed by United Nations Security Council under chapter VI of UN charter, which unfortunately is 'non binding' and has 'no mandatory enforceability'. So, armed with a resolution without any 'teeth', doesn't the *Hurriyat*'s decision to repose consummate faith in the UN amount to nothing more than just 'great expectations'? And in light of this, is the observation of Prof Abdul Gani Bhat that the UN resolutions are no more "relevant" as these have now become "impracticable" and "obsolete "really unfounded?

"Why is *Hurriyat* so adamant in clinging on to UN resolutions which have failed to deliver even after more than six decades? Why our leaders expect us to believe that the recent statement of the UN Secretary General Ban Ki-Moon asking New Delhi to resolve Kashmir problem is a 'victory' for the people of Kashmir and not just 'lip service' by the UN, which people have got sick of listening to right since 1948? Why is the *Hurriyat* conveniently brushing the 'fine print' of this resolution (which renders its implementation virtually impossible) under the carpet? And what is compelling the *Hurriyat* to indulge in self deception by castigating Bhat for stating the obvious?

"The 'impracticality' of implementing the UN resolution is not limited merely to its inherent lack of 'mandatory enforceability'. *Hurriyat* has never cared to enlighten us on how does it believe that Pakistan will agree to fulfill the first UN stipulated pre-condition before plebiscite takes place-that of withdrawing its troops from those areas of J&K presently under its control and allowing India to send in its army there to "keep civil order". Further, we have not been told of what will be the status of non-Kashmiris who have been allowed to settle in Pakistan administered Kashmir in terms of voting rights for the plebiscite and how will this complex issue be resolved?"[16]

Qureshi is of the opinion that the *Hurriyat* leaders must realize that the old days have gone by and the present generation, being more discerning, can no longer be swayed by emotions and sentiments alone. She has identified what she calls the three congenital ailments that afflict the *Hurriyat* amalgam. These are:

- The existence of deep ideological fissures within the conglomerate.
- Its blatant intolerance towards considering new alternatives.
- Its inexplicable refusal to accept ground realities.

The Kashmiri Hindu Factor

Possibly the single biggest blunder of the *Azaadi* movement was the targeting, hounding out and the consequent alienation of the Kashmiri Pandit (or Hindu) community. This was the primary reason that the demand for independence has lost its legitimacy. The two nation theory was founded on the assumption that the interests of the minority community would be ignored in a Hindu majority India and therefore the creation of Pakistan was justified. Subsequent historical events proved that this theory was flawed when Bangladesh was created. The case of Jammu and Kashmir is unique, in that, it is the only Muslim-majority State in the Union of India. Those of the view that the interests of the Muslims of Jammu and Kashmir were neglected in a Hindu majority India are now faced with the uncomfortable truth that the interests of minorities would be even more so compromised in an independent Jammu and Kashmir.

It is the ultimate irony that Article 370 which guarantees a special status to the State of Jammu and Kashmir and the proposal for an independent Jammu and Kashmir were both the brain children of the Kashmiri Pundits, and yet they were the one community to lose home and hearth in the struggle for these very same entities. The brains trust behind the independence movement did not take into account the importance of this community, not in terms of numbers but in terms of the sheer clout wielded by it. This is the community which has given independent India two prime ministers (three, if one were to include Rajiv Gandhi), many governors, chief justices of the highest courts, a chief of army staff, a chief of the air force and scores of doyens and luminaries who have occupied the highest rungs of civil administration and have been the pillars of society in every possible sphere.

This community has always been politically inclined and has always considered itself to be an indispensable part of the political milieu of the state right from the earliest times. They always considered themselves Kashmiris first and any other denomination later. Right from the times of the *Rajatarangini*, the Kashmiri Pundit always saw himself as king-maker rather than king. In fact, throughout the various dynasties which have ruled Kashmir, his presence as a courtier and advisor to the ruler has been a constant. Only once in history has a ruler tried to dispense with the services of his Hindu advisers and administrators. That was in the time of Sultan Sikandar, when a merciless pogrom was unleashed against the Hindus and those who did not convert to Islam had to flee for their lives. In the absence of able governance, the kingdom degenerated into chaos and a successor of Sultan Sikandar, Sultan Zain-ul-Abedin, on realizing the reason for the pathetic state of affairs, was constrained to invite all the Hindus who chose to return, to their former positions of prominence.

Santayana said, "Those who neglect the lessons of history are condemned to repeat it." Similar has been the case of the exodus of the Kashmiri Hindus. Had they been handled with sensitivity and accorded due importance in the scheme of the independence struggle, there is every possibility that there might have emerged a sizeable section of population within the Kashmiri Hindus in favour of an independent Jammu and Kashmir, according the required legitimacy to a popular cause. This is not such a far-fetched scenario as it may appear, because in the ultimate analysis, the ordinary citizen, whether Muslim or Hindu is looking for peace, tranquillity and a good quality of life. There are thousands of Kashmiris who have settled in Europe and North America and have taken on citizenship of their adopted country. They have done so, not because they are traitors to the land of their birth, but for better prospects for themselves and especially so for the generations to follow. With a realistic promise of similar living conditions and prospects of growth in their own land, why would they not have supported the cause of an independent State?

Kashmiri society has always stood on two pillars – the Kashmiri Muslim and the Kashmiri Hindu. The latter can certainly not survive without the former, but once before in history, some segments of the former mistakenly thought that the Kashmiri Hindus were irrelevant and could be dispensed with. History proved them wrong and years later Sultan Zain-ul-Abedin was constrained to send a delegation to fetch the Kashmiri Hindus back to save the Valley from anarchy. History repeated itself in 1989 and the majority of the Kashmiri Hindus are homeless once again. But that does not mean it is the end of *Kashmiriyat*. With enlightened and resolute leadership and some practical and innovative steps, a mutually acceptable compromise can be worked out that will restore the harmonious relationship which was the hallmark of the two communities in Kashmir.

NOTES

1. PNK Bamzai in his book *History of Kashmir,* (1962) writes that "His land settlement in the State marks a turning point in the economic and social history of its people". p. 44.
2. Lawrence, Walter, *The Valley of Kashmir*, p. 286.
3. Manisha Gangahar, *Decoding Violence in Kashmir* (Economic and Political Weekly Vol XLVIII No. 04, January 26, 2013).
4. Ibid.
5. Akbar MJ, *Kashmir behind the Vale,* Roli Publications, New Delhi, 2003.
6. Prithivi Nath Kaul Bamzai, *History of Kashmir* (1962) p. 671.
7. Knight, Frederick Edward, *Where 3 Empires Meet,* Nabu Press, 1895.
8. Nehru, *The Discovery of India*, Oxford University Press, 2002 Edition, p. 235.
9. Lawrence, Walter, *The Valley of Kashmir*, p. 286
10. Prithivi Nath Kaul Bamzai *History of Kashmir* (1962) p. 671.
11. Khan, Nyla Ali, *Islam, Women and Violence in Kashmir : Between India and Pakistan*, Tulika Books, New Delhi, 2009, p. 40.
12. In the author's inter-action with a lady professor in Srinagar, who prefers not to be quoted, *Kashmiriyat* is now a dirty word for the hardliners. *Kashmiriyat* is today taken as a sign of weakness. They claim that *Kashmiriyat* is being forced upon them by "Hindu India" to dilute the identity of Kashmiri people of Islamic origin. They wish to disassociate themselves with the ancient and medieval history of Kashmir. As per them, the history of Kashmir begins with Shah-i-Hamdan.
13. Manisha Gangahar, *Decoding Violence in Kashmir [Economic and Political Weekly,* Vol. XLVIII No. 04, January 26, 2013]
14. Ibid.
15. Syeda Saiyidain Hameed, *On regaining Kashmiriyat,* Tribune, Chandigarh, March 2, 2003
16. Niloofar Qureshi, *Three Congenital Ailments of Hurriyat* 08 Jun 2012 (Rising Kashmir).

3

Stake Holders

"The fact of the matter is that India wields a terribly disproportionate share of power in the South Asian region and, when it comes to settlement in Kashmir, cannot be treated as an equal of Pakistan, much less of Kashmir."

—Robert Wirsing

It is necessary, at this stage, to identify the stakeholders in the present impasse and to further identify their aspirations so that common points of interest and points of conflict may be ascertained. The legality of the stands of the two main antagonists in the conflict is also studied briefly. The main stakeholders in the conflict are:

- Citizens of the undivided state of Jammu and Kashmir
- India
- Pakistan
- China (to the extent that it is in illegal occupation of territory)
- The security forces
- The terrorist groups

Position of Stake Holders

Indian Position on Kashmir[1]. If indeed, the desire of the world community is to ensure peace and stability and to permit the people of Jammu and Kashmir the right to determine their own destiny in an atmosphere of freedom, this can only be achieved under the democratic framework of modern India and not under the kind of extremist, obscurantist polity that the ideology of the terrorist and mercenary groups seeks to impose on the people of the State. Accordingly, the Indian position, in the face of Pakistan's propaganda over the years has remained consistent.

- The accession of the State of Jammu and Kashmir took place as per the provisions of the India Independence Act and is final and legal and cannot be disputed. The States that acceded to Pakistan did so in the same manner and the Ruler's decision was accepted. Pakistan made no attempt to ascertain the will of the people of these states. If there is any "unfinished" business of partition it is the requirement that Pakistan relinquish control of that part of Jammu and Kashmir that it illegally occupies.
- The UN Resolutions calling for the will of the people to be ascertained are no longer tenable because Pakistan has not fulfilled the precondition of withdrawal from the territory it occupied through aggression. This resulted in a long delay in the implementation of the Security Council Resolutions and led Mr. Gunnar Jarring, the Representative of Sweden on the UN Security Council and the President of the Council, who had been requested by the Council to explore options of arriving at a solution through discussions with India and Pakistan, to observe in his 1957 report to the President of the Security Council that "... The Council will, furthermore, be aware of the fact that the implementation of international agreements of an ad hoc character, which has not been achieved fairly speedily, may become progressively more difficult because the situation with which they were to cope has tended to change ..." In the meantime, the will of the people of J&K has been repeatedly determined through elections in India.
- After Pakistan's attempts to alter the *status quo* by force of war in 1965 it has forfeited the right to invoke the UN Resolutions. The fact that the Council stopped recalling the resolutions of 1948 and 1949 underscored the irrelevance of those resolutions with the passage of time.
- The will of the people does not need to be ascertained only through a plebiscite. Democratic elections are a recognised means of ascertaining the wishes of the people and the people of the State of Jammu and Kashmir have repeatedly participated in such elections. The same cannot be said of the parts under the occupation of Pakistan where, in the Northern Areas, adult franchise has still not been granted.
- Kashmir is not an Islamic or a religious issue and the two nation theory has been seen to be irrelevant. A sizable Muslim community chose to live in India at the time of partition rather than move to Pakistan. The most prominent Kashmiri political party, the National Conference, headed by a popular Muslim leader, Sheikh Abdullah sought and endorsed the accession of Jammu and Kashmir to India.

The emergence of Bangladesh as an independent nation proved conclusively, if further proof were needed, that the notion that all Muslims of the sub-continent would wish to be a part of Pakistan, which is the basis of Pakistan's claim to Jammu and Kashmir, was a fallacy.

- The extremist structure that Pakistan wishes to impose on Kashmir is alien to the Kashmiri ethos which has been one of tolerance and coexistence with its origins in the Sufi expression of Islam that is Kashmir's heritage.
- The problem of Kashmir today is one of terrorism sponsored by Pakistan. The targets are Muslims in Kashmir, belying Pakistan's argument that it is concerned about the welfare of Muslims in Kashmir. The international community must impress upon Pakistan to desist from such terrorism so that the democratic political process, which India has restored to the state, is not held hostage by terrorists who, even now, continue to target political leaders, the majority of whom are Muslims.
- The internal situation of Jammu and Kashmir is, by the will of its people, strictly India's affair and there is no call for any international intervention.
- India wants to resolve all outstanding issues with Pakistan and has started a dialogue for this purpose. However the integrity and sovereignty of India cannot be a matter for discussion. India is committed to protecting the human rights of all its citizens and for this purpose militancy must be eradicated.
- Every State has the duty to protect the life and property of its citizens and cannot countenance their security being threatened by armed terrorists. Any discussion of the question of human rights must take into account the environment in which the state authorities have to function. Jammu and Kashmir has been a target of Pakistan sponsored terrorism for years and this aspect is fundamental to any discussion of human rights. The Indian Government has sought to maintain transparency in the state. International and Indian media personnel, foreign diplomats, the International Committee or the Red Cross, all have free access to Jammu and Kashmir. The National Human Rights Commission of India and the Jammu and Kashmir State Human Rights Commission are performing a stellar role in taking cognizance of, and enquiring into, allegations of human rights violations. The NHRC has undertaken, at its own discretion, investigations into incidents where human rights were reported to have been violated and where these have been substantiated, it has called for punitive action.

Pakistani Position on Kashmir[2]. The official Pakistani Position on Kashmir as explained in the Pakistan Embassy website is as follows:

- Kashmir is a disputed territory. Accession of Jammu and Kashmir to India is disputed because Maharaja Hari Singh acceded to India under duress without consulting the wishes of the people. Kashmir is a case of unfinished partition. The promised plebiscite was never held by India.
- Kashmir is the jugular vein of Pakistan. Kashmir is the core political dispute between India and Pakistan and it runs in our blood.
- Pakistan is only providing moral and diplomatic support for the freedom struggle in Kashmir. The *Mujahedeen* who fight for their suffering Muslim brethren in Kashmir may cross the LoC, we cannot guarantee an end to all infiltration.
- Implementation of UN resolutions. The solution to the dispute requires a unitary plebiscite for the whole of Jammu and Kashmir under international auspices. UN resolutions call for the holding of a plebiscite to determine the wishes of the Kashmiri people.

Chatham House Study Report[3]

Detractors of India, notably Pakistan and some Islamic countries, spare no effort to spread the canard that the Kashmiri population is compelled by force of arms to stay within the Union of India. As per them, given a choice Kashmiris would opt for Pakistan or for Independence. As proof, they cite India's refusal to abide by the provisions of the 1948 UN resolution to ascertain the will of the public by means of a plebiscite.

For long, Western scholars also believed that the Kashmiri population have been held hostage in India against their will. In the absence of a neutral fact-finding body with access to data on both sides of the Line of Control, it was difficult to establish the truth. India has always resisted third party intervention, on the grounds that it is a bilateral matter between India and Pakistan and that there is no need for any arbitration. Pakistan on the other hand, despite according it the euphemism of '*Azad* Jammu and Kashmir' has never allowed proper democracy to grow roots in Pakistan occupied Kashmir. Local self government has been all but non-existent and all major decisions are taken in Islamabad.

To get the factual position as existing on both sides of the Line of Control, an opinion poll was commissioned in May 2009 at the Chatham House by Dr Saif al Islam al Qadhafi (son of the Libyan dictator). Chatham House is the home of the Royal Institute of International Affairs, London, a world-leading source of independent analysis, informed debate and influential ideas on how to build a prosperous and secure world for all. This was the first poll to be conducted on both sides of the LC. The purpose of the poll was to establish current attitudes in Kashmir on both sides of the LC to alternative scenarios for the resolution of the conflict. The poll took as its starting point the assumption that Kashmiri opinion represents a vital foundation for the region's political future peace and stability, and for wider global security. The survey was conducted by Robert W Bradnock (of King's College London and Associate Fellow, Asia Programme) in the entire erstwhile princely state of Jammu and Kashmir with the exception of the areas under Chinese occupation and the Gilgit-Baltistan area of POK. No reason was given by the Commission for excluding the region of Gilgit-Baltistan from the survey. The sample size of the population interviewed was 2374 and 1400 respectively for J&K State and POK. The respondents were asked a series of questions, the basic one being, 'What do you think are the main problems facing people in Jammu and Kashmir/POK?' The other questions related to their preference for independence, merger with India or Pakistan and other related issues.

The survey found that the majority of the respondents from Jammu and Kashmir were against independence, and that support for independence was concentrated solely in the Kashmir Valley, with very minimal support in Jammu or Ladakh. Although 43% of the total population of the undivided state said they would vote for independence, in only five (one in POK and four in the Kashmir Valley) out of eighteen districts was there a majority preference for the independence of the whole of Kashmir. It is evident, therefore, that the demand for independence of the State comes from the Kashmir Valley, relatively small in terms of acreage but with a high density of population. In the other five districts of Jammu & Kashmir, support for independence is 1% or less.

There is even less support across the whole of undivided Jammu & Kashmir for joining Pakistan. In POK the intention to vote for this option is barely 50% while, in Jammu and Kashmir it is just 2%. Legally speaking, the poll results render the demand for independence irrelevant because the UN resolution on Jammu and Kashmir offers one of only two options that is merger with India or merger with Pakistan. As the results of the study indicate that, while 21% of the population of the undivided State preferred merger with India, only 15% of the population preferred merger with Pakistan.

In an analysis of the study report titled 'Jammu and Kashmir: Governance is the key', Smruti S. Pattanaik concluded that:[4]

- This poll, in common with the two preceding polls in Indian Jammu and Kashmir, shows that, setting aside all other political obstacles, it is difficult to see how the plebiscite proposed in the UN resolutions of 1948/49 could play any part today in the resolution of the dispute. There is no clear majority for independence either. These results support the already widespread view that the plebiscite option is likely to offer no solution to the dispute. Nor is there evidence that an independence option could offer a straightforward alternative. Any solution will depend on the Indian and Pakistani governments' commitment to achieving a permanent settlement. The poll suggests that such a settlement will depend critically on engaging fully with all shades of Kashmiri political opinion.

- There is an overwhelming wish for change and resolution of the dispute.
- The Human Development Index is more important to the people of the State than the politics and violence of *Azaadi.* The common citizen wants a clean and effective administration with less corruption and more governance. Human rights are an issue which needs immediate attention of the powers that be.
- Improvement of infrastructure and generation of employment should be the key focus areas of the government.
- Conjointly with the above, it is essential that the terror machinery in the State be never allowed to disrupt the functioning of government. To ensure this, the State has to develop the police capabilities of intelligence gathering, surveillance of anti-national elements and retaliation capability as and when any terrorist activity occurs.

The intention behind the commissioning of the report was evident. The timing coincided with the Libyan resolution tabled at the UN in September 2009 advocating an independent Jammu and Kashmir. The findings of the Report were intended to be cited in support of the resolution. That may also explain why Gilgit-Baltistan was excluded from the study. Given the level of marginalization of the indigenous population and its hostility towards the Pakistani State, one can be reasonably certain that the results from this region would not have been favorable from the Pakistani perspective. Unfortunately for the sponsors, the survey delivered surprising results, more pleasant from the Indian point of view than the Pakistani. Another spanner in the works turned out to be the release of the 2009 edition of the Freedom in the World Report by the United Nations High Commissioner for Refugees.[5] The report was released around the same time as the Libyan resolution on Jammu and Kashmir. This report rated Jammu and Kashmir as "Partly Free", whereas in comparison, POK was rated as "Not Free." Hence the UN resolution turned out to be a non-starter.

Mainstream Political Parties

Like all the states of India, Jammu and Kashmir has a multi-party democratic system of governance. Main political parties and prominent leaders of the state include:

- J&K National Conference (NC) : pro-autonomy
- Indian National Congress (Congress) : pro-India
- J&K People's Democratic Party (PDP) : pro-autonomy
- Bharatiya Janata Party (BJP) : pro-India
- CPI (M) : pro- autonomy
- J&K Panther's Party : pro-India

Prominent Political Leaders from the State

Farooq Abdullah. He is the son of Shaikh Abdullah, and his nominated heir to lead the National Conference. He has served as Chief Minister of Jammu and Kashmir on several occasions since 1982 and also as a Union Minister in the Government of India. Though he has handed over the reins of the state leadership to his son, Omar, he still remains one of the most influential and media savvy politicians from J&K. Farooq has been consistent in his stand for the restoration of autonomy to Jammu and Kashmir while yet remaining an integral part of India. He is of the opinion that the state of Jammu and Kashmir should revert to its pre-1947 undivided status. Some of his relevant quotes are: "It is time to tell Pakistan that it should return to India parts of Kashmir under its control and the area it has gifted to China" and "Kashmir has not acceded to India by force... It chose to become a part of the India belonging to Gandhi and Nehru".

In a debate in parliament on 26 Aug 2010, he had this to say,[6] "During the regime of NDA, I also brought the autonomy proposal, but that had also been rejected. I had requested the then Prime Minister that we were ready to change the points which they thought could weaken India. But, our request had not been considered.... We do not want to secede from India. Nobody wants to secede from India. People who want to secede from India do not know the situation on the other side. They think everything is green on the other side. I would like to request all the honourable members, please try to understand that we want to find a solution within India, not within Pakistan or China or America. So, if we want to find a solution, let us sit down rather than have an obstruction that Article 370 will go and we will have a better India. There will never be a better India unless hearts and minds of people are won. To win the hearts and minds of the people, hearts and brains should be opened and people's views should be accommodated. The federal structure of the country should be strengthened. A true federal structure means that every State will have its powers and the Centre will have its own. If the Centre has to be made powerful, then the States must be made powerful. The success of the people and the success of our nation depends if we work together. Therefore, let us sit together, let us find out is there a way forward where we can win the hearts and minds of these young people. At the same time, when our Prime Minister goes across the border or their Prime Minister comes here, it is made abundantly clear to them that not only is 'this' Jammu and Kashmir ours, 'that' Jammu and Kashmir is also ours. I would make my earnest request to the media that it should not put the things in such a manner that creates hatred."

Omar Abdullah. He is the scion of the first family of the State, son of Farooq Abdullah and grandson of the Shaikh. He became the 11th and the youngest Chief Minister of Jammu and Kashmir, after forming a government in coalition with the Congress party, on 5 January 2009. Prior to that, he was a member of the 14th Lok Sabha, representing the Srinagar constituency of Jammu and Kashmir. He was a Union Minister of State for External affairs 23 July 2001 to 23 December 2002.

Mufti Mohammad Sayeed. He is one of the most prominent politicians from the Kashmir Valley and the current Chief Minister heading the government in coalition with the BJP. He was a member of the Indian National Congress party until 1987, when he quit the Congress party to join V.P. Singh's Jan Morcha, and was appointed the first Muslim Minister for Home Affairs in the Union Cabinet of India in 1989. In 1999 along with Master Tasadiq Hussain, he decided to form his own party, The Jammu and Kashmir People's Democratic Party (PDP). Within three years of its formation, the PDP participated in the 2002 assembly election and won 18 assembly seats. He went on to form a coalition government with the Indian National Congress, and was sworn in as the Chief Minister of Jammu and Kashmir for a term of three years.

Mehbooba Mufti Sayeed. She is the President of the PDP and the daughter of Mufti Mohammad Sayeed. She is a prominent and influential politician in her own right.

Ghulam Nabi Azad. He is a politician from the Indian National Congress and the current Minister of Health and Family Welfare. He is unique in the fact that he is the only politician who has served as the Chief Minister of Jammu and Kashmir but does not belong to the Valley. He was appointed Chief Minister of the state in 2008, but chose not to face the vote of confidence as his ally, the PDP, withdrew support at the last moment.

Sajjad Gani Lone. He is the youngest son of Abdul Ghani Lone, who was killed in a rally in Srinagar in 2002. After the assassination of his father, Lone became the chairman of People's Conference. In the last few years, it appears that he has been convinced that the prosperity of the Kashmiri people is dependent on development and progress rather than an armed struggle. He is eloquent and charismatic and seen by many as a future Chief Minister. He is one of few Kashmiri politicians who has been able to strike a personal chord with Prime Minister Modi without displaying signs of sycophancy. In the 2014 state elections, Lone was elected as MLA of Handwara.

Other political leaders of note from Kashmir are:

- Peerzada Mohammed Sayeed - Congress
- Abdul Gani Vakil - Congress
- Taj Moiuddin - Congress
- Muzzaffar Beig - PDP
- Mehboob Beig - NC
- M Y Tarigami - CPI (M)

Separatist/Terrorist Groups

There are a number of separatist/terrorist groups operating in Jammu and Kashmir. A brief write up on the main ones who have impacted counter terrorist/police operations at some time in the last two decades is given in the succeeding paragraphs. The material has been sourced from the official website of the South Asia Terrorism Portal[7] and the book, "Militant Groups in South Asia"[8].

Hizb-ul-Mujahideen (HM)

The HM (Party of Holy Warriors) also known as the *Hizb* is claimed to be one of the largest militant outfits operating in J&K. It came into being in the Kashmir Valley in September 1989. It was reportedly set up as the militant wing of the *Jamaat-e-Islami* (JeI) at the behest of the ISI to counter the JKLF, which had advocated complete independence of the State. Many of its early cadres were former JKLF members. The *Hizb* reportedly has a substantial support base in the Kashmir Valley and in the Doda, Rajouri, Poonch districts and parts of Udhampur district in the Jammu region.

The HM is headed by an ethnic Kashmiri Muslim, Syed Mohammed

Yusuf Shah, who fled the Valley after losing the assembly elections in 1987 in questionable circumstances and assumed the *nom de guerre*, Syed Salahuddin. Headquartered at Muzaffarabad in POK, the HM stands for the integration of J&K with Pakistan. Since its inception, the HM has also campaigned for the Islamisation of Kashmir. It is one of the 32 outfits proscribed under POTA 2002.

The HM has its own news agency, Kashmir Press International, and a women's wing, Banat-ul-Islam. It is closely linked to the Jamaat-e-Islami, both in the Kashmir Valley and in Pakistan. Overseas, it is allegedly backed by Ghulam Nabi Fai's Kashmir American Council and Ayub Thakur's World Kashmir Freedom Movement in the USA. Early in its history, the Hizb had established contacts with Afghan Mujahideen groups such as *Hizb-e-Islami*, under which some of its cadre is alleged to have received arms training. SIMI is also believed to have links with the *Hizb-ul-Mujahideen*.

The HM is reported to have a close association with the ISI, the United Jehad Council (UJC), and other terrorist organizations operating out of Pakistan. Its chief Syed Salahuddin also heads the UJC.

Harkat-ul-Jihad-al-Islami (Movement of Islamic Holy War)

The *Harkat-ul-Jihad-al-Islami* (HuJI) is a Pakistan-based terrorist group with an affiliate in Bangladesh. While the exact formation date of the group is not known, its origin is traced to the Soviet-Afghan war.

The HuJI continued to exist after the Soviet withdrawal from Afghanistan in 1989 by merging with another Pakistani militant group known as the *Harkat-ul-Mujahideen*, to form the Harkat-ul-Ansar which subsequently began terrorist operations in J&K. In order to avoid the ramifications of the U.S. designation of Harkat-ul-Ansar as a Foreign Terrorist Organization in 1997, it renamed itself as *Harkat-ul-Mujahideen* in certain areas while its Bangladesh-based unit (formed in 1992) is known as the HuJI Bangladesh (HuJI-B).

The HuJI belongs to the Deobandi school of thought and its recruits are indoctrinated in the mould of radical Islam. By describing itself as the "second line of defence for every Muslim", it aims to establish Islamic rule by waging war. It draws inspiration from Osama bin Laden and the Taliban. The HuJI supports, like the other Pakistan-based terrorist groups, the secession of J&K from India and its eventual accession to Pakistan, essentially through violence. It also propagates the idea of Islamic rule over all parts of India. Although there is no authoritative information on the actual cadre strength, some reports mention it to be around 500-750.

The HuJI's operations in J&K began in 1991 and it was reportedly managed by a semi-autonomous unit led by 'chief commander' Muhammad Ilyas Kashmiri. According to an estimate, 650 HuJI cadres were killed in 2002: 190 belonging to both sides of Kashmir, nearly 200 belonging to Pakistani Punjab, 49 to Sindh, 29 to Balochistan, 70 to Afghanistan, 5 to Turkey, and 49 collectively to Uzbekistan, Bangladesh and the Arab world. However, the HuJI activities in Jammu and Kashmir have progressively declined since 9/11.

The HuJI is closely linked to the Inter-Services Intelligence, the Taliban and *Al Qaeda*. The outfit is believed to have been behind the February 2007 Samjhauta Express bomb blast and the May 2007 Hyderabad blasts It has a strong network ranging across western Uttar Pradesh, Maharashtra, Andhra Pradesh, Rajasthan and Bangladesh from where the group's anti-India operations are planned.

The HuJI maintains links with militant groups operating in India's Northeast, including the Assam-based United Liberation Front of Asom (ULFA) and the Manipur-based People's United Liberation Front (PULF). The HuJI is reportedly running some of ULFA's camps situated in the Chittagong Hill Tracts in Bangladesh along the border of Tripura.

The HuJI is a banned terrorist organisation in India under The Unlawful Activities (Prevention) Act, 2004. The US State Department designated the HuJI as a Foreign Terrorist Organisation in March 2008. Earlier, the US administration had classified the HuJI in the 'Other Terrorist Organisations' list in 2003.

Harkat ul-Ansar (Now known as *Harkat ul-Mujahideen*)

The *Harkat ul-Ansar* was formed by the merger of two Pakistani groups, *Harkat ul-Jihad al-Islami* and *Harkat ul-Mujahedin*, as depicted in the chart below. The merger of these two political groups and its transformation into a militant group came about as part of the Afghan *jihad*. With a pan-Islamic ideology, the outfit strove to achieve the secession of Jammu and Kashmir from India through violent means and its eventual merger with Pakistan. About 60 per cent of its estimated 1000 strong cadre were Pakistanis and Afghans.

The *Harkat-ul-Ansar* was termed a terrorist organization by the US in 1997. To escape the impact of the repercussions of the US ban, the group was recast as the *Harkat ul-Mujahideen* in 1998.

Based in Muzaffarabad, the *Harkat ul-Ansar* has participated in insurgent and terrorist operations in Kashmir, Myanmar, Tajikistan, Bosnia and Herzegovina. In Kashmir, the outfit carried out several operations against Indian troops besides attacks on civilian targets. In the process, several of its top leaders including Masood Azhar (General Secretary and top idologue), Sajjad Afghani (Commander of the *Harkat ul-Ansar* in Jammu and Kashmir) and Nasarullah Manzoor Langaryal (commander of the erstwhile *Harkat-ul Mujahedin*) were captured by Indian security forces.

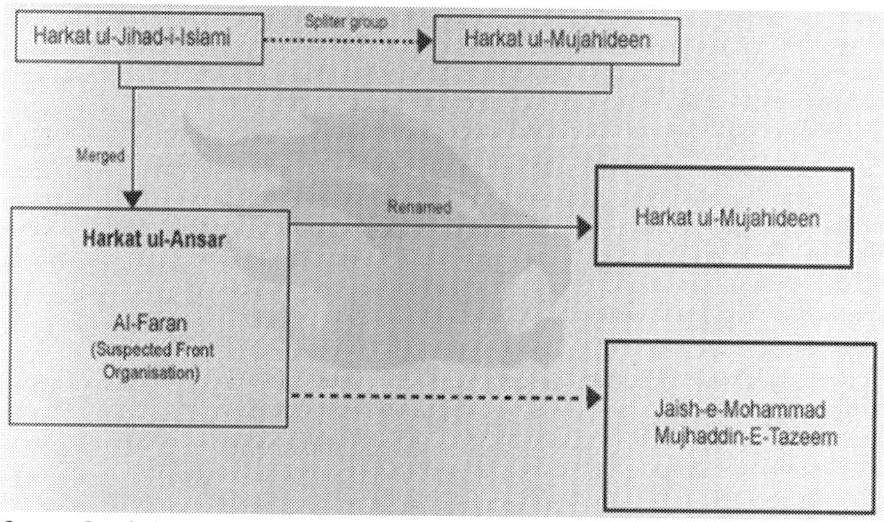

Source: South Asia Terrorism Portal Website

With all these arrests, the outfit gradually lost its influence in the State's militancy. The outfit's controlling body, Pakistan's ISI ensured that most of the cadre were transferred to the *Lashkar-e-Toiba*, which enlarged the latter's role in the State's militancy.

The US ban made it difficult for the *Harkat-ul-Ansar's* Pakistani sponsors to continue their support. Fund raising activities in Western countries too were affected. Hence, the *Harkat-ul-Ansar* was officially closed and a new militant outfit *Harkat ul-Mujahideen* was formed.

With the near total loss of its top leadership, the cadre base and Pakistani sponsorship, the *Harkat-ul-Ansar* appears to have collapsed and is no longer active in the State's insurgency

Lashkar-e-Toiba (Army of the Pure)

Formed in 1990 in the Kunar province of Afghanistan, the Lashkar-e-Toiba (also known as Jama'at-ud-Da'awa) is based in Muridke near Lahore in Pakistan and is headed by Hafiz Muhammad Saeed.

Its first presence in Jammu and Kashmir (J&K) was recorded in 1993 when 12 Pakistani and Afghan mercenaries infiltrated across the Line of Control (LoC) in tandem with the *Islami Inquilabi Mahaz*, a terrorist outfit then active in the Poonch district of J&K.

The LeT is outlawed in India under the Unlawful Activities (Prevention) Act. It was included in the Terrorist Exclusion List by the US Government on December 5, 2001. The US administration designated the Lashkar-e-Toiba as a FTO (Foreign Terrorist Organization) on December 26, 2001. It is also a banned organization in Britain since March 30, 2001. The group was proscribed by the United Nations in May 2005. Pakistan The military regime of Gen. Pervez Musharraf banned the LeT in January 2002.

The LeT's professed ideology goes beyond merely challenging India's sovereignty over the State of Jammu and Kashmir. The Lashkar's 'agenda', as outlined in a pamphlet titled, 'Why are we waging *jihad*' includes the restoration of Islamic rule over all parts of India. Further, the outfit seeks to bring about a union of all Muslim majority regions in countries that surround Pakistan. Towards that end, it is active in J&K, Chechnya and other parts of Central Asia.

Hafiz Saeed, a scholar of Islam, has said that the purpose of *jihad* is to carry out a sustained struggle for the dominance of Islam in the entire world and to eliminate the evil forces and the ignorant. He considers India, Israel and US to be his prime enemies.

The LeT does not believe in democracy and nationalism. According to its ideology, it is the duty of every *'Momin'* to protect and defend the interests of Muslims all over the world where Muslims are under the rule of non-Muslim in the democratic system. It has, thus chosen the path of Jihad as the suited means to achieve its goal. Cadres are drawn from the Wahabi school of thought. The LeT has consistently advocated the use of force and vowed that it would plant the 'flag of Islam' in Washington, Tel Aviv and New Delhi.

The outfit's headquarters at Muridke, 30 kms from Lahore, was built with contributions and donations from the Middle East, with Saudi Arabia being the biggest benefactor. The headquarters houses a *madrassa*, a hospital, a market, a large residential area for 'scholars' and faculty members, a fish farm and agricultural tracts. The LeT also reportedly operates 16 Islamic institutions, 135 secondary schools, an ambulance service, mobile clinics, blood banks and several *madrassas* across Pakistan.

LeT publishes its views and opinion through its Website (http://

www.jamatuddawa.org/), an Urdu monthly journal, *Al-Dawa*, which has a circulation of 80,000, and an Urdu weekly, *Gazwa*. It also publishes Voice of Islam, an English monthly, and Al-Rabat—monthly in Arabic, *Mujala-e-Tulba* - Urdu monthly for students, Jehad Times—Urdu Weekly.

While the primary area of operations of the LeT is Jammu and Kashmir, the outfit has carried out attacks in other parts of India, including in New Delhi, Mumbai, Bangalore, Hyderabad, Varanasi, Kolkata, Gujarat and other places. It reportedly has cells in many cities/towns outside Jammu and Kashmir.

The LeT has been able to network with several Islamist extremist organizations across India, especially in J&K, Andhra Pradesh, Tamil Nadu, Karnataka, Maharashtra and Gujarat. LeT is actively engaged in subversive activities in the States of Maharashtra, West Bengal, Bihar, Hyderabad, Delhi, Haryana and Uttar Pradesh at the instance of ISI to expand the frontier of violence outside J&K by subverting fringe elements. Of all the Pakistan-based terrorist groups, the LeT is the only group with support bases across India.

The LeT has training camps spread across Pakistan and POK. Its camps, recruitment centres/offices are spread across the length and breadth of Pakistan and PoK in Muzaffarabad, Lahore, Peshawar, Islamabad, Rawalpindi, Karachi, Multan, Quetta, Gujranwala, Sialkot, Gilgit and other places. LeT reportedly has 2,200 offices across Pakistan. LeT has an extensive network that run across Pakistan and India with branches in Saudi Arabia, United Kingdom, Bangladesh and South East Asia. It has allegedly set up sleeper cells in the U.S. and Australia, trained terrorists from other countries and has entered new theatres of Jihad like Iraq. It also has links with the International Sikh Youth Federation.

The outfit provides training to both militant cadres and the *Ulema* (religious scholars). Its militant cadres are given two months training in the handling of AK series rifles, LMGs, pistols, rocket launchers and hand grenades. It also provides a 21-day training programme called *Daura-e-Aam* and a three months specialized training programme called *Daura-e-Khas*.

LeT is credited for having initiated the strategy of *Fidayeen* (suicide squad) attacks in J&K. It has formed two sub-groups called *Jaan-e-Fidai* and *Ibn-e-Tayamiah*. While the first group consists of highly motivated terrorists, the second comprises terrorists suffering from incurable diseases.

Compared to other terrorist outfits in J&K, the LeT has commanded significant attention primarily due to two reasons; first, for its well planned and executed attacks on security force (SF) targets and secondly, for the massacres of non-Muslim civilians. It is closely linked to the Pakistani Inter-Services Intelligence, the Taliban and al Qaeda.

India's National Security Adviser M.K. Narayanan described the group to be as powerful as any international terror network. "It is as big and as omnipotent as *Al Qaeda* in every sense of the term. It is the most visible manifestation of the *Al Qaeda* in India."[4]

Jaish-e-Mohammed (Army of the Prophet)

The *Jaish-e-Mohammed* (JeM) has been held responsible for the December 13, 2001 terrorist attack on the Indian Parliament in New Delhi. The outfit has been banned by the Indian government under provisions of the POTA on October 25, 2001. The US Secretary of State, Colin Powell, in a notification on December 26, 2001, designated the outfit as a foreign terrorist organisation.

The JeM is a relatively new terrorist outfit, compared to other major outfits active in Jammu and Kashmir (J&K). Like the LeT, the JeM too is an outfit formed, controlled and manned by Pakistan. The outfit was launched on January 31, 2000, by Maulana Masood Azhar in Karachi after he was released from an Indian jail during the terrorists for hostage swap of December 31, 1999, following the hijacking of the Indian Airlines Flight IC 814. (See the chart showing the evolution of the *Harkat ul Ansar*)

The outfit's creation can be linked to the popularity surrounding Masood Azhar after his release from India. Maulana Masood Azhar was the general secretary of the newly established Harkat-ul-Ansar (HuA) in 1994 and was on a 'mission' in J&K when he was arrested on February 11. When he was released, the HuA had been included in the US list of Foreign Terrorist Organisations which had compelled the outfit to rename itself as the *Harkat-ul-Mujahideen* (HuM). However, Masood Azhar decided to float the new outfit JeM rather than rejoin his old outfit. He was also reported to have received assistance in setting up the JeM from Pakistan's Inter-Services Intelligence ISI, the then Taliban regime in Afghanistan, Osama bin Laden and several Sunni sectarian outfits of Pakistan.

The JeM is part of the Islamist terror network with its base in Pakistan and active in the terrorist violence in J&K. The outfit, like other terrorist outfits in J&K, claims to using violence to force a withdrawal of Indian security forces from J&K. In its fight against India, he added that the outfit would not only "liberate" Kashmir, but also would take control of Delhi, Amritsar and the Babri Masjid in Ayodhya.

Most Jaish-e-Mohammed attacks have been described as *fidayeen* (suicide terrorist) attacks. In this mode, terrorists of the outfit storm a high security target, including security forces' bases, camps and convoys. After storming, they either fortify themselves within the target, killing as many security force personnel and civilians as possible before they are killed by retaliatory action. In other cases, they kill and injure as many as possible before attempting to escape.

JeM chief, Masood Azhar was released by Indian authorities in Kandahar and has reportedly met Taliban and Al Qaeda leaders in Afghanistan on various occasions. The JeM is also reported to have links with Sunni terrorist outfits operating in Pakistan such as the *Sipah-e-Sahaba* Pakistan (SSP) and *Lashkar-e-Jhangvi* (LeJ).

Jammu and Kashmir Liberation Front (JKLF)

There are two distinct outfits, each of which identifies itself by the name JKLF. Amanullah Khan heads the first, while Yasin Malik, who parted ways with Amanullah Khan and formed another JKLF, heads the other. In May 1994, Yasin Malik who was released from jail (after his arrest in August 1990) declared that his faction would renounce violence as a tool to achieve the goal of "Independence". In March 1996, the last surviving members of the Amanullah faction who were based in J&K under the leadership of Shabbir Siddiqui were killed in two encounters.

Both the Fronts trace their origin to the Jammu and Kashmir National Liberation Front (JKNLF). The JKNLF was an offshoot of the Plebiscite Front. After the Sheikh-Indira Accord was signed, militant, pro-independence elements within the Plebiscite Front walked out to continue with the movement to secede from India.

The JKLF was set up in the United Kingdom, in May 1977, by one of the co-founders of the JKNLF, Amanullah Khan. Another JKLF, a splinter group headed by Yasin Malik, was founded in September 1995, after Malik split from Khan over differences on the strategy to be pursued to achieve perceived goals.

While both the JKLFs share a common goal, self-determination for the people of Jammu and Kashmir, the Yasin Malik faction has renounced the use of violence to attain this goal. It lays emphasis on adopting non-violent means and mobilising public opinion in India and Pakistan in favour of its objectives. It is a constituent of the All Party Huriyat Conference.

Amanullah Khan's JKLF promotes itself as an outfit conducting the struggle on three fronts—political, which implies mobilisation of public opinion; diplomatic, which implies lobbying with third countries; and armed struggle against Indian security forces in Jammu & Kashmir (J&K).

In the seventies and early eighties, the JKLF operated mostly from London and PoK, with Amanullah Khan and Hashim Qureshi directing from London unit and Farooq Haider and Mohammed Muzzafar holding fort in PoK. Their activities were, in large measure, confined to propagating the cause of a plebiscite in J&K and mobilising international support for this objective.

Even before the inception of JKLF, its leaders under various other banners had indulged in terrorist activities. One such instance was the hijacking of an Indian Airlines aircraft in 1971; Altaf and Hashim Qureshi, two prominent leaders, hijacked the plane. Maqbool Butt, one of the co-founders of the outfit and who had escaped from an Indian jail in December 1968, was reportedly involved in planning the hijacking.

After elections were held to the State Legislature in 1987, which were allegedly rigged, several youth crossed the LoC and received arms training. Simultaneously, the JKLF established its network in Srinagar and, in 1988, initiated the present phase of armed insurgency in the State with two bomb blasts in the capital city of Srinagar.

All through its history the JKLF has demanded conducting a plebiscite in J&K, but has made no effort to conceal its preference for an independent, sovereign State. This latter position is in direct conflict with Pakistan's contention that Kashmir, in its entirety, belongs to it. Pakistan has been consistent in its refusal to include the option of independence in the plebiscite narrative (the other options are: accession to either India or Pakistan). Another cause of friction between the JKLF and its mentors is the status of Gilgit-Baltistan. While JKLF maintains that this region is a part of J&K, Pakistan's position is that this region is separate from the State and its accession to Pakistan is final and irrevocable.

Analysts hold that, despite these differences, the ISI had to depend upon the JKLF in the initial stages of the insurgency as it lacked its own network in J&K. Once the JKLF began bringing in people for training, the ISI gradually weaned away a considerable section of them from the JKLF. Using money and weapon supplies as baits, the ISI bought the loyalty of several militants. By 1991, with ISI's help the pro-Pakistan *Hizb-ul-Mujahideen* gained greater terror potential as compared to the JKLF. Moreover, the formation of *Harkat-ul-Ansar, Lashkar-e-Toiba* and numerous other smaller outfits contributed to the marginalisation of JKLF. Besides this, JKLF has been directly targeted by the ISI and the outfits that were controlled by it with armed attacks, such as the killing of two JKLF cadres in July 1997 in Muzaffarabad and the forcible attempt to close a JKLF training camp in PoK, in February 1998.

Dukhtaran-e-Millat

An all-woman outfit, the *Dukhtaraan-e-Millat* (DeM) can be categorized as a soft-terrorist outfit in the sense that it uses extra-legal means including threats to impose its doctrines but has not taken to arms so far. The outfit, formed in 1987 has claimed that the Kashmir issue is primarily a religious issue and *jehad* is mandatory. It also supports the accession of the Kashmir valley with Pakistan. The DeM primarily operates in the Kashmir valley and its present strength is reported to be approximately 350.

The outfit has grabbed attention in spurts due to controversial remarks made by its leader, Ayesha Andrabi, a conservative Muslim and radical feminist, who has been running an aggressive campaign exhorting Kashmiri Muslim women to adopt the strict Islamic dress code. The DeM has sought to work in tandem with the insurgency which broke out in 1989. During the 1990's, the outfit was active in organising protests against Kashmiri women who did not adhere to the *burqa* system. In May 1993, the DeM issued warnings to the women in Srinagar not to venture outside their houses without wearing the *burqa*. It also organises protests against the alleged display of objectionable literature in Jammu and Kashmir. Another issue that the outfit periodically raises is alleged excess of security forces conducting counter-insurgency operations in the State. It has regularly co-operated with the APHC in organising protest demonstrations on this issue.

The DeM has not been accused of any instances of terrorist violence, though they are suspected of acting as couriers of arms and funds for various terrorist outfits operating in the State. The U.S. State Department Report of 1995, held a *Dukhtaran-e-Millat* activist responsible for a parcel bomb blast at the BBC office in Srinagar in which one person was killed and another two injured.

The DeM has also been accused of being linked with cases of money laundering, and allegedly receiving money from the ISI through hawala channels for later distributing the same to different terrorist groups.

Al Badr

The *Al Badr*, currently an active terrorist outfit in Jammu and Kashmir, was proscribed by the Government of India on April 1, 2002, under the POTA. It is also designated as a Foreign Terrorist Organization in the United States.

Al Badr was formed in June 1998 with the professed goal of strengthening the "Kashmiri freedom struggle" and to "liberate" the Indian

State of Jammu and Kashmir and merge it with Pakistan. The outfit advocates that Kashmiris should be given the right of self-determination in accordance with the United Nations resolutions.

Al Badr reportedly traces its origins to 1971 when a group of the same name carried out attacks on Bengalis in what was then known as East Pakistan. The group also operated as part of the *Hizb-e-Islami* (HIG) of warlord Gulbuddin Hekmatyar in Afghanistan during the 1980s.

While advocating the idea of a sovereign Kashmir it is also critical of the moderate Kashmiri organisations, such as the Jammu and Kashmir Liberation Front (JKLF). The current *Al Badr* leadership is also opposed to the United States, Israel and the regime of Saudi Arabia. The outfit has in the past indicated that it perceives Kashmir to be the 'gateway of India' and describes its objective as the 'liberation' of Muslims in the rest of India after 'occupying' Kashmir.

The outfit is headquartered at Mansehra in Pakistan. It is also reported to have a camp office in Muzaffarabad, PoK.

Al Badr is active in the Anantnag, Baramulla, Budgam, Srinagar and Kupwara districts of the Kashmir Valley. It also has a presence in the Poonch and Rajouri districts of Jammu region.

The *Al Badr* is part of the United Jehad Council (UJC), a coalition of Pakistan-based terrorist groups active in Jammu and Kashmir.

The outfit is opposed to the amicable settlement of the Kashmir issue, and has requested Pakistan to refrain from initiating any steps that would undermine the "freedom movement" in Jammu and Kashmir.

Muttahida Jehad Council (Also known as the United Jehad Council)

The *Muttahida Jehad* Council (MJC), a conglomerate of Pakistan-based *Jehadi* outfits, was formed in November 1990 to bring under a single platform all the outfits involved in the terrorist violence in Jammu and Kashmir (J&K).

The MJC, for long an alliance of 13 *Jehadi* organizations led by Syed Salahuddin of the HM, has reportedly been restructured and three Pakistan-based groups, the LeT, JeM and *Al-Badr Mujahideen* have been brought into the MJC. This new adjustment is called *Muwakhaat* ('agreement on the basis of brotherhood') that is aimed at putting an end to the internal differences among the groups waging the Kashmir *Jehad*.

According to reports, reorganizing the command and control structure of the HM-led MJC was part of a strategy change to enable the ISI to have tighter control over its functioning. With the restructuring, no component member of the UJC would now be allowed to launch an attack in J&K, unless approved by the Council. To this end, most of the smaller groups, which had reportedly become irritants for the ISI, have been merged to reduce the number of their representation in the Jehad Council from thirteen to five. *Al Barq*, Tehreek-e-Jehad, *Islamic Front*, Brigade 313 and the Kashmiri component of *Harkat-ul-Mujahideen (HuM)* have been merged to form the Kashmir Freedom Force, which would be led by Farooq Qureshi of the *Al Barq*. The Muslim *Janbaz* Force, *Al Jehad* Force, *Al Fateh* Force, *Hizbullah and JuM* (JuM) have also been merged to form the Kashmir Resistance Force which would be led by Ghulam Rasool Shah.

The headquarters of the MJC is at Muzaffarabad in POK. At the time of inception, all the terrorist outfits operating in J&K were required to register with the MJC. The council aims at joining forces and resources to augment the terrorist operations in J&K. The Muttahida Jehad Council also acts as the primary public voice of the terrorist outfits currently active in the State of Jammu and Kashmir.

In December 1995, Syed Salahuddin, 'Supreme Commander' of the HM was appointed the Chief of the conglomerate. The following terrorist outfits are currently members of the *Muttahida Jehad* Council:

1. *Hizb-ul-Mujahideen*
2. Jammu Kashmir Liberation Front
3. *Harkat-ul-Ansar*
4. *Tehrik-e-Jehad*
5. *Tehreek-ul-Mujahideen*
6. *Jamiat-ul-Mujahideen*
7. *Al Jehad*
8. *Al Umar Mujahideen*
9. Jammu Kashmir Islamic Front
10. Muslim *Janbaz* Force
11. *Hizbullah*
12. *Al Fatah*
13. *Hizb-ul-Momineen*
14. *Lashkar-e-Toiba*
15. *Jaish-e-Mohammed*
16. *Al-Badr Mujahideen*

Jamiat-ul-Mujahideen

The *Jamiat-ul-Mujahideen* (JUM) is a break away faction formed out of the HM in 1990. Its followers are mostly Kashmiris from the *Ahle Sunnat* (Deoband) school.

The JUM is organised along military lines and a political *Amir* heads the organisation. It has a 'Commander-in-chief' and a 'Vice Commander-in-chief' who commands four 'Divisional Commanders' who in turn command the various 'District Commanders' and 'Area Commanders'. It publishes a monthly magazine *Mahaz-e-Kashmir* in which it enumerates its terrorist operations systematically.

Unlike the other terrorist organisations who draw support along sectarian lines, the outfit recruits terrorists from all sects. But, it has not been able to grow into a larger outfit. The JuM played a significant role in the early years of militancy in Jammu and Kashmir. However, it has not been able to maintain its momentum, despite remaining active in several parts of the State over the years.

The JuM considers itself as being a 'pure' Kashmiri organization and according to the leadership, all other terrorist outfits have either been suppressed or have accepted Pakistani-recruited cadres in their midst. However, recent reports indicate that as the inflow of Kashmiri youth from Jammu and Kashmir is decreasing, the JUM now needs to recruit Pakistani youth into its ranks.

The JuM is opposed to the APHC which they describe as a danger for the terrorist movement in Jammu and Kashmir. They consider the APHC an obstacle in the way of the imposition of Islamic laws in the State. The *Hurriyat*, according to the JUM, has no right to represent the terrorists in Jammu and Kashmir. The outfit has come out strongly against the recent peace initiatives of both India and Pakistan as it considers violence as the only means to settle the Kashmir issue. The JUM also supports the accession of Jammu and Kashmir with Pakistan.

Lashkar-e-Jabbar

The existence of *Lashkar-e-Jabbar* (LJ) was first reported by the local media in Jammu and Kashmir in August 2001 following two incidents. In the first incident, two unidentified youth poured diluted acid on two school teachers in Srinagar. The next day, an armed terrorist threatened all students and teachers of a girls school in Srinagar with violence unless they adopt 'Islamic' dress codes. Thereafter the *Lashkar-e-Jabbar* claimed responsibility for these attacks warning that Muslim women must always wear the *burqa* in public. The outfit also released a statement asking non-Muslim women to wear identifying marks such as *'bindis'* on their foreheads or saffron *duppatas* or to dress in yellow clothes.

For an outfit that has cornered publicity on a large scale, little is known of its origin or character. There has only been speculation. Some news reports speculate that it is a creation of the DeM, which had failed in the early nineties in its attempt to force women to accept Islamic dress codes. Another news report claiming to cite intelligence reports said that the outfit was promoted by other terrorist outfits to make the use of burqas widespread and consequently to use these for launching attacks on security forces.

Most terrorists outfits active in the State, including the HM and the LeT initially condemned the outfit, alleging that there was no such terrorist outfit and that its appearance on the scene signified a deep conspiracy against the 'Kashmiri freedom movement'. Later, however, the group's changed their opposition and welcomed the outfit's activities.

The All Party *Hurriyat* Conference and several other Islamic organisations in the State such as the *Jamiat-Ulema Hind, Jamiat-e-Islami Hind* and the All India Muslim *Majlis-e-Mushawarat* denounced the "coercive tactics" to make women wear veils, by saying that Islam does not permit use of force to implement dress codes. Other organizations condemned the use of coercive measures to implement 'Islamic values'.

Tehreek-ul-Mujahideen (TuM)

The *Tehreek-ul-Mujahideen* was formed in June 1990 with the aim of merging Jammu and Kashmir with Pakistan and to promote a pan-Islamist identity.

The outfit has a two-tier structure with the apex level consisting of *Amir, Naib Amir* (Deputy Chief), 'Operations Chief', Military Adviser', 'Intelligence Chief' and 'District Commanders' and the field level consisting 'Divisional Commanders' and 'Regiment Commanders'.

The TuM is dominated by foreign mercenaries recruited from Pakistan and PoK although a certain percentage of its cadres are also drawn from J&K. It operates primarily in the Kashmir Valley, especially in the Beeru belt of Budgam district, Ganderbal and downtown localities of Srinagar, Pulwama and Anantnag districts. In 1990, it opened an office in POK and sent its cadres for training in arms.

The outfit receives funds from Pakistan, Bangladesh, Saudi Arabia, UK, USA and Gulf Countries primarily through organisations subscribing to the *Ahle Hadith* tradition.

The outfit has a close association with *Lashkar-e-Toiba* (LeT), another *Jehadi* group of the *Ahle Hadith* tradition. It is one of the members of the Muzaffarabad-based UJC. Are the BCEE are

Though the outfit has a limited presence in the Kashmir Valley and its activities declined in comparison to the bigger groups like the HM (HM), LeT and the Jaish-e-Mohammed (JeM), the smaller outfits have been encouraged to claim responsibility for terrorist actions conducted by the major terrorist groups as part of the ISI's new operational strategy in J&K, to ease international pressure on the larger groups. From 1995 onwards, the ISI started to route funds to the LeT through the TuM.

Terrorist/Extremist/Insurgent Groups in Jammu and Kashmir (Data Updated till July 7, 2013)

Proscribed Terrorist/ Extremist Groups	*Active Terrorist/ Insurgent Groups*	*Inactive Terrorist/ Insurgent Groups*
Hizb-ul-Mujahideen	*Lashkar-e-Omar*	*Al Barq*
Harkat-ul-Ansar (presently known as *Harkat-ul Mujahideen)*	*Lashkar-e-Jabbar*	*Al Jehad*
Lashkar-e-Toiba	*Tehrik-ul-Mujahideen*	J&K National Liberation Army
Jaish-e-Mohammed	Jammu & Kashmir Liberation Front	Muslim *Janbaz* Force
Harkat-ul Mujahideen (previously known as *Harkat-ul-Ansar)*	All Parties Hurriyat Conference	Kashmir *Jehad* Force
Al BadrJamiat-ul-Mujahideen	*Mutahida Jehad Council*	*Al Jehad* Force
Harkat-ul-Jehad-al-Islami		*Mahaz-e-Azadi*
Al Umar Mujahideen		*Islami Jamaat-e-Tulba*
Dukhtaran-e-Millat		J&K Students Liberation Front
Front Organisations of Terrorist Groups Active in Jammu and Kashmir		*Ikhwan-ul-Mujahideen*
		Islamic Students League
		Tehrik-e-Hurriat-e-Kashmir
		Al Mustafa Liberation Fighters
		Tehrik-e-Jehad-e-Islami
		Muslim Mujahideen
		Al Mujahid Force
		Tehrik-e-Jehad
		Islami Inquilabi Mahaz

Source: South Asia Terrorism Portal.

Front Organisations of Terrorist Groups Active in Jammu & Kashmir

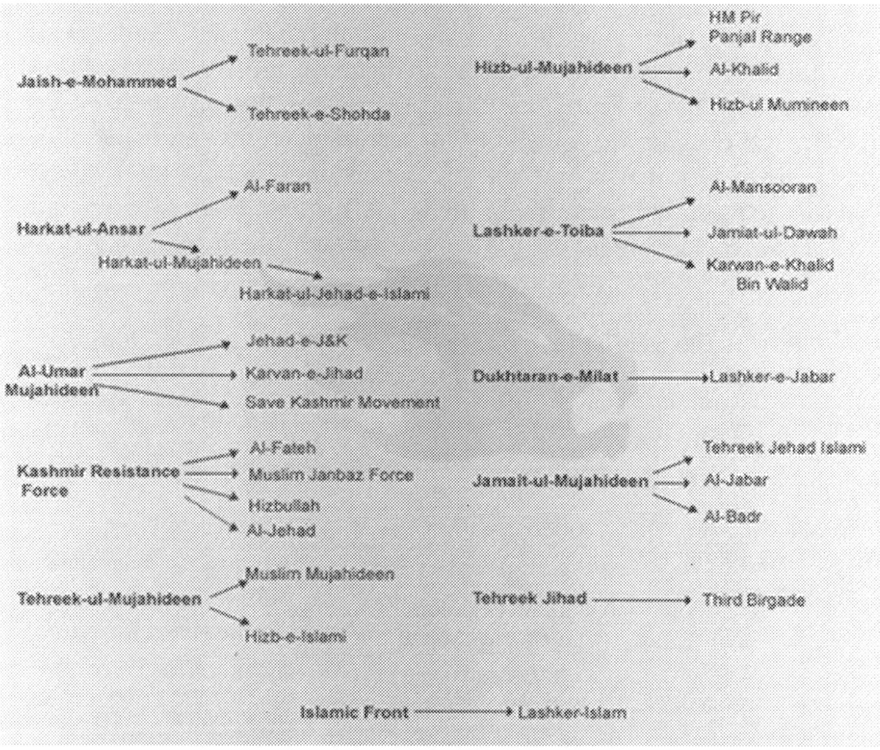

Source: South Asia Terrorism Portal.

Separatists/Secessionist and Other Leaders who Refuse to Join Mainstream Polity

All Party *Hurriyat* Conference (APHC)

The *Hurriyat* conference is an umbrella organization of over 20 political, social and religious groups founded in 1993, and is the political face of the Kashmiri separatist movement with reasonable support in the Valley, if one goes by the compliance of the Valley in response to APHC's calls for strikes and protests. However, in great part this compliance can also be attributed to the fear induced by the actual power behind the *Hurriyat*'s call for *bundh*, i.e. the armed groups who call the shots. Members of the Executive Council of the original APHC were:

- Syed Ali Shah Geelani of the *Jamat-e-Islami*
- Mirwaiz Umar Farooq of the Awami Action Committee

- Sheikh Abdul Aziz of the People's League
- Moulvi Abbas Ansari of the *Itehad-ul-Muslimeen*
- Abdul Ghani Bhat of the Muslim Conference
- Yasin Malik of the JKLF
- Abdul Ghani Lone of the People's League

The *Hurriyat* is committed to self-determination for Kashmiris and fighting Indian rule by peaceful means and has thus far refused to participate in Jammu & Kashmir's elections, although it is deeply divided in whether the ultimate objective is independence or accession to Pakistan. The hardliners insist that talks with India must include Pakistan, an option India completely rejects. The *Hurriyat* claims to represent the whole State, however it has refused to indicate the future status of various regions and communities within the proposed state. The *Hurriyat* has scant support outside the Kashmir Valley and in POK. The main leaders of the *Hurriyat* Conference and their respective stands are given in the subsequent paragraphs.

Syed Ali Shah Geelani. Syed Ali Shah Geelani is a hardliner who places the Kashmiri struggle within the Islamist discursive framework. According to his ideology, the concept of nation or nationalism is antithetical to Islam. He advocates merger of the state with Pakistan.

Yasin Malik. He is the Chairman of the JKLF and a pro-independence *Hurriyat* leader. He was a military commander of the JKLF before becoming a politician with the JKLF cease-fire in 1994, which he claims to have largely brokered. He has also consistently claimed to have spoken for minorities. But this aspect has been visible only after he forswore the use of an armed struggle. Prior to that, he and his outfit were primarily responsible, through selective killings of prominent leaders, for deepening the sense of insecurity within the minority community and their subsequent hounding out of the Valley.

Umar Farooq. He is seen as the liberal face of the *Hurriyat*. Farooq is also one of the few mainstream leaders from the *Hurriyat* Conference who has consistently raised questions about Kashmiri minority communities.

Mohammad Abbas Ansari. He is a prominent political leader and Shia cleric from Srinagar. He is the ex-chairman of the All Parties *Hurriyat* Conference, and founder of the Jammu & Kashmir *Ittihadul Muslimeen* (JKIM) political party. He is considered a moderate and has called for an end to violence.

Sheikh Abdul Aziz. A former militant commander turned politician, he was Chairman of the Jammu Kashmir Peoples League and a prominent member of the All Parties *Hurriyat* Conference. He supported the accession of Jammu and Kashmir with Pakistan. He died in August 2008.

Abdul Ghani Lone. He made his first entry into politics serving in the state assembly as a Congress candidate in 1967. In 1978, he formed a separatist organization called the People's Conference dedicated to "the restoration of 'internal autonomy' in Kashmir". He was assassinated on May 21, 2002. After his death, his son Sajjad, became the chairman of People's Conference. Sajjad has since become a prominent mainstream politician who successfully contested the state assembly elections in 2014.

Syed Asiya Andrabi. Asiya Andrabi is the chief of the all-women *jihadi* outfit *Dukhtaran-e-Millat*. She trashes the idea of Kashmiri nationalism saying that Islam is the basis of identity for Muslims and says: "We believe in a two-nation theory. One of the Muslims, the other of non-Muslims. Kashmir, sooner or later, will be an Islamic state"[8].

Masarat Alam Bhat. He is the chairman of the Jammu Kashmir Muslim League and also the general secretary of the *Hurriyat*. He is one of the most prominent leaders of the younger generation and is emerging as one of the prime successors to Syed Ali Shah Geelani's political mantle. Telephone transcripts of his conversations indicting him in taking instructions from and giving periodic feedback to unidentified "masters/ controllers" during the stone-pelting phase in 2010 somewhat eroded his credibility and took the sheen off his halo. His influence and ability to create mischief cannot be underestimated. His driving force is ambition and steadfast belief. He was released from prison in March 2015 and immediately commenced indulging in anti-India activities and whipping up mass hysteria. He is a person who appears willing to make any pact with anti-Indian entities to further his own ambitions and is therefore somebody whom the intelligence agencies need to keep under close surveillance.

NOTES

1. Indian embassy website (http: //www.indianembassy.org /policy/ Kashmir/ Kashmir_ MEA/Indian_Position.html)
2. Pak Embassy Website (http://www.mofa.gov.pk/pages/ Brief.htm. It is a snapshot of the page as it appeared on Jul 1, 2010)
3. Bradnock Robert W, *Kashmir: Paths to Peace*, Chatham House (the Royal Institute of International Affairs), May 2010

4. http://www.idsa.in/idsacomments/JammuandKashmirGovernanceisthekey_sspattanaik_070710
5. *Freedom in the World 2009 – Kashmir (India)*, Freedom House. 16 July 2009
6. Parliament debate records for 26 Aug 2010
7. Official Website of the South Asia Terrorism Portal.
8. Surinder K Sharma and Anshuman Behera, *Militant Groups in South Asia*, IDSA, 2014, Pentagon Press, New Delhi.
9. Manisha Gangahar, *Violence in Kashmir (Economic and Political Weekly Vol - XLVIII No. 04, January 26, 2013)*

4

Overview and Assessment of the Situation

In this section, we will assess the situation as prevailing in the State at present. We will also assess the impact that the cycle of insurgency and counter-insurgency has had on the State. We will see that there has been an overall decline in the levels of violence and infiltration. We will examine the steps that have been initiated by the State and Central Governments and their effectiveness in the long run.

Impact of Terrorism in Jammu and Kashmir

Infiltration

Estimated Infiltration in Jammu and Kashmir

Year	*Total*
2001	2417
2002	1504
2003	1373
2004	537
2005	597
2006	573
2007	535
2008	342
2009	485
2010	489
2011	247
2012	264
2013	277
2014	222

Source: Annx-II,.Annual Reports, Ministry of Home Affairs.

As can be discerned from figures given in the table above, there has been considerable drop in the numbers of successful infiltrations into the state in this decade. By the year 2011, measures to curb infiltration were successful in containing the figures within manageable levels. However, intelligence reports indicate that the infrastructure for training terrorist elements across the border remains intact and efforts to infiltrate militants into the State continue unabated. The available information reveals that the infiltration that consistently decreased since 2004 was reversed in the year 2009 and increased substantially when compared to 2008. During the period from January to December 2011, infiltration attempts have shown a downward trend compared to the corresponding period in 2010. The number of infiltration attempts for the period up to December 2011 is 247 compared to 489 during the same period in 2010, a decline of 49.5%.

Year	*Number of Incidents*	*Numbers Killed*			
		Civilians	*Security Forces*	*Terrorists*	*Foreign Terrorists*
1990	4158	461	155	550	14
1991	3765	382	173	844	12
1992	4817	634	189	819	14
1993	5247	747	198	1310	90
1994	5829	820	200	1596	122
1995	5938	1031	237	1332	85
1996	5014	1341	184	1209	139
1997	3420	971	193	1075	197
1998	2932	889	236	999	319
1999	3071	873	355	1082	305
2000	3074	847	397	1520	436
2001	4522	996	536	2020	625
2002	4038	1008	453	1707	508
2003	3401	795	314	1494	470
2004	2565	707	281	976	60
2005	1990	557	189	917	*
2006	1667	389	151	591	*
2007	1092	158	110	472	*
2008	708	91	75	339	*
2009	4 99	78	64	239	*
2010	488	47	69	232	*
2011	340	31	33	100	*
2012	220	11	38	50	*
2013	170	15	53	67	*
2014	222	28	47	110	*
Total	67747	13853	4792	21423	3396

Source: Annx-II, MHA Annual Reports, 2011-12/14-15.
*Details not available from any credible source.

Loss of Life. Terrorism in Jammu & Kashmir has taken a toll of over 40,000 lives during the period since the onset of violence in 1990, including more than 13,000 civilians and about 21,000 terrorists. In addition, it has caused enormous damage to the Kashmiri people, their age-old syncretic culture and to the economy of the State. The figures in the table below indicate the heavy loss of life in the two decades of unending mindless violence.

Destruction of Public and Private Property. In addition to the loss of life, there has been considerable loss and damage to government and private property. This has been consequent to the attempt of the terrorists to impose their writ on the local population and to prevent the administrative machinery from functioning efficiently and lowering the morale of government personnel. The table below indicates the widespread and wanton destruction of public and private property during the worst phase of the insurgency.

Destruction of Property by Terrorists

Year	*Govt Bldg*	*Edn Inst*	*Bridge*	*Hosps*	*Pvt Shop*	*Bldg*	*Houses*
1990	646	501	129	172	0	1242	202
1991	391	45	24	24	0	819	83
1992	564	65	57	28	0	2312	200
1993	662	98	46	34	0	1110	400
1994	606	172	119	46	4	666	162
1995	688	127	133	16	2	1814	402
1996	482	52	68	2	3	602	161
1997	259	13	11	5	1	437	67
1998	177	13	15	1	0	273	66
1999	136	7	9	2	0	284	6
2000	129	14	6	1	0	330	107
2001	274	30	16	2	1	419	77
2002	255	14	10	4	0	421	20
2003	205	6	5	2	0	259	9
2004 1st qr	38	1	0	0	0	40	20
Total	5512	1158	648	339	11	11028	1982

Source: MHA Annual Report 2003-04, Chapter III, Para 3.10

Recovery of Arms, Ammunition and Explosives. If proof was ever required to dispel the notion that the insurgents had declared war on the legitimate government of the state of Jammu and Kashmir, one just has to look at the quantum of arms and ammunition seized from the terrorists. The number of rifles alone seized from them is more than required to arm 40 infantry battalions of the Indian army. The figures given in the tables below indicate the recovery of arms, ammunition and explosives from the terrorists during the period 1990 to the period when the armed struggle was subdued to within manageable limits.

Recovery of Arms from Terrorists/Militants

Year	*AK Rifles & Pistols*	*UMGs*	*Rocket Launchers*
1990	1991	77	108
1991	3169	130	29
1992	4260	164	62
1993	3130	142	36
1994	3136	127	31
1995	3020	67	36
1996	3202	84	43
1997	2749	64	81
1998	2104	71	140
1999	1629	28	42
2000	1887	21	59
2001	2016	10	39
2002	1879	3	36
2003	1784	8	30
2004 1st qr	317	0	2
Total	36273	996	774

Source: Annx-III, Annual Report, Ministry of Home Affairs 2003-04.

Recovery of Explosive Materials from Terrorists/Militants

Year	*RDX (kg)*	*Explosives*	*IED*	*Grenades*	*Rockets*
1990	0	231	0	2502	296
1991	0	274	18	1784	256
1992	0	285	86	2391	245
1993	0	2950	136	4263	135
1994	0	1342	126	2603	395
1995	0	1484	811	2870	170
1996	166	2381	245	3949	378
1997	342	6448	1033	5124	479
1998	769	2922	514	5883	375
1999	886	2182	466	4093	332
2000	1508	1798	718	4807	555
2001	2547	1009	450	4152	397
2002	647	912	211	2701	138
2003	1624	861	229	3733	144
2004 [1st qr]	428	197	44	593	23
Total	8917	25276	5087	51548	4343

Source: Annx-III, Annual Report, Ministry of Home Affairs 2003-04.

Trends in Terrorist Tactics[1]

Once it was clear to the masterminds of the sponsors of terrorism in Jammu and Kashmir that the tactics of waging an all-out insurgency against the Indian State was proving counter-productive in terms of popular support and costly in terms of losses of leadership and manpower, it was decided to adopt a change in the approach to terrorism. Military and paramilitary locations were targeted taking care to ensure that there was no civilian casualty as a result of a terrorist action. Some important trends in the terrorism post 2003 in the State emerged as follows:

- Selective targeting of political workers at grassroots level, volunteer civilian members of Village Defence Committees and Special Police Officers.
- Targeted killing of surrendered militants.
- Reactivating and energizing the OGWs for the following activities:
  - Recruiting local youth to join terrorist ranks.
  - Collecting funds for sustaining terrorist activities.
  - Forced recruitment of local boys, if sufficient volunteers were not forthcoming.
  - Extending logistical support to the terrorists.
  - Publicize and highlight alleged human rights violations.
  - Instigating people to demonstrate on trivial grounds in order to demoralize and discredit the security forces.

The Situation in the Early 2011

By early 2011 the situation had seen a gradual restoration of normalcy, after the mayhem of the summer of 2010. The state administration, government functionaries, police and the security forces had once again become effective. It was evident that the common man was no longer interested in protests. It appeared that the writ of the Hurriyat Conference as well as that of Mr Geelani was on the decline. Not wishing to lose out on the momentum that the movement had gathered in 2010, there was a sudden impetus in the infiltration and terrorist activities at the instance of the Pakistani backed separatist groups. The militants and the separatists were under considerable pressure to revive the unrest.

Meanwhile, the interlocutors had commenced their interaction with all segments of society. The earnestness with which they went about their task was received well by the population and everyone was keen to meet and convey their grievances to them. The appointment of the interlocutors had another positive fallout. There was now a greater degree of interaction between the government agencies and the people through the interlocutors who gave an accurate and real time feedback on action needed to be implemented immediately.

The key instigators of the violence were put behind bars so that they could not foment further trouble. Successful conduct of *Panchayat* polls also electrified the people. Local self government was at last taking root and the mood was upbeat in the entire Valley. Going by the report of the newspapers, there was a positive trend in the attitude of the citizens and an overall improvement in the atmosphere.

This state of affairs did not sit kindly with the separatists. A new plan was implemented to strike fear into the heart of the common man and leaders at the grassroots level. An edict was issued prohibiting people from contesting the *Panchayat* elections. A number of *sarpanches* were executed in cold blood as a warning to others. This turn of events presented a new challenge to the government as it meant providing security that even the lowest level of village administration.

The Present Situation

Overall Assessment. With the restoration of normalcy and the writ of the separatists on the decline, there is an air of optimism in the atmosphere. All arms of the state machinery are functioning efficiently. Militancy has been contained to a great extent, but it cannot be said to have been eradicated. As such that is no room for complacency on the part of the security forces. It is clear that the common man is only interested in leading a normal life and is not interested in protests, violence and disturbances. At the same time, it is also clear that the vested interests are under pressure to revive the unrest. They are looking for the trigger which can reactivate the violence. Hence, a cautious approach is the need of the hour.

Separatists. The support for the separatists in the Valley is on the wane as they have no substantial issue apart from Independence, which the population has realized is an extremely difficult goal to attain. It appears that the leadership is awaiting another opportunity to provoke a strong reaction from the police forces with substantial collateral damage which can then be used as the trigger to provoke further unrest. This is precisely the scenario which the security forces should anticipate and avoid reacting to any provocation with disproportionate force. It must be borne in mind that though support may have waned across the length and breadth of the Valley, the separatists are still capable of massing considerable numbers of raucous supporters especially from the youth and projecting the protests in the media as a mass uprising.

Locals. The Kashmiris are tired of the endless cycle of protests and violence. Their sentiments are hurt and they are yearning for a change so that they can live their life with dignity and in peace. They display a state of apathy towards the state police and the CRPF, and a state of resigned acceptance towards the Indian Army and the Rashtriya Rifles. However, a slow but definite change is discernible in the attitude of the people as well as in the reporting trend of the print media.

Army. The Indian Army has achieved the objectives that were set before them in the winter of 1989-90. The situation has been brought under control and there is no need for them to be employed in routine duties involving maintenance of law and order, for which there are adequate number of state and central police forces. Whenever there is need to call in the army, they should conduct operations in a surgical manner and only on specific intelligence. As far as possible, the army should remain confined to its barracks, with minimum interaction with the common man. And whenever there is interaction, it should be polite yet firm, so that a positive image is always conveyed. They need to continue to adopt a humane approach to influence the Kashmiri mind with the theme of "The Heart is my Weapon". Sadbhavana was a good initiative of the army. It had two components; assistance in improving local infrastructure and WHAM. The former should be handed over to the local administration while the Army should concentrate on continuing with the latter. Initiatives like taking youngsters on a tour of the Indian mainland go a long way in bridging the gap between the State, in particular the Valley and other inaccessible areas, and the rest of the country.

Terrorism. With the elimination of the top militant cadres, the main terrorist organizations such as the LeT appear to be on the back foot. They seem to be waiting for favorable conditions before they can re-commence their operations. Intelligence reports seem to suggest that efforts are on for the revival of the HM and the reactivation of the JeM. The security forces can invariably expect a sudden increase in infiltration prior to the setting in of winter.

Political Class and Government Machinery. After the successful conduct of the *Panchayat* polls, the ground has been laid for better interaction between government agencies and the people in the quest to provide good governance. Positive political activity has to be resumed so that no political space is provided for the separatists and fundamentalists. The longstanding promises made by the Prime Minister viz employment opportunities and improvement in infrastructure need to be fulfilled at the earliest, before it is dismissed as hollow talk and despondency sets in.

The recommendations of the interlocutors should be considered seriously and implemented wherever it is felt that a positive outcome will accrue. Proper investigation into outstanding cases of human rights violations and custodial deaths should commence expeditiously.

Removal of the AFSPA is an emotive issue and addressing this in a practical manner would pay rich dividends in the long run. A bold approach is required as a timid approach fearing the doomsday scenario would be counter-productive. Less disturbed districts of the State can be identified and considered for removal of AFSPA after discussions with all the concerned parties. Of course, diluting the provisions is not within the powers of the state government and will require an act of parliament to do the same.

Comments

Where are we after over two decades of violence? Is there a winner? Can there be a winner? Colossal losses have been recorded on either side. An entire generation has been lost to the cause of terrorism. The damage in terms of lost opportunities, damage to infrastructure, weakening of the fabric of a society, dislocation of lakhs of people and scarring of the psyche of an entire populace is incalculable.

Who is right? Can the blame be placed squarely at the doorstep of the security forces? Definitely not; because, despite the alleged excesses, they are only doing their job in the maintaining the integrity of the nation. Their methods may be faulted, not their actions, because once you are faced with an armed opponent, it is a war for all purposes but in name. But can the same be said of those who take to arms against the state? No matter what the provocation, they have to answer for the deaths of thousands of their fellow citizens because the miseries that afflicted their lives was as a direct consequence of their decision to challenge, by armed might, the authority of the legitimate government. The security forces are merely an instrument of enforcing the political will. If the solution to the problem is political, the depressing fact is that the root cause of the problem was also political.

NOTES

1. Ministry of Home Affairs, Annual Report 2004-05, Ch - 3.33

5

Feedback and Interviews

Ordinarily, feedback and interviews would form part of the research data and be confined to an annexure. However, in the absence of prior research and published material on the subject, the author was compelled to rely on the opinion of experts in the field and feedback from the persons interacted with, to arrive at relevant and implementable recommendations. Hence this has been included as a regular chapter.

Methodology of Obtaining Feedback

Two questionnaires were circulated within the public at large as well as to persons occupying positions of responsibility and power, including the Honorable Chief Minister. The first questionnaire pertains to the basic subject ie demilitarisation and is relevant to all the stake-holders including the security forces. The second questionnaire is more generic and pertains to the concept of *Kashmiriyat* and relevant only to the Kashmiri population. The distribution of the second questionnaire was therefore limited to sections of the population in Kashmir, Jammu and Ladakh. The text of the circulated questionnaires is given at Annexure 1.

Feedback

It was disappointing that the majority of the respondents, including the then Honorable Chief Minister, to whom the questionnaires were circulated for comments chose, for whatever their reasons, not to respond in writing. Most, though quite voluble in airing their views in personal conversation or in a group discussion, were wary of disclosing their identity. Hence the findings of the feedback are based mostly on the author's personal notes and the audio recordings of some conversations.

The gist of the feedback to the questionnaires as well as personal conversations and group discussions are given in the succeeding paragraphs.

Kashmir University

In the interaction with students of the Political Science Department of the Kashmir University, the common refrain was that daily existence has become a nightmare for the ordinary citizen because the number of security personnel on the streets of Srinagar was way in excess of the numbers required to maintain law and order effectively. When asked to elaborate exactly how excess security personnel on the street was affecting everyday life, the most common reasons that emerged were

- Frequent security checks.
- Rude and humiliating behavior of the security personnel.
- Disruption of traffic during the convoy movements, especially the convoys on the Srinagar-Leh highway

Conversation with a Senior Professor at the Department of Political Science, Kashmir University

- Conflict resolution should be by dialogue and not by recourse to arms. An excellent example available to us is that of Sweden and Finland, who were able to resolve their territorial dispute through talks.
- The demand for demilitarisation in the Kashmiri context would be basically confined to the opening of civilian space.
- Non-reduction of forces results in the loss of good will. When there are barely 400 militants remaining in the state, why should the Indian Army risk losing so much of goodwill?
- In my opinion, demilitarisation will not create a vacuum as suggested in the questionnaire. So there is no requirement of any additional troops.
- The various task force elements operating in the State have become a law unto themselves. They need to be brought under control. (Here, the Professor was referring to the Ikhwani outfits that have become extremely unpopular with the local community and are perceived as turncoats.)
- Power breeds arrogance which in turn leads to the mistrust of the law-enforcing machinery by the locals.

- The Indian Army must not lose out on the opportunity to exploit the gains arising out of normalcy and must build upon it.
- Generally there are no protests against military presence, these happen only when there is an encroachment in public space. When that happens, only the appropriate amount of force should be used.
- There should be a comprehensive approach to the resolution of the problem. Adhering to the following commandments would pay rich dividends:
  - Ensure no further alienation.
  - The rule of law should prevail. Do not make Kashmir an exception.
  - Kashmiris are by nature a peace loving people. They can be an example for Muslims all over the world.
- His passionate plea: "Feel for us. In the worst days of militancy we still retained elements of humanity."

Interaction with the Students Department of Political Science, Kashmir University

The author had a long session with students of the Department of Political Science. Given their background and choice of subject, the students had strong opinions and were highly politically aware. Naturally, the discussion was lively and, at times, passionate. Their response to various questions posed to them, are given below.

Q 1. "What does the term demilitarisation mean to you? What actions do you visualize being taken on ground?"

- Removal of troops from the rear areas and moving them either to the borders or out of Kashmir.
- Reduction of troops from both sides of the Kashmir border.
- Disbanding of the special action groups.
- Trust the Kashmiris and give them some space so they can get some relief.
- Free Kashmir from both India and Pakistan.
- The Government of India should come clean about the number of troops in Jammu and Kashmir.
- People in Baramulla and Kupwara Districts need more relief.
- Demilitarisation is not just reduction of weapons and personnel. It is an ideology. It implies a change in approach, image and behavior of the military, police and the paramilitary forces. It would mean an end to exploitation and harassment.

- If demilitarisation happens half the problem of Kashmir would be resolved.
- Demilitarisation would result in automatic de-alienation.

Q 2. If you are asked to suggest the first step in the demilitarisation process, what would your recommendation be?

- AFSPA needs to be done away with. It has given the security forces 'license to hunt and kill'.
- Discontinue the movement of convoys during daylight hours.
- Withdrawal of Draconian laws (read AFSPA) should be the first step.
- Demilitarise the Indian mind set which always treats Kashmir as an exception to the rule (sic).

Q 3. How long, in your opinion, should the process of demilitarisation last?

- Just one month.
- The time it takes for the military to hand over the reins to the police.

Q 4. How should the process of demilitarisation commence?

Create zones of peace under Kashmiri leadership and then engage in talks with all parties involved.

Q 5. What has been your personal experience ever since the onset of militancy?

- Kashmiris are being subjected to brutality day in and out.
- One never gets any peace of mind.

Conversation with a recently Retired Senior Army Officer at Jammu

During a visit to Jammu and Udhampur, the author had a long discussion with a retired Major General. The general officer was very knowledgeable on the subject of Jammu and Kashmir, being a keen student of the geopolitics of the region and having been posted in the State at various stages during his service. The main points which emerged from the interaction are summarized below:

- Till 1953, there was no major constituency for freedom or separation from India. This constituency has been steadily fuelled, stoked, fanned and at times allowed to rage in an uncontrolled manner by various people with their own agenda.
- Quoting a former corps commander who had also served as Advisor to the Government of Jammu and Kashmir, he said, "*Yahan to dheel hi dheel hai*" meaning that the politicians had been given too loose a rope and could get away with anything. He was of the

opinion that they should be no soft pedaling in case it was proven that an individual had acted in a patently anti-national or subversive manner. Politicians need to realize that there are some *Laxman Rekhas* (limits) which they should not transgress.

- The Kashmir problem has been fuelled and kept alive by constant rigging of elections.
- The military is part of the solution and not the problem.
- By and large people still have faith in the military.
- There are many tools to be put into place before demilitarisation can take place. Before we consider demilitarisation, it has to be assessed whether the Jammu and Kashmir Police are capable of maintaining law and order in the absence of central security forces. If not, an alternate force capable of doing the job effectively has to be identified, recruited, trained and equipped. The composition of the new force has to be properly thought out. This is a time consuming process and will take anything between 5 to 10 years to implement.
- Much as everyone claims that they want a speedy solution to the Kashmir problem, the fact on ground is that the problem is a source of considerable funds. This has resulted in the problem becoming a well orchestrated game. No one wants to kill the proverbial golden goose by solving the problem.
- Structurally, the systems for administering the state efficiently are in place, but the delivery is highly weak.
- Considering the situation, there are not too many human rights violations. However, since the situation is fluid there are new challenges every day, the army is on a constant learning curve and the code of conduct is under constant revision.
- There is a need to retrain our forces. Different types of threats require different types of response. And hence the need for differently trained troops.
- There is a case for emulating what the US is doing in Afghanistan. It is attempting to develop the local police capability to maintain law and order once the US forces de-induct. If the United States, which is an occupation force, can consider this, there is no reason why we cannot do so in our own State. After all other states also have elite police personnel engaged in counter-insurgency operations.
- The mainstream political parties in the State need to be strengthened and developed.

Interaction with an Expert on Kashmir Affairs

- Cessation of violence became the primary objective post the Agra summit.
- Post Vajpayee's second tenure as PM, it became evident that peace negotiations were imperative.
- The first serious role of civilian society in conflict resolution commenced in 2004.
- **Role of the Media.** The media has become a factor in the conflict rather than the reflector of the truth. They do not check their facts; misreporting has often become the norm. Freedom of media must go hand in hand with their duties and responsibilities.
- **Demilitarisation is a Goal.** In each goal there are phases. The level of forces increased after 1989. The armed conflict is almost over. It is entirely logical that there should be a discussion on re-deployment. It is being discussed at every forum. Steps have already been initiated. 14 bunkers have been removed. Two parts reduction of the paramilitary forces and re-deployment of the army is being considered. The army is more or less in the barracks and is focused on the LOC and counter insurgency. Since reduction in insurgency is a fact, the security establishment is seriously considering reduction in forces. Ultimate demilitarisation in its true sense can only take place once the Indo-Pakistan conflict is resolved.
- **On Police Brutality.** In armed conflicts all sides tend to behave badly. Few abide by the Geneva conventions. The Jammu and Kashmir Police are being trained in and getting ethical orientation.

Interview with Lt Gen (Retd) Mukesh Sabharwal, Renowned Military Strategist and ex Corps Commander, 15 Corps.

Q. What are the problems that you faced in the functioning of the police forces in conjunction with the CRPF?

There was always a clash of interests, and naturally so. The senior most officer of the CRPF, whatever his rank, reports back to his DGP. But while he is in the State, he has to work under the local police. So there is always a clash of personalities and conflict of interests, because he is veritably following a dual channel of command. On the one hand he has to listen to his own headquarters, whereas at the same time he may get contrary orders from the local police boss. So you may have any amount of outside forces, but they will never be able to function effectively because of the clash of interests. To cite a recent incident, orders were issued, probably at the behest of the Chief Minister's office that all police personnel, including the CRPF, will operate without arms and only with *lathis*. This is contradictory to the basic rules of operating in a counter-insurgency environment and reduces the police personnel to sitting ducks. Unnecessary loss of lives could have been avoided if this politically motivated order had not been issued.

There is also a basic difference in operational ethos. The CRPF is an apolitical force and everyone has a nationalist outlook whereas, police operations are highly influenced by political leanings. In Jammu and Kashmir because of the special status conferred by Article 370, the politicians are always conveying conflicting signals. Sometimes they're pro-India, sometimes pro-autonomy and at times they are even pro-separatist. They are constantly playing to the gallery. There's no consistency of approach and that is where the problem lies. The political class is always sending conflicting signals which leaves the police forces confused and diffident. The CRPF does not face this kind of convenient politics in other states. And where there is a clash of interests, there is bound to be trouble.

Ultimately, the answer is to raise a local police force to replace the central police forces operating in the state. This force has to be specially trained in counter terrorist operations and modern methods of crowd control. I am aware that such an exercise is already underway. What is more important, however, is not the quantum of troops but the quality of manpower and training which, in the ultimate analysis, will make all the difference.

Q. What are your thoughts on the conversion of the Rashtriya Rifles into a sort of commando force and placed at the disposal of the state government as a counter terrorist force?

I don't think it is a great idea. The Rashtriya Rifles are doing a great job and we should not disturb with their operations and their structure of command and control.

Q. Is it possible that your view is clouded by the fact that you have seen them operate at maximum efficiency and you would not like to see their performance degraded by converting it into a local police force and subjecting it to unwarranted political pulls and pressures?

The moment you put any force under the security apparatus of the state, you are ruining it.

Q. That I accept; but what will you do with so many battalions that had been raised? Surely so many are not required now that the counter insurgency has been brought under control?

I have a number of suggestions as to how they could be utilized.

The Rashtriya Rifles were designed for a particular purpose and they have achieved a lot. But now you should think of expanding their role in other spheres. We cannot afford to lose the expertise which they have gained in counter terrorism. Jammu and Kashmir is one state where the Army and the BSF operate hand in hand all along the international border and the line of control. Unfortunately, the BSF often operates at cross purposes with the Army because their roles and line of reporting are different. This is especially evident when it comes to the sharing of intelligence and monitoring and preventing cross border intrusion. There are about 13 battalions of BSF located in the Jammu and Kashmir. Their task can be easily be handed over to the Rashtriya rifles. In any case the LC is supposed to be under the control of the Indian army as per the decision of the Group of Ministers. So where is the need to have the BSF there? They can be replaced by the Rashtriya Rifles who in any case are better trained in border sealing operations.

The Rashtriya Rifles have a lot of scope to be used in a varied number of roles. Their composition is so structured that they can take on any kind of role be it infantry or all arms. Apart from employment in the counter insurgency role, they can be used equally effectively in the conventional infantry role. Hence, another option is to keep only that amount of force which is actually required in the interiors, while the balance can be pushed up to the line of control or the international border. Thereby you do not lose out on a potent force.

The very thought of reduction of the Rashtriya Rifles units is dangerous. No better organization exists to combat militancy and terrorism. Insurgency has not ended. It has diminished, but will rise and ebb a number of times over the years until it completely peters out. So, one can be sure till the foreseeable future, the Rashtriya Rifles battalions will be summoned for counter-insurgency tasks on a regular basis. From the Army point of view this is good because of two reasons, first because it provides good training for the soldiers as there is no better training than under fire; and second because it is good for the career progression of the soldiers, especially those from other arms and services, since they acquire a valuable experience in operational conditions, which they otherwise would not have been available to them.

They can also be used to replace the reserve offensive formations that are operationally deployed there and enable them to be spared for training, rest and refit. In fact they can also be used to be a relief for some battalions located on the line of control.

In times of operations they can relieve the infantry battalions in the defenses as to free them for offensive operations they can also be used for shallow infiltration during offensive operations and for occupying the ground behind the minefields during defensive operations.

The SD Directorate faces major problems in ensuring that an infantry battalion gets a minimum of 2 to 2½ years of peace tenure after a hard field tenure. By utilizing the Rashtriya Rifles battalions to give relief on the line of control to normal infantry battalions, you are automatically helping the SD Directorate in the relief planning process. What I mean to say is that since the problem in the hinterland has reduced, we can always push the Rashtriya rifles battalions to the LC. As it is, we have already done that earlier and that has been a big, big success. So, if you put them on the line of control, and instead of four companies you have six, and they can perform the infantry task as well, if not better, because they have more personnel to do the same job.

Another task, for which they can be utilized, is maintaining the strategic lines of communication. This is linked with the partial revocation of the AFSPA which is being repeatedly recommended by the state government. That action is fraught with danger because our strategic lines of communication pass through the districts which are intended to be declared as 'not disturbed'. We cannot afford to leave the road opening process in the hands of a unionized force like the Jammu and Kashmir Police. That is just too much at stake, not just in terms of lives but also in the fact that our winter stocking is dependent on free and unhindered movement along the highways. The Rashtriya Rifles, being a multi-tasked force, can easily be employed on tasks like road opening.

Q. There is talk that some Rashtriya Rifles battalions may be moved out of the state to combat terrorism in the Maoist infected areas. What is your opinion on this development?

That is a totally different ballgame, and if we can avoid it will be better. The moment we do it once, even an innocuous move of one battalion at that time, there is bound to be a precipitation of some nature and those troops were actually meant to combat the situation, such as the CRPF, would just step aside and request for additional troops and consequently more Rashtriya Rifles troops will be sucked in. After that there will be no end to it, and the force raised primarily for counter terrorist operations in the state of Jammu and Kashmir would lose its lethality and punch.

If, however, there is no other option and we have to spare Rashtriya rifles units for operations in the Maoist infected areas, we could reduce the number of companies from 6 to 4 and thereby raise some additional 10 battalions for the purpose.

Q. Is there anything else that you would like to add on the operation of the state and central police forces?

It is high time to initiate the police reforms which have been on the anvil for many years. Until the police force is freed from the clutches of the politician, it will never be able to enforce the rule of law in a fair and unbiased manner.

The Unified Command is unified only in name. Different security forces operating in the State have created their own fiefdoms. A dangerous trend which has set in is the attempt at gradual reduction of the relevance of the Indian Army in the State. The politicians with the tacit approval of the Ministry of Home Affairs are withdrawing departments which were earlier the domain of the forces. An example is that of cyber war.

There also needs to be a change of thinking. You first have to think of India and determine the contours of the emerging situation, whether it is converging or diverging from the concept of a united India, and then act accordingly. The problem in Jammu and Kashmir can be compared with the problem in the Northeast, in that even after 60 years the problem has not been resolved. But at least the Assam Rifles grid established over the years has succeeded in checkmating China and Bangladesh on a number of occasions. A similar permanence has to be sought for Jammu and Kashmir in terms of the Rashtriya Rifles.

Interaction with a Retired Bureaucrat

- The conflict is bleeding India both in terms of casualties and financially. So far the Government of India has spent over Rs 10,00,00,00,00,000 on Kashmir (There is no government confirmation of this figure - Author). An early end to the conflict is the need of the hour. But in no case must we negotiate from a perceived point of weakness.
- There are 79 families in the Valley for whom the conflict has become a cottage industry and are thriving because of it. Quite naturally, it is in their interest to keep the conflict alive; else their source of income would dry up. It is their wings that must be clipped, the earlier the better. The intelligence agencies need to focus their attention on them especially on the money trail emanating from their varied businesses.
- The demands of the separatists are unacceptable and this needs to

be hammered home as frequently as necessary. At the same time, the negotiables can and should be discussed. Independence, merger with Pakistan and any action that disturbs the secular fabric of society are non-negotiable; anything else is fair game.
- The philosophy of the third force is relevant.

Conversation with a Counter-insurgency Expert

It is a tragedy that in the last couple of decades there has been a deliberate and systematic erosion of the *Sufi* tradition and radicalization of the brand of Islam as being practiced in the Valley today.

The stone pelting incidents of 2010 were not random and spontaneous outbursts. It was a well thought out strategy to provoke a disproportionately strong reaction from the security forces. It took quite some time for the security forces to realize that they were reacting to pre-planned events.

I concur that some form of demilitarisation is needed. An elite force drawn out of the J&K Police itself, specially trained to react to armed incidents will be ideal. One battalion of such a force, properly led, can achieve infinitely more than what five times the number of ordinary policemen cannot. Add to that the force-multiplication factor of increased intelligence gathering capability that such local units inherently bring with them, and the resultant effect would be spectacular.

I agree that the Rashtriya Rifles are the best force to be entrusted with the task of normalizing the situation whenever it gets out of hand. I am of the opinion that the local content of troops should be increased. There are adequate numbers of troops hailing from the state that can be sent on ERE (extra regimental employment) to the force. It is but natural that the citizenry would react in a less hostile manner when confronted by troops who speak their language.

Conversation with a Counter-espionage Agent

In the course of meetings with the common citizens of Srinagar, the author got an opportunity to interview a counter-espionage agent whose name has been withheld. He is a reformed terrorist, who had crossed over into POK and received training in arms and explosives at the hands of Pakistani instructors. He was very soon disillusioned with the treatment that he and his colleagues received at the hands of the trainers. He said that they treated them like an inferior species, with disdain and totally without respect. He was also surprised to see that the so-called *Azad* Kashmir, was independent only in name. On getting the opportunity, he returned home and became a counter-espionage agent.

He spoke on a number of subjects ranging from the current situation in Jammu and Kashmir to the possibility of fanning an insurgent movement in POK. He was of the opinion that it was a mistake to hang Maqbool Bhat and that the government should not repeat the mistake by hanging Afzal Guru (the conversation took place before the event). The main points of the conversation are summarized below:

- India must actively support the concept of *Aar Paar Azadi*, which involves launching a pro-independence struggle in POK. This will add to the discomfiture of Pakistan and is an appropriate payback for its unabashed support for the anti-India movement in Jammu and Kashmir. If adequately funded, he was willing to mobilize his contacts across the LOC and launch ananti-Pakistan movement in POK.
- India made a tactical error in preventing the processions from proceeding beyond Uri during the 2010 protests. He said that the protestors should have been allowed to enter POK via the Uri Bridge and left it to the Pakistani forces to block their entry. The Pakistani Border Guards would certainly have been constrained to fire upon them, as they cannot risk permitting pro-*Azaadi* sloganeering in POK for fear of the separatist sentiment gathering momentum in POK also.
- The younger generation is not as scared of the security forces as the older generation because they have grown up in the shadow of the gun.
- The general public is not in favour of converting to the radical brand of Islam because, thanks to the television, they are aware of what is happening in Pakistan and Afghanistan after talibanisation.
- The security forces must be careful in their interaction with the public. They need to realize that arresting and mistreating innocents has an adverse effect, because once a person has been wrongly detained and brutalized, he becomes automatic fodder for the separatist cause.
- He opines that the government gives in too easily to Syed Ali Shah Gilani. They should concentrate on cultivating leaders like Maulvi Umar Farooq, Yasin Malik and Shabbir Shah and isolate Gilani.
- The Indian Government has consistently supported and placed their trust in just three or four political families. These families have been ruling the State, in turn despite their growing unpopularity,

over the last 60 years. This was a mistake and should be rectified at the earliest. The central government should promote genuine grassroots leadership and nurture them, thereby widening its support base.

- Once the central government supports a leader, it should not give up on him; otherwise he is a marked man.
- Political advisers to the Governor should be appointed from amongst the locals.

Conversation with a Senior Journalist from Srinagar

Q. What are your views on the role of the media in Jammu and Kashmir? Do you feel that measures to curb the freedom of the press and imposition of a measure of censorship are in order?

I am not in favour of censoring the media. Attempts to suppress the media invariably prove to be counter-productive. Here, I must quote what Lindsay Ross, Executive Director, Commonwealth Press Union, said in an interview to the Hindu. "Journalists have a major responsibility and must audit themselves. As journalists have the ability to change history, they carry a major responsibility and must, therefore, be scrupulous in auditing themselves. They must understand the necessity of verifying facts and maintaining standards. It is absolutely imperative for every journalist to self-analyze and self-reflect on a regular basis."

Q. What then, needs to be done?

What is really needed is greater transparency. Feed the media truth and not lies. Everyone understands that there are limits beyond which the media cannot intrude into operational conditions, but to the extent possible they should be given credible information and they should be made to understand what is going on. A positive approach will be helpful in bringing people around, in getting public support and giving satisfaction to the public that the armed forces are in fact engaged in the right thing and in the right way. To prevent misreporting the US forces follow the practice of co-opting journalists with them into operations. However, when it comes to the media in Jammu and Kashmir, we fight shy of trusting of journalists.

Q. Isn't there a code of conduct within the bounds of which the media is supposed to operate?

The Editors' Guild of India recently conducted a conclave for senior editors on developmental issues and role of media. It was accepted that critical issues like contempt of court, reporting of matters which are *sub judice*, trial by media, reporting practices, use and abuse of the freedom of press and the need of a code of conduct must be addressed by the Guild. Regular defaulters stand the risk of having their license revoked.

Q. What other social role can the media perform apart from just reporting/misreporting news?

The media needs to raise its voice for development. The media can perform its rightful role by publishing correct information thereby contributing to development. At the same time, the media needs to desist from sensationalizing news and views. To be fair to the administration, I must admit that by and large, no one in the administration really wants to gag the media. They only want the press to be fair in reporting on sensitive issues and report the version of both sides.

With the advent of latest technology, readers' and viewers' expectations from the media have increased, thereby enhancing the responsibility of the media. Higher viewership and TRPs should not be the criteria; instead the main news channels should be more sensitive to their responsibilities.

Conversation with Another Journalist

The propaganda which the general public in the Kashmir Valley believes is that the Amarnath agitation of 2008 and related violence in Jammu was funded by the Kashmiri Hindus. The Amarnath agitation provided the opportunity to the Hurriyat to spread the canard that the Government of India intended to revoke Article 370 and to resettle Indians masquerading as Kashmiri Hindus on land acquired from the Muslims.

It is also widely believed by the public that Governor Jagmohan pushed the Kashmiri Pandits out of Kashmir in 1990 so that he could unleash "genocide" in the Valley. This impression was never strongly countered convincingly enough by successive regimes. Resultantly, the masses still believe that the events of 1989-90 were part of a larger Indian conspiracy.

In support of his theory that the Centre was pulling all the strings in the State, he cited the example that there was not a single Kashmiri Hindu on the Amarnath Shrine Board. (This was an incorrect assertion. What he probably meant was that none of the board members was Valley-based, which is not surprising considering the fact that over 95% of the Kashmiri Hindus, and 100% of the prominent ones, were forced to flee for their lives in 1989-90).

Conversation with some Hindus who did not flee the Carnage of 1989-90

The conditions prevailing in the winter of 1989-90 were extremely scary and we cannot blame our brethren for having fled to safer areas. There was no rule of law and the streets were taken over by rampaging mobs. No one felt secure. Even our neighbours, with whom we have had excellent and practically familial relations for generations, were helpless and scared themselves. No one dared to say anything. You were either for the movement or against it. There was no third choice. The immediate answer to a dissenting opinion was a bullet. Those of us who stayed on, did so out of compulsion, not choice. We were unwilling to leave our home and hearth to go and rough it out in a refugee camp. As a precaution, many of us sent our women away to safer locations and called them back only once the situation improved.

It is unlikely that majority of the Pundits who fled will return, despite all the assurances given by the politicians and even their erstwhile neighbours. Once bitten, twice shy. The only feasible option appears to be the setting up of dwelling units in an independent township with all the amenities for day to day existence catered for. Even then, it is unlikely that the younger generation will return, because the State does not have adequate job opportunities for a cent percent literate community.

It would be an incorrect move to create yet another refugee camp in the Valley. No one would be tempted to return if it just meant exchanging a room in Jammu with two rooms in Srinagar. There has to be honour in the return. And that can only happen if the new abode and conditions are attractive enough.

The government, both at state level and at the centre, is responsible for our plight because they were not able to prevent the exodus. Therefore, it is incumbent on the government of the day to ensure an honourable return of the refugees and to establish the secular credentials of the country.

Conversation with a Lawyer representing the Indian Army

The JAG Branch needs to improve its professional competence and provide better advice on legal matters to commanders in the field.

The judiciary at district level, bar and bench, are scared of the terrorists. They are unwilling to take on government cases for fear of incurring their wrath.

A considerable number of police personnel are involved deeply with the "cause". There have been a number of occasions where the security forces have made an arrest based on the information provided by the police, only to have the police later retract under pressure from the militant groups or politicians beholden to them.

Some security personnel have a tendency of getting photographed to garner publicity and gain mileage. This tendency can backfire because it provides a face and name with the incident which can be exploited at a later date by Human Rights activists.

Conversation with a Town Planner and Author with Kashmiri Roots

For most of the world's population, life is a daily struggle for survival, a way of living by one's wits within the confinements of a social order not of their making. Kashmiri people are no different from the rest of their compatriots throughout the civilized world. What an average citizen wants is to own a home, to find a job that bring him a decent income, to have access to clean air, water, modern sanitation and affordable health care, to send his children to good schools, to commute expeditiously to and from work, to live in a clean, green, safe and culturally vibrant environment, to feel he is truly a stakeholder in his own destiny. These are not my words, but basically the findings of a draft world report Empirica 2000.

For this to happen, good governance has to be the instrument for promoting the common goal of development. Decisive local political action, in cooperation with civil society, is the need of the hour. To be truly successful and to achieve faster results, a greater degree of autonomy is required within an acceptable framework. A new balance of power needs to be established to replace the present norm of over-centralized government.

Comments

Interaction with the local population by way of interviews and casual conversation provided the author with a fund of invaluable information not available in books and study reports. By and large, it was evident that the ire of the locals was not so much against the presence of the security forces in Kashmir as with the curtailment of civil liberties. The average citizen agrees that violence can only be neutralised by violence, but that everyone must be treated as a potential terrorist is hugely resented. AFSPA invariably evokes strong sentiments. Much of this is related to the restriction of mobility within the cities and the frequent checks by security personnel. If a way can be found by which the citizens can proceed with their normal daily lives without the overbearing presence of the uniform, much of the civil unrest would abate. Many implementable measures were suggested by the interviews and have formed the basis of many a recommendation subsequently in the book.

All security personnel who are likely to come into contact with civilians should be put through a training capsule on dealing with the public. It is evident that the presence of non-Kashmiri security personnel creates great resentment. It stands to reason, therefore, that the interaction between security personnel and the ordinary citizen should be kept to a minimum, and wherever possible it should be by someone who speaks or at least understands the local language. This will reduce the possibility of potentially grievous misunderstanding due to the language barrier.

Steps should be initiated to streamline the movement of convoys through the city so as to cause the minimum disturbance to the citizens. Opening of civilian space would be a good beginning of the process of demilitarization.

6

Force Levels of Uniformed Personnel Operating in Jammu and Kashmir

In this section we will review the forces, both state level and central, at the disposal of the State Government for maintenance of law and order and for the conduct of counter-insurgency operations. A brief history on each will also help the reader to appreciate the reasons for increase in the force levels from modest beginnings at the time of independence to present day levels. Brief comments/recommendations follow at the end of the write up on each entity.

J&K POLICE

History[1]

The J&K Police, in its modern avatar, was established at the turn of the century. Between the years 1913 to 1947, with a solitary exception, a British Imperial Police officer on deputation served as Inspector General of the State Police. The first Indian Police Chief took over on 1st June 1946. Since then, the Police in J&K has undergone several re-organizations, The strength of Police in J&K gradually rose from 1040 in 1889-90, to 1570 in 1903 and to 3179 in 1943-44. The present strength of J&K Police is more than 83000.

Police Formations

Jammu & Kashmir Executive Police

The command and control of the J&K Police vests with the Director General of Police, J&K, (DGP) who is in-charge of the entire gamut of Police

Administration viz operations, recruitment, discipline, internal economy and administration in the State of J&K. Besides being the head of the Police Department, the DGP is also the Advisor to the Government on all matters connected with the Police.

Police Wings

The state police has been organized into various wings each headed by an officer of the rank of inspector general. A brief description of the wings of the state police is given in the subsequent paragraphs:

- **Police Headquarters**. This wing deals with various facets of administration, coordination, control, logistics, establishment and policy planning.
- **Crime Branch.** This wing is responsible for investigating cases of public importance, collection and consolidation of crime data, supervision of State Crime Records Bureau (SCRB), Crime Photograph Cell and maintenance of the Dog Squad.
- **Railway Wing.** This wing was carved out of the erstwhile Department of Crime and Railways. The Railway Police deals with criminal cases at railway platforms and tracks besides ensuring protection of Railway property.
- **Technical Wing.** This wing is responsible for installation, functioning and maintenance of police telecommunication grid in the State linking police stations, control rooms, district headquarters and other police wings.
- **Security Wing.** The Security Wing has the charter of providing security to protected persons, vital installations and to secure venues during sensitive events. The role of the wing has assumed more significant since onset of militancy in the State and personnel of the wing are mostly deployed with various categorized protected persons for providing physical security to them and their immediate family members.
- **Special Security Group.** The Special Security Group (SSG) is responsible for the protection of the Chief Minister, ex-chief ministers and their immediate family members.
- **Jammu & Kashmir Armed Police**. The Armed Police is a specialized force to deal with the maintenance of law and order and to combat militancy. It is not deployed for routine duties. The Armed Police is also utilized for manning static guards at protected places, vital installations, and vulnerable areas besides striking force to meet any eventuality. There are at present 11 Armed and 20 IRP Battalions in the State.

- **CID Wing.** CID is the premier intelligence wing of J&K Police and functions as the eyes and ears of the Government. The Special Branch deals with collection, collation and dissemination of intelligence while the Counter Intelligence branch is basically an anti-militancy set-up for collection of intelligence to counter the threat of anti-national, subversion, espionage, smuggling of contrabands and trans-border activities. Apart from these functions, the CID also carries out verification for the purpose of service, passports, threat perception, VISA clearance, NORI, migration relief cases and other allied verifications. The CID also maintains liaison with the Government of India on intelligence having bearing on law and order, security and terrorist activities.
- **Training Wing.** The Training Wing imparts Induction Training, on the job and specialized training so as to enhance professional competence and enabling the police personnel to acquire the requisite skills required to handle any kind of situation. The State Police Academy at Udhampur runs induction courses, promotion courses and specialized courses for various ranks. In addition, there are five subsidiary training schools at Kathua and Talwara (Jammu Region) and Zewan, Manigam, Lethpora and Sheeri (Kashmir Region) and an Intelligence and Security Training School at Vijaypur, Jammu.
- **J&K Civil Defence, Home Guard & State Disaster Response Force.** This Auxiliary Police force discharges multifarious duties such as assisting the civil Police in traffic control/regulation, maintenance of law and order and protection of life and property. The Auxiliary Police Battalions also organize training of Civil Defence and Home Guard Volunteers to meet any eventuality and extend a helping hand during emergencies like natural disasters.

In addition to the wings mentioned above, the Prosecution Branch, the Forensic Science Laboratories and the Police Housing Corporation function as independent entities.

Police Zones

For efficient police functioning, J&K State has been divided into two Zones, Jammu Zone and Kashmir Zone, each headed by a Zonal Inspector General of Police (IGP) who is overall In-charge of law and order situation in the respective zone. The two zones are further sub-divided into Ranges, each headed by an officer of the rank of a Dy. Inspector General of Police (DIG). The Range DIsG supervise the police administration in the Districts, each of which is headed by an officer of the rank of Superintendent of Police (SP)/ Sr. Superintendent of Police (SSP).

Police Ranges

Jammu Zone – 4

- Jammu-Kathua
- Rajouri-Poonch
- Udhampur-Reasi
- Doda-Kishtwar

Kashmir Zone – 3

- Central Kashmir
- North Kashmir
- South Kashmir

Police Districts

- **Jammu Zone**—10 (Jammu, Samba, Kathua, Udhampur, Reasi, Rajouri, Poonch, Doda, Kishtwar and Ramban Districts)
- **Kashmir Zone**—15 (Srinagar, Ganderbal, Budgam, Pulwama, Anantang, Kulgam, Shopian, Awantipora, Baramulla, Sopore, Bandipora, Kupwara, Handwara, Leh and Kargil Districts).

Districts have further been divided into Sub divisions, Police Stations and Police Posts/Divisions. The sub-Divisions are headed by officers of the rank of Assistant/Deputy Superintendent of Police.

Presently, there are 193 Police Stations (including two Women Police Stations one each at Srinagar and Jammu) and 158 Police Posts/Divisions in the State of J&K manned by Police personnel of the rank of Inspectors, Sub-Inspectors, Assistant Sub-Inspectors, Head Constables, Selection Grade Constables and Constables.

At Headquarters of each district, an Armed Reserve contingent under an officer of the rank of Deputy SP is maintained to cater for contingencies like leave/sickness etc. and to perform other miscellaneous duties in the district like armed and unarmed guards, escort of treasuries, prisoners/ under trials and the like.

Impact of Insurgency

In the aftermath of the disturbances, which began with the rioting and civil disobedience from 1989 onwards and culminated in the onset of a full scale insurgency in the early 1990s, the moral authority of the Jammu and Kashmir Police was badly eroded. The force was totally unable to enforce the will of the administration. The situation was handed over to the Indian Army and thereafter, for over a decade, the police force played second fiddle to the military authorities.

Once the situation was brought under control and a semblance of law and order was evident, the authorities decided that it was time to restore the situation to the state police. It was evident then that this would be a long and tedious process because the force was highly demoralized and totally dominated by the ruffian elements of society. In addition, the force had been penetrated by informers of the anti-national elements and terrorist organizations. Hence there was a trust deficit between the state police and the central police forces which needed to be bridged before the situation could be fully handed over to the J&K Police. However, there was no doubt in anyone's mind that ultimately the situation had to be handed over to the local administration, and only once this was achieved, could the situation be really termed to be normal.

This was the reiterated in 2009 by the Union Home Minister P. Chidambaram during his visit to Srinagar that the Centre would like the Jammu and Kashmir Police to play the primary role in maintaining law and order in the State. He said that the Central Government would prefer to see paramilitary forces like CRPF in a secondary role to the J&K Police. The Home Minister instructed the heads of the CRPF and the State Police to jointly work out a strategy for gradual substitution of CRPF by J&K Police in the essential duties that should ordinarily be performed by the Police. Advocating a step by step approach, he said, "We would like to take small, baby steps one by one and no great leap in Kashmir." [2]

The stone throwing agitation of 2010 is an important milestone in the history of the agitational politics of the State as it marked a shift in strategy by the separatists. Once they realized that despite all help from Pakistan, the Indian State machinery was far too strong to be dislodged by direct conflict and that it was next to impossible for them to achieve their goals by violent means, they decided to cash in on the unpopularity of the police forces by confronting them in massive numbers and use stones as missiles. The stones were meant to provoke the police forces into retaliation. Unfortunately, the police force at hand reacted in the worst possible way and fell directly into the trap set out for them by the separatist leaders. 'Bullet for stone' despite the provocation, can never be justified. It took many weeks for the CRPF and J&K Police to realize that they were facing a different style of agitation and that there was a definite method behind the apparently sporadic outbursts of mass agitations. By that time the damage was done. Apart from the civilian casualties of over 100 deaths, for the first time questions began to be raised about the legitimacy of the presence of Indian security forces in Kashmir, not just abroad but also within certain circles of the Indian intelligentsia some of whom began to openly advocate the right to self-determination of the Kashmiris.

It took a tragedy of such mammoth proportions for the state and central police leadership to realize that there was a pressing need to prepare and re-train its personnel on appropriate crowd control and the urgency to shift to non-lethal response measures.

Modernisation of the Jammu and Kashmir Police Forces

India's police forces are governed by an out-dated Police Act which is more than 150 years old. As 'Police' and 'Law & Order' are state subjects as per the VIIth Schedule to the Constitution of India, it is the responsibility of the States to provide an effective, competent and responsible police force for its citizens. The states are also competent to raise additional police forces as per their law and order, internal security and other requirements. After Independence, most states adopted the 1861 Act without change, while others have passed laws heavily based on the 1861 Act.

The Central Government has been supplementing the efforts of State Governments, especially frontline states like Jammu and Kashmir, in modernizing their police forces in terms of infrastructure, to meet challenges to Internal Security, effectively and to reduce their dependence on Central Police Forces.

Raising of the IRP Battalions

With a view to strengthening the capabilities of the States, and reducing their dependence upon CPFs to deal with various types of Law and Order and internal security situations, a scheme of raising India Reserve Police (IRP) Battalions in the States was introduced in the early 1970s. The objective was to create a well trained armed police force in the States with specialized skills and equipment to deal with various types of challenges posed by extremists and terrorists.

The advantage of raising such battalions is that the police force is augmented by an armed auxiliary composed of recruits from among the local population who possess an extensive knowledge of the local terrain and other peculiar conditions. This also serves the additional purpose of providing increased employment, thereby reducing one of the main complaints of the local population.

The number of IRP battalions in the state as under:[3]

- In existence till 2009—15.
- Raised between 2009 and 2011—5.

Apart from being armed with conventional weapons, the IRP has also been equipped with non-lethal state of art equipment to minimize casualties to unarmed protesters. Priority has been given for training the IRP personnel in effective crowd-control and in operating in a counter-insurgency environment. Standard Operating Procedures have been formulated for every conceivable contingency to prevent a recurrence of the 2010 type of situation.

In February 2011, the central government ordered the pull out of 133 CRPF companies[4] (amounting to approximately 13,000 personnel) from Jammu and Kashmir, as part of the process off reduction of security forces in the State. It is expected that a further reduction will follow as the local police takes complete charge of the situation and IRP battalions are fully operationalised in their new role.

Village Defence Committees (VDCs)

A system of VDCs has also been put in place to encourage and equip the village community for self-defence against the menace of terrorism and supplement the ongoing efforts of the Security Forces. This was required as due to poor communications in the remote areas, the response time for the security forces to an emergency was inordinately high. Invariably, the police team would arrive hours after the incident.

The aim of the VDCs is to organise the village community for self-defence against terrorism and to supplement the ongoing efforts of the security forces. These volunteers, known as Special Police Officers (SPOs) are paid a monthly honorarium and used for operational purposes. They remain attached to the VDCs or the local Police. Success of this effort is a manifestation of the will of the people to actively participate in the fight against terrorism.

Conclusion

Only an efficient, honest, professional and de-politicized police force is capable of providing a sense of security to the common man on the street. The police force needs to be diligent and fair in its dealings. Only then will the force be able to enjoy the trust and confidence of the citizens. Going by the figures reflected in the section on human rights elsewhere in this report, it is quite evident that such a force exists nowhere in the country. Urgent police reforms are the need of the hour.

In an article titled, *Police Accountability in India: Policing Contaminated by Politics*[5], GP Joshi mentions that, the reforms package must include the establishment of statutory institutional arrangements, which would ensure that the power of superintendence of the state government over the police force is limited to guarantee that police performance is in strict accordance with law. In other words, the police function to establish rule of law and not the rule of politics. This would require insulating them from outside illegitimate control and giving them functional autonomy. Once the police are given functional independence, they must be held accountable for the wrongs they do. The existing mechanisms of accountability must be strengthened and improved. In addition, new mechanisms, working independently to monitor the functioning of the police and to inquire into public complaints against the police, must be established.

CRPF

The CRPF is the largest paramilitary organisation of the country and is actively looking after the internal security in every part of India and are even operating abroad as part of United Nations peacekeeping missions. It performs a variety of duties ranging from VIP security to election duties, from guarding of vital installations to counter-terrorism and anti-naxal operations.

The CRPF is headed by an IPS officer of the rank of Director General. The force is divided into ten administrative sectors, each headed by an Inspector General. Each Sector consists of one or more administrative and/or Operational Ranges, headed by an officer of the rank of Deputy Inspector General (DIG) of Police. Group Centres are also headed by DIGs.

There are 222 CRPF battalions of approximately 1200 constables each. Each battalion is commanded by an officer designated as Commandant, and consists of seven CRPF companies, of 135 men each. A company is headed by an Assistant Commandant. The Home Ministry is planning to increase the strength of the force by adding 35 more battalions (30,000 personnel approx) in the coming years.[6]

CRPF in Jammu & Kashmir[7]

Pre-1989

CRPF was first deployed in Kashmir 1950, when a detachment of three companies of 1st battalion was deployed on law and order duty in Srinagar. They were withdrawn in early 1954 but in 1956 they were again deployed and moved out only in 1959. It was tasked to manage the Praja Parishad agitation besides some small assignments to check trans-LC crimes and crossovers. The 3rd Battalion was fully deployed in Kashmir in February 1957 and it remained within the state till July 1966. Duties of the CRPF included guarding the vital installations and the jails including the Kud Jail where Sheikh Abdullah was imprisoned.

By the mid-fifties, it was quite apparent that CRPF deployed in J&K was going to be a permanent feature. Three battalions were raised in 1956 under CRPF exclusively for duties in J&K. They were later merged in to CRPF (4, 5 & 6 battalions). While two of them (4, 6) were deployed in J&K after the requisite training, fifth was sent to Nagaland. In 1965 Indo-Pak war, CRPF fought pitched battles for safety of the bridges. In 1967 one more battalion (2nd) was moved into J&K and later three more units were added given the turmoil in the state. At any given time, there were four to six battalions in the state mainly for law and order duties till the rise of militancy during 1989. The Force has traditionally played an important role in the arrangement for the annual Amarnath Yatra in the state.

Post 1989

Till this period the CRPF was not unpopular with the local population. This was to change once the agitation turned violent and terrorism replaced the civil unrest, and the decision was taken to induct central forces in large numbers into the Valley. At the peak of militancy, CRPF had up to 129 battalions posted in Kashmir.

The CRPF has had a chequered tenure in the state, particularly in the Valley. They have often been accused of human rights violations, high-handedness and arbitrary behavior. Many incidents are on record but foremost among them are the incidents of molestation of women in Chanpora locality in 2006, and the firing on funeral procession of Mirwaiz Mohammad Farooq on May 21, 1990. The latter incident was highly unfortunate because it diverted the attention and anger of the population against the killers of the Mirwaiz and instead directed their fury totally against the Indian establishment and any and everything that stood for India. In fact, it is this incident that is held directly responsible for having led to the resignation of Mr. Jagmohan as Governor and forced re-assessment of the situation by the central government as a result of which the BSF started being deployed in phases.

By 1992 the effective strength of the CRPF was reduced to 89 companies and they were mostly utilized for guarding vital installations and VIPs. During this period the counter-insurgency operations were conducted by units of the Indian Army, Rashtriya Rifles, the BSF and elements of the special operations group.

The Kargil war of 1999 led to a reappraisal of the situation. Most of the units on the counter-insurgency operational role were withdrawn and sent to Kargil as reinforcements, leading to serious voids in the security matrix. A Group of Ministers (GoM) was tasked to review the system. The recommendations of the fresh plan envisaged a scenario under which, as far as possible, each organization was expected to be employed in its basic role. The army was tasked to continue ensuring the sanctity of the international borders. The BSF was tasked to go to the borders while the CRPF was tasked to take over the law and order situation in the state. The Rashtriya Rifles (RR) would continue to be employed in the counter insurgency role, the role for which it was specifically raised.

The process of de-induction of the BSF and induction of the CRPF started in 2003 and was supposed to be complete by October 2004. However, the process was delayed because it was considered vital to carry out prior training of the CRPF before assuming the new assignment. Over 5,000 CRPF men who replaced the BSF in September 2005 underwent training in Srinagar for over two months.

However, there was a serious flaw in the type of training imparted to the CRPF. They were basically trained to fight terrorists alongside the state police and the SOG. So long as the CRPF was facing armed militants or engaged in routine law and order duties, there were no problems. It was the stone throwing agitation in the summer of 2010 that exposed the serious weaknesses in the training of the CRPF. It was evident that the police force, which includes the J&K police and the CRPF, were neither physically equipped for, nor mentally prepared for the control of violent but unarmed mobs. It would not be incorrect to state that the police forces did not have a clue as to how to respond to the stone throwing youth.

A senior police officer admitted as much: "When the CRPF was deployed in 1990 they knew how to tackle routine law and order situations. Later when they were re-inducted, they were trained to fight militants but the situation demanded plain policing to take care of crowds. They over-reacted in most of the cases and led to many deaths. The CRPF alone is not to be blamed. For the last two decades, tackling militancy is the top of the priority for the government. Hence the troops were trained in counterinsurgency tactics and not in the mechanics of crowd control."[8] He added that the previous three batches of the Kashmir Police Service recruits knew more about neutralizing militants than crowd management.

Comments

No force involved in the counter-insurgency has evoked such strong emotions in the minds of the civil population as the CRPF. This cannot be attributed merely to the ruthlessness of the force. Prolonged deployment of the force and constant contact with the population coupled with the unfamiliarity with the language and local customs tends to breed distrust and contempt. The same treatment meted out by a local force would probably meet with considerably less resentment, and the locals and the leaders would be more understanding and be willing to consider it as part of duty by a uniformed force entrusted with the maintenance of law and order.

BORDER SECURITY FORCE (BSF)

The BSF is a paramilitary force charged with guarding India's land borders during peace time and preventing trans-border crime. Established in December 1965, it operates under the administrative control of Ministry of Home Affairs. It is one of primary law enforcement agencies of India and currently stands as the world's largest border guarding force. The current strength of the BSF is 186 Battalions or approximately 2,22,000 personnel.[9]

The tasks of the BSF are as under:

- *Peace time.*
    - Promote a sense of security among the people living in the border areas.
    - Prevent trans-border crimes and unauthorized entry into or exit from the territory of India.
    - Prevent smuggling and any other illegal activity.
- *War Time.*
    - Holding ground in less threatened sectors.
    - Protection of vital installations.
    - Assistance in control of refugees.
    - Anti-infiltration duties in specified areas.

In the last few years the BSF has, in addition to the above duties, been deployed for counter insurgency and internal security duties.

BSF in J&K

BSF has been deployed in Jammu and Kashmir ever since its inception in 1965. The newly embodied units were deployed along the International Border and on Line of Control. BSF units gave a creditable account of themselves during the war of 1971.

Although originally charged with guarding India's external boundaries, the BSF was entrusted with the task of counter-insurgency and counter-terrorism operations. When the insurgency in Jammu and Kashmir broke out in 1989, the Jammu and Kashmir state police and the thinly-deployed Central Reserve Police Force struggled to cope with the spiraling violence. The Indian government took the decision to deploy the BSF in Jammu and Kashmir to combat terrorism. The BSF, with a strength of six battalions, was inducted into the anti-insurgency operations in the strife-torn Kashmir Valley in 1990. The strength of the BSF in the State rose to 34 battalions from 1993 onwards.

The BSF initially suffered heavy casualties from insurgent attacks but later saw successes, including the arrest of militant leaders, after setting up an intelligence network and working with local civilians. The Kashmir chief of the BSF claimed that since 1990, the BSF had killed 2,700 ANEs and arrested over 10,000 of them.[10] He also claimed to have killed 38 top guerrilla commanders during this period. Despite the BSF's success in a counter-terrorism role, many in the government felt that this additional burden was leading to a dilution of the BSF's mandate and degrading the force's ability to perform its primary role of guarding the country's borders.

Pursuant to a GoM recommendation, in 2005 the Government decided to implement recommendations to restrict each security agency to its mandate. Thus the 16 BSF battalions in Jammu and Kashmir were gradually withdrawn from counter-insurgency duties and sent back to guard the borders. They were replaced by fresh units from the Central Reserve Police Force that have undergone specialized training in counter-terrorism.

CRPF replaced the BSF in Kashmir in September 2005. The de-induction started in 2003 and initially eight battalions were withdrawn from north Kashmir. As per the Director General, the complete withdrawal of BSF was planned to be achieved by 2007. Only one battalion of the BSF would continue to function in Srinagar for the security of the Raj Bhawan and the politically sensitive Gupkar Road.

Comments

After almost total de-induction from the counter insurgency role, the BSF had limited role in the counter-insurgency operations in the Valley and practically no role after 2009 as the CRPF had completely take over the counter insurgency duties from the BSF and the BSF reverted to its designated role of guarding the international border/LOC and preventing trans-border crimes/infiltration.

ITBP

ITBP was raised on 24 Oct 1962 in the wake of the Indo-Chinese conflict in 1962. It is deployed from the north-western extremity of the India-China border up to the tri-junction of India, China and Myanmar covering 3,488 km of mountainous terrain. The force is deployed at altitudes ranging from 9000 ft to 18,600 ft.

ITBPF is a specialized mountain oriented force and most of the officers and men are professionally trained mountaineers and skiers. It is also the first responder for natural disasters in the Himalayas and has conducted numerous rescue and relief operations.

ITBP was raised with 4 service battalions. Today there are 43 Service Battalions assisted by 4 specialized battalions with a total strength of 70,523. In order to cover the existing gaps along Indo-China border and to enhance surveillance capabilities of the Force, the Government of India has approved the re-structuring proposal of the Force which is to be implemented in a phased manner as under:[11]

Phase-I

2011-12

- Conversion of 20 Battalions from a 4 Company to a 6 Company pattern.
- Augmentation of strength of Intelligence set-up.
- Augmentation of strength of FHQ, SHQ, BOPs and the Directorate General.
- Creation of a Water Wing, Sub-Depot and Field Arms Workshop.

2012-13

- Raising of 4 Battalions alongwith one FHQ and One SHQ
- Establishment of Training Institutes.

Phase-II

2013-15

Raising of the remaining 9 Battalions and 2 Sector HQ.

Modernization. A five year perspective plan for modernization for the year 2011-16 amounting to Rs 786 crore is under process of finalisation.

Assessment. The value of the ITBP in terms of local knowledge of terrain, rapport with the locals and fighting ability in the rarefied atmosphere of their areas of deployment cannot be overemphasized. What, however, needs fine tuning is their command and control structure in times of conflict and their responsibility to respond to incidents of infiltration and deliberate violation of the LOC by the PLA. This is particularly applicable to the units deployed in Ladakh.

THE RASHTRIYA RIFLES

By mid-1990 it was apparent that the troops of the Indian Army deployed within the state were inadequate to meet the emerging challenge posed by the insurgency. The army which until then was the custodian of the international border and the line of control had been called in to assist in the counter-insurgency operations and help bring the situation under control. The army had already inducted a large number of formations from outside the state and was also constrained to thin out troops from the international border and the LC for counter-insurgency duties. This was not, obviously, acceptable for a longer period of time. Hence the army saw the need to create a specialized counter insurgency force which was christened the Rashtriya Rifles. These battalions were meant to help the Army to withdraw its regular troops from the counter insurgency role and free them for their primary role viz defence of the territorial integrity of the nation against external aggression.

The Central Government accorded approval to create the Rashtriya Rifles in 1990. The initial sanction was for two Sector Head Quarters of three battalions each. The then Chief of Army Staff, General BC Joshi supported the thinking in army circles that India was now involved in an extended counter-insurgency in Jammu and Kashmir like it was in the North-East. Hence a new force - akin to the Assam Rifles - was needed, which could be permanently located in the area to counter the insurgents. He maintained that using regular frontline army formations for counter insurgency would be playing into Pakistani hands. He pushed for setting up 10 more Rashtriya Rifles Sector HQ ie 30 battalions or the equivalent of three divisions. It was also felt that in the bargain the Army would have three additional battle-hardened divisions, ready for rear guard action during war. In 1994, the government gave a conditional go-ahead for a period of three years. In 2000, the Government accorded in-principle approval, to raise 30 more Rashtriya Rifles battalions, to bring up the total strength of the Rashtriya Rifles to five Force Headquarters, 17 Sector Headquarters and 66 Rashtriya Rifles Battalions by 2005.[12]

Rashtriya Rifles was raised as a paramilitary force as it was envisaged that personnel posted to Rashtriya Rifles would comprise regular Army volunteers on deputation, ex-servicemen and lateral inductees from various paramilitary forces and central police organisations. However, ever since its inception this force has comprised hundred per cent regular Army troops on ERE.

The Rashtriya Rifles has an organization structure tailor-made for counter insurgency operations. Each battalion has six infantry companies with approximately 1150 officers and men. Also unlike regular army units which are rotated out of the Valley regularly, the Rashtriya Rifles concept was to rotate personnel after a two years deputation. The Rashtriya Rifles units are permanently located in 'sectors', with each sector being the equivalent of a brigade with three battalions. To create a distinct identity, the Rashtriya Rifles has its own dress, special insignia and flag.

The Rashtriya Rifles units come under five CI Force HQs with areas of jurisdiction as shown below:

Kashmir Province	
Kilo Force	Srinagar, Kupwara and Baramulla districts.
Victor Force	Badgam, Anantnag and Pulwana districts.
Jammu Province	
Delta Force	Doda district.
Romeo Force	Poonch and Rajouri districts.
Uniform Force	Udhampur and Banihal Districts.

Source: Wikipedia.

The Force Headquarters come under the operational control of the regional Corps. Each force is headed by a GOC of the rank of a Major General. In terms of their operational use, each of the units and sectors is inter-changeable with a regular, equivalent army formation.

Once the government approval to raise the Rashtriya Rifles was accorded, the army decided to milk its existing units by 10-20% of their personnel to set up it up quickly. The officers and men came on deputation from all branches of the army. The infantry contributes approximately 50% strength of the Rashtriya Rifles, the other arms 40% while the services make up 10% of the strength.

Each regimental center was given the task of raising 1-2 battalions within a year. During this period, the units were raised and sent to the Northern Command where they got another 4 to 6 weeks to consolidate. All of them went through a structured 8 week course in special counter insurgency schools. They were then given another month to stabilize and then sent to the more dormant sectors of Kashmir and to the Punjab. To provide an experience base, 6 Rashtriya Rifles battalions were exchanged for 6 Assam Rifles units.

In raising the Rashtriya Rifles to full strength, the Army also had to dig into its war-wastage reserves, with the best available vehicles, weapons and radio sets going to the RR. In fact the Rashtriya Rifles units were even the first to receive bullet-proof jackets and *patkas*. With manpower drawn from all its arms and services, the Army has had to deal with serious shortages in many of its conventional units, for Rashtriya Rifles battalions are maintained at full authorized strength.

The Rashtriya Rifles battalions were initially raised on an All-India-All-Class basis with troops from all over the Army. The logic being that since the units were going to fight an insurgency, there should be no scope for vested interests in accusing a battalion of bias based on a class or regional attributes. However, this system was abandoned in favor of maintaining the individual identity of infantry units to instill a sense of camaraderie, cohesion and belonging among troops and thereby to reduce problems of administration and indiscipline. Instead of its units comprising of troops from all over the Army, two Rashtriya Rifles battalions were made an integral part of each of the infantry regiments and other arms. Now not only are majority of troops of the two Rashtriya Rifles battalions drawn from the other units of the Regiment, but their Commanding Officer or the 2IC, is from the same regiment. This ensures not only functional cohesion but also the regimental esprit-de-corps. This experiment has produced excellent results even while the units were deployed in the most difficult areas.

The induction of the Rashtriya Rifles in Jammu & Kashmir proved to be extremely effective from the very beginning. This fact is supported by the Rashtriya Rifles casualty figures rose from 3 out of 44 army casualties in 1991 to 82 out of 150 in 1996. By September 1997 by the combined efforts of the Army, RR, and other paramilitary forces, the situation in Kashmir had stabilized to the extent that the army decided to de-induct two brigades from the Kashmir Valley over a two-year period.[13]

In the spring of 1999, the Pakistani Army intruded into the Kargil heights. To deal with the situation, the army had to withdraw troops from counter-insurgency operations in J&K. During this period, the Rashtriya Rifles held the fort with the help of other paramilitary forces keeping the road and lines of communications open, fighting the terrorists, taking land mine blasts. Apart from that, Rashtriya Rifles units also actively contributed to operations in the Kargil heights where they fought shoulder-to-shoulder with units of the regular army at heights of 16,000 feet and above.

By moving regular army units to the Kargil theatre, the counter-insurgency grid was definitely weakened and this set the timetable for normalization back by at least one year. Keeping this in mind, after the Kargil battle, the Government decided to immediately raise 12 more battalions of the Rashtriya Rifles and 20 more battalions of the Assam Rifles. Also sanctioned were the force headquarters Kilo and Romeo. It was also decided in the post-Kargil scenario, that counter-insurgency operations will be undertaken now mainly by the Rashtriya Rifles supplemented by other paramilitary forces such as the BSF and CRPF. The Army is to be used only in extreme situations.[14]

The formal clearance for the Rashtriya Rifles is only till 2013. To implement and fine tune the new structure, the government will have to redefine the role of the Rashtriya Rifles as a regular force and not keep it hanging as an ad hoc formation. Its contribution to bring back peace and stability and Jammu and Kashmir is immense. The force has been able to create a situation conducive for good governance in coordination with the local population, police and the civil administration.[15]

A case has been taken up to raise up to 100 Rashtriya Rifles battalions and apply the balance 37 in the red zone. The army is opposed to this move. It does not want to move any battalion to the Naxal the affected areas as it does not want to disturb the counter-insurgency grid in Jammu and Kashmir.[16]

Miscellaneous Activities[17]

Goodwill Missions. Rashtriya Rifles troops have undertaken a number of goodwill missions in their respective areas to project the humane face of the army and to win the hearts and minds of locals. These include running of schools, organizing friendly matches between Army and locals and prize distribution. There has been overwhelming response from the people for such programmes, which has generated tremendous goodwill toward Rashtriya Rifles troops.

Development Works. Rashtriya Rifles troops have undertaken a number of development works including constructions of roads, water supply, education, model village, dispensary, children park, community hall, shopping complex etc under 'Operation Sadbhavna' in Jammu and Kashmir.

Medical Camps. As part of people friendly civic action projects, medical and veterinary camps for general public of remote villages were organised every month. A team of specialist doctors including physicians, ophthalmologists, gynaecologists, dentists and veterinary doctors worked in close cooperation with Army doctors to make the medical camps a big success. The camps provided services of the Army and civilians medical officers for immunization and the name family planning programmes.

Rashtriya Rifles troops maintained law and order, provided safety to general public and created conditions conducive to the local populace participating in elections. Such laudable achievements and sacrifices of all ranks will go a long way towards marginalization of militancy in J&K and in further enhancing the image of the Rashtriya Rifles and the Indian Army as a whole in the years to come.

Assessment of Impact

The reputation of Rashtriya Rifles as a specialized anti-terrorist force has had a tremendous impact on the psyche of the terrorists. Due to proactive operations conducted by well-trained and well-equipped troops, the Rashtriya Rifles have been able to maintain continuous pressure in a relentless manner on the terrorists who lost a number of their cadres, arms and equipment and now tend to avoid direct confrontation with Rashtriya Rifles troops.

As there is more permanence in the deployment of Rashtriya Rifles formations and units, they have a better rapport with the locals to gain more authentic flow of intelligence. As a result of all these factors, the junior leaders of Rashtriya Rifles battalions are able to take greater risks, often at the cost of their own lives to attain their operational goals. They always lead from the front, thereby setting an example for others to emulate. The fact that they have neutralised more than 7000 terrorists, captured more than 6000 weapons of all types and won more than 2000 honours and awards speaks volumes of this organisation.

The relationship of the Rashtriya Rifles with the local people, civil administration and law-enforcing agencies has been of an exceptionally high order. This has been possible due to regular interaction with the locals by Rashtriya Rifles formations, units and even companies. Various core group meetings are held periodically wherein the problems of the people are looked into and acted upon with compassion. Numerous civic action programmes like construction of water points, community centres and improvement of schools, mosques, roads and tracks have been undertaken. Hundreds of school children have been taken on various Rashtriya Rifles sponsored educational-cum-cultural tours to various historical places in India.

Other successes of this force include successful conduct of parliamentary and state assembly elections in 1997 and 1998 respectively, management of entire counter-insurgency and rear area security operations in J&K during Op Vijay, elimination of over 2700 militants since its raising, capture of large quantities of arms, ammunition and warlike stores, causing confusion and disarray amidst various militant cadres and improving the quality of life of the local public in their respective areas of responsibility.

Rashtriya Rifles has supplemented the work of the Army and the Central Para Military forces in J&K over the years. Its role in aid to civil authorities and maintenance of law and order has also had a significant impact. The modernization of the Rashtriya Rifles through weapons and equipment for sustained CT operations was approved during the year. This will include improved mobility and protection to personnel through mine protective vehicles, light bullet proof vehicles, hardened Army buses apart from ambulances and civil vehicles.[18]

The Rashtriya Rifles have also played a role in winning the heart and minds of people by providing assistance in health and education and carrying out relief and rescue operations during natural calamities.

Rashtriya Rifles remains the Counter insurgency/Counter Terrorist Arm of the Indian Army. The kind of surgical operations being carried out now-a-days has resulted in drastic reduction in own casualties. Operational performance of Rashtriya Rifles has been exemplary. Due to sustained pressure of Rashtriya Rifles, terrorist organizations have lost their cohesion resulting in in-fighting amongst various groups. This has been possible due to high motivation level of troops, a good intelligence network and an excellent rapport with local population and civil administration. However, success in proxy war has not been without a cost. Many gallant officers and men of Rashtriya Rifles have made the supreme sacrifice in the relentless pursuit of their objective.

There is scope for even further reorientation of the Rashtriya Rifles to make them more effective. Tackling insurgency and terrorism is heavily dependent on intelligence gathering, frequent shifting of units engaged in the conflict should be avoided. While combating low intensity conflicts, most actions are either at the platoon or the section level and it is important to have the best trained and seasoned 'junior leaders' leading the men into the fray. In a lot of places, they are pitted against highly motivated & trained mercenaries, who are guided by locals familiar with the terrain and topography.

One unforeseen consequence of the Rashtriya Rifles being a counter insurgency force is that it has led to command & control problems with other police organisations. The latter started arguing that the Rashtriya Rifles was in effect now a central police organisation, just like the BSF and the CRPF, under the MHA. However, that argument does not cut ice with the Indian Army. The force is at par with other army formations in terms of staffing, training and professionalism.

THE INDIAN ARMY

Increase in Indian Army Force Levels since 1947

Quantum of troops deployed in the state has increased in direct proportion to the perception of threat from across the borders post the wars of 1948, 1962, 1965, 1971 and 1998 and from within post 1989. The requirement of troops has always been linked to the varying nature of threats. Jammu and Kashmir being a frontline state, the Indian government would always prefer to err on the positive and therefore position more troops than may actually be required.

It is an oft repeated argument that the density of troops in the state of Jammu and Kashmir is extremely high and that there is a need for considerable reduction in force levels. The Indian Army, in particular, has been singled out in this criticism. The force levels of the regular Indian Army in the state of Jammu and Kashmir have, indeed, increased manifold since Independence. However, this increase cannot be attributed purely to the internal turmoil that has plagued the state over the last two decades. In fact, most of the troops which were inducted into the state in the late 1980s and early 1990s to combat the insurgency, have since been de-inducted to other areas of the country. The increase has invariably been as a direct response to a hostile action by an unfriendly neighbor coveting land which was not his, and willing to employ any form of deceit and subterfuge in order to grab the same. The increase in the force levels of the Indian Army since independence is outlined in the succeeding paragraphs.

J&K State Forces[19]

At the time of independence, the Maharaja of Kashmir maintained a larger number of State Forces than any other Ruler of an Indian State under the British Raj. These forces were organized into the Jammu and Kashmir Brigades. They comprised one Bodyguard Cavalry regiment, two Mountain Batteries, seven active and one training battalions of Infantry and a Transport unit consisting of both pack and mechanized transport. The strength of the Kashmir State forces was approximately 9000, of which roughly 2000 were Muslims.

The disposition of state forces of J&K on 22 October 1947 was as under:

Jammu Brigade
- Bde HQ
- J&K Infantry (KI) Regt Centre—Jammu
- 5 J&K Infantry (KI) Bn
- J&K Bodyguard Cavalry less one squadron
- Four garrison police companies

Kashmir Brigade
- Bde HQ
- J&K Infantry (KI) Trg School
- One squadron J and K Bodyguard Cavalry
- 7 J&K Infantry (KI) Bn less two companies—Srinagar
- 4 J&K Infantry (KI) Bn less two companies—Domel
- Company—Kohala
- Company—Spread in gen area Keran
- 6 J&K Infantry (KI) Bn less two companies—Bunji
- Company less one platoon—Leh
- Two Platoons—Kargil
- Company less one platoon—Skardu

Poonch Area
- Force HQ—Poonch
- 1 J&K Infantry (KI) Bn—Spread in base area
- 8 J&K Infantry (KI) Bn (relieving 1 Bn)
- 9 J&K Infantry (KI) Bn
- Two Companies 7 J&K Infantry (KI) Bn—Rawalkot (spread in sub-units)

Mirpur Brigade
- Bde HQ
- One Platoon J&K Infantry (KI) Bn
- One Platoon 3 J&K Infantry (KI) Bn
- One garrison police company—Dharamsal-Jhangar
- 2 J&K Infantry (KI) Bn less one platoon—Naushara and its outposts
- 3 J&K Infantry (KI) Bn—Mirpur and its outposts

**Note:* The J&K Infantry (KI) battalions mentioned above were later merged with the regular Indian Army and formed the Jammu and Kashmir Rifles. The J&K Militia was converted into the Jammu and Kashmir Light Infantry.

From the above it is evident that the force was largely ceremonial in nature and totally incapable of providing serious defence of any territory much less that of a state the size of a large European country. The State, therefore, had the mouthwatering potential of rich pickings in terms of pillage and loot for any marauder. Pakistan was quick to seize the opportunity and unleashed the Pashtun tribesmen on the unsuspecting and unprepared Kashmiri population. The subsequent events as to how the Indian Army was inducted to check the advance of the raiders once the Maharaja signed the Instrument of Accession are too well documented to bear repetition.

Orbat of Troops in J&K after the 1947-48 Indo-Pak War[20]

During the course of the war, a sizeable portion of the Indian Army was engaged in combating Pakistan. At the time of signing the ceasefire agreement, the disposition of Indian troops in Jammu and Kashmir State was as under:

Div HQ-2

- Jammu Div
- Srinagar Div

Jammu Div

- Five infantry bdes
- Jammu SF

Srinagar Div

- Four infantry bdes
- Srinagar SF
- L of C Sub Area (responsible for protecting the L of C from Pathankot to Srinagar)

Thus the total force level in the state at the end of the 1947-48 war stood at 2 Divisions, 12 Infantry Brigades, 50 Infantry Battalions (including Indian State Forces Battalions) and 14 Battalions of J&K and East Punjab Militia. Subsequent events would prove that this force level was also highly inadequate for the defence of such a large territory.

Forces in Ladakh during 1962 Sino-Indian War[21]

By the late 1950s, it had become evident that a serious border issue with China was likely to erupt. In anticipation of hostilities, it was decided to increase the quantum of troops in the Ladakh province, the defence of which was till then entrusted to the J and K Militia. Accordingly, an independent brigade was raised in 1959 at Leh for the defense of Ladakh. The border was handed over to the Army in April 1960. The Brigade initially had just two battalions for the defence of the 480-kilometer long sector. Even with the additional inductions, troops were still so thinly spread out that the vital Chushul airfield could be spared only two platoons. An additional battalion was inducted into the sector in September 1962 just prior to the commencement of hostilities. In the early phases of the fighting, the whole of Ladakh had merely one brigade group consisting of four battalions. 3 Mountain Division was raised at Leh in October 1962.

By the end of the Sino-Indian war of 1962, the force level in Ladakh was:

- HQ 3 Mountain Division
- Three infantry brigades

Force Levels in Jammu and Kashmir during the 1965 Indo-Pak War[22]

15 Corps. Located at Srinagar, the Corps controlled Indian forces in Ladakh, Kashmir, and Jammu. At approximately 950 kilometers, this Corps probably had one of the longest frontages of any in the history of warfare, particularly so because the 750 km front with Pakistan was live. The Corps had to be prepared to go to war at a moment's notice: its front was not some forgotten backwater overgrown with the moss of decades of inactivity and neglect, but one where Indian and Pakistani forces faced off on a daily basis. The disposition of troops under HQ 15 Corps was as under:

Headquarters 15 Corps (Srinagar)

- **3 Mountain Division** (for the defence of Ladakh province) comprising two infantry brigades.
- **An Independent Infantry Brigade Group** (for the defence of Dras and Kargil) comprising two infantry battalions.
- **19 Infantry Division** (for the defence of Kashmir Province) comprising four infantry brigades.
- **25 Infantry Division** (for the defence of the mountainous regions of Jammu Province) comprising four infantry brigades.
- **HQ 10 Infantry Division.** A newly raised HQ with 30% of its establishment, was transferred from Hyderabad/Secunderabad as war became imminent. It had no troops of its own. It took over existing formations on the ground and was responsible for the defence of the riverine and low hills sector of Jammu Province.
- **26 Infantry Division** (for the defence of the plains sector of Jammu province)
- An infantry brigade group as a reserve formation.
- **Srinagar Force** – Originally set up to protect Srinagar area from

infiltrators entering under Pakistan's Operation Gibraltar, as 15 Corps's infantry divisions were busy on the border. It had the following troops under command:

- HQ Srinagar Force
- An infantry brigade less an infantry battalion ex 3 Mountain Division
- HQ 31 Communication Zone Sub-Area
- HQ J And K Militia With A Battalion Less Two Companies

Force Levels in Jammu and Kashmir During the 1971 Indo-Pak War[23]

Indian strategy aimed at strategic defence in the Western Theatre while conducting offensive operations in East Pakistan.

In Jammu and Kashmir, 15 Corps comprising 3, 19, 25, 10 and 26 Infantry Divisions and an independent armoured brigade was committed to static defence along the ceasefire line and to covering the routes of ingress to sensitive areas. The troop levels and areas of responsibility generally remained the same as in 1965. One infantry brigade of 3 Infantry Division was detached and moved to the desert sector in Rajasthan.

Raising of Northern Command[24]

During the 1971 war, it was realized that the geographical spread of Western Command was too extensive for effective real time control in operational scenarios. A decision was therefore taken for raising another command to exclusively look after the state of Jammu and Kashmir. Accordingly, in 1971, duplicate headquarters with duplicated staff were set up at Shimla and Bhatinda.

Raising of 16 Corps

It was decided in June 1972 to raise Northern Command at Udhampur, with two Corps under it, to look after the defence of Jammu, Kashmir and Ladakh. The area of responsibility of 15 Corps was confined to Kashmir and Ladakh and a new Corps, viz 16 Corps, was raised at Nagrota to cater to the defence of Jammu Province.

Occupation of the Siachen Heights (Op Meghdoot)[25]

Roots of the Siachen conflict lie in the non-demarcation of the Line of Control between India and Pakistan on the map of J&K beyond point NJ9842. The 1949 Karachi agreement and the 1972 Shimla pact presumed that it was not feasible for human habitation to survive beyond NJ9842. By the watershed principle the glacier lies on the Indian side; since the Nubra River rising out of the glacier flows into Ladakh and joins the Indus River. However, in defiance of this principle and in a clear violation of the Shimla pact, the Pakistanis claimed the entire glacier and the adjoining mountain ranges up to the Karakorum Pass as theirs. The Pakistanis used various means, such as clearing international mountaineering expeditions for scaling peaks in the Siachen region, to legitimize their claim over the Siachen Glacier. In 1984, the Indian Army intelligence came to know of the Pakistani Army's intentions to occupy the Siachen Heights. The Indian Army therefore launched Op Meghdoot to secure the glacier and adjoining heights from Pakistani aggression. The responsibility for the defence of the Siachen Glacier is that of 102 Brigade of the 3 Infantry Division.

Onset of Insurgency and the Induction of the Rashtriya Rifles[26]

With the sudden flare up of insurgency in 1990, the state was beset with a flood of terrorists from across the border. Large numbers of misguided youth from the state were recruited by the Pakistani ISI to be trained in camps established across the LC in POK and pushed back into the state of the having been armed, indoctrinated and given the minimum training required to combat the Indian Security forces. The situation in 1990 was quite critical and required drastic measures to stem the cycle of violence, breakdown in the law and order machinery and total anarchy. To make matters worse, Hindus of the Valley began fleeing in droves in response to threats by fundamentalist organizations to either join the fight for *Azaadi* or be liquidated.

The local administration was in no condition to handle the protests and violence. Once the situation was handed over to the Indian Army, immediate steps were taken to induct additional troops into the state of Jammu and Kashmir from the rest of India. 8 Mountain Division and other formations were inducted into the state to bring the situation under control. In addition to the additional units of the regular army, it was also decided at the government level to raise a specialist counter insurgency force called the Rashtriya Rifles.

Technically, however, the Rashtriya Rifles are paramilitary forces under the home ministry and not part of the regular army, even though the manpower has been drawn from the regular army. The raising, induction, strength and impact of the Rashtriya Rifles is discussed in a separate chapter.

The induction of the Rashtriya Rifles in Jammu & Kashmir proved to be extremely effective from the very beginning. By September 1997 by the combined efforts of the Army, Rashtriya Rifles, and other paramilitary forces, the situation in Kashmir had stabilized to the extent that the army decided to de-induct 13 battalions (12,000 troops) including two brigades from the Kashmir Valley over a two-year period. In fact up to Spring 1999, the army had already withdrawn nine battalions (8000 troops) including a brigade from the Kashmir Valley without replacements. The last batch of 4 battalions (about 4000 troops) along with a brigade HQ commenced de-inducting in April 1999 and was supposed to complete by mid-summer 1999. However, the Pakistani perfidy in Kargil added another dimension to the already complex problem in Jammu and Kashmir, and the entire process of de-induction of the Indian Army came to a grinding halt.

Raising of 14 Corps

The Pakistani intrusions in 1999 in the Kargil sector underscored the requirement of more troops for defence of this hithertofore dormant sector. A Mountain Division was rushed there from Srinagar Valley after the intrusions were detected. With the induction of the second division into this sector, it was the next logical step to raise a Corps headquarters for better command, control and coordination. Accordingly, 14 Corps was raised for the defence of Ladakh and Kargil. While 8 Mountain Division was given the responsibility of guarding 150 kilometers of the border in the Kargil sector, 3 Infantry Division had the responsibility of the Siachen and the Aksai Chin border.

Assessment

From the above, it can be seen that the increase in force levels has been as a direct consequence to an aggressive action by a belligerent neighbor. Except for brief periods in the early 1990s, other inductions have been the result of heightened threat perception. It is axiomatic, therefore, that de-induction can only take place when the threat perception reduces. For that to happen, improvement in relations with Pakistan and China is a necessity. It would take a very fool hardy leadership to agree to a substantial troop pullout thereby weakening the defensive posture, in the absence of tangible and credible measures and assurances from across the borders.

NOTES

1. Official website of the J&K Police.
2. Interview of the Home Minister - 2009.
3. Annual Report 2010-11, Ministry of Home Affairs.

4. February 2011 withdrawal of 153 CRPF companies.
5. GP Joshi, *Police Accountability in India: Policing Contaminated by Politics*, Insight, 29 April 2005.
6. Annual Report 2010-11, Ministry of Home Affairs.
7. Official website of the CRPF.
8. Interview of a senior CRPF officer.
9. Official website of the BSF.
10. Interview of a senior BSF officer.
11. Official website of the ITBP.
12. http://www.globalsecurity.org /military/world/india/rashtriya-rifles.html
13. Bhattacharya, B, *"The Rashtriya Rifles"*, Bharat Rakshak Monitor - Volume 3(2), Sep - Oct 2000.
14. Ibid.
15. Nitin Gokhale, Defence Forum India.com the/forum/indian-army.
16. Sishir Gupta, Hindustan Times Dec 2, 2011.
17. Annual Report 2003-04, Ministry of Defence.
18. Ibid.
19. Major General KS Bajwa, Jammu *And Kashmir War (1947-48): Political And Military Perspective*, 2003, Har-Anand Publications Private Limited, F 1211, Chittaranjan Park, New Delhi 110019.
20. *Operations in Jammu & Kashmir*, History Division, Ministry of Defence, Governmentof India, Nataraj Publishers, Reprinted edition 2005, quoted on page 136 of the Autumn 2012 issue of Scholar Warrior.
21. *History of the Conflict with China, 1962* by Dr. PB Sinha and Colonel AA Athale Beria Chief Editor SN Prasad . History Division, Ministry of Defence, Government of India, New Delhi, 1992).
22. *Indian XV Corps, Kashmir 1965* v.1.0 April 7, 2002, Ravi Rikhye & Dave Sandhu. As per the authors this orbat may be wrong in some respects because units were being shifted between formations all the time.
23. *War in the Western Theatre 1971* - Maj Gen Dhruv C Katoch.
24. *Global Security.org*
25. *horsesandswords* (blogspot.com/2006/03/op meghdoot.html, Mar26,2006))
26. *The Rashtriya Rifles*, B Bhattacharya, Bharat Rakshak Monitor, Vol. 3(2), September-October 2000).

7

AFSPA

"Revocation of the AFSPA is more in the hands of the Hurriyat, the insurgents and their mentors in Pakistan than in the hands of the government. The day the former forgoes the option of violence against the state machinery, there would be no AFSPA"

—Author

Probably no other issue evokes such strong sentiments from all sections of Kashmiri society and also the security forces, for differing reasons of course, as the revocation of the AFSPA. It has become a symbol of all that is wrong and repressive about the presence of the central security forces in the state. Its removal is prescribed as the panacea for all the evils that beset the state. At the same time, the security forces have legitimate concerns about the removal of the AFSPA while they are still expected to conduct operations. Before we discuss differing points of view, it would be in order to understand the provisions of the Act and why it had to be enacted in the first place. Extracts from an article[1] by Lt Gen Mukesh Sabharwal, a former Corps Commander in the Valley, are reproduced in the succeeding paragraphs.

Genesis

The Armed Forces Special Powers Act (AFSPA), 1958 was enacted by the Parliament on September 11, 1958, to provide necessary powers and legal protection to the Armed Forces while carrying out proactive operations against the insurgents in a highly hostile environment. Since then, the Armed Forces have been able to effectively contain insurgency and establish stability in the region. With the ongoing insurgency in the North East, the AFSPA-1958, is currently applicable in the States of Assam, Manipur, Meghalaya, Mizoram, Nagaland, Tripura, as also Tirap and Changlang districts of Arunachal Pradesh. Subsequently, the Parliament enacted the Armed Forces (Jammu and Kashmir) Special Powers Act, 1990 for the state of Jammu & Kashmir, which came into effect on July 05, 1990.

Initially, the Government had declared areas falling within 20 kms of the Line of Control (LC) in the districts of Rajouri and Poonch as also the districts of Anantnag, Baramulla, Budgam, Kupwara, Pulwama and Srinagar as disturbed. Subsequently, in August 2001, the AFSPA was extended to the districts of Jammu, Kathua, Udhampur, Poonch, Rajouri and Doda, when these were also declared 'disturbed'.

Need for Legal Protection

The Armed Forces are required to operate in varied terrain such as thick forests, in far flung areas and also in the built up areas ranging from small hutments and villages to towns and cities, where the insurgents have established their training camps and support bases. Not only do the troops operate in hostile terrain, they also work in an unfriendly population environment exposing themselves to grave dangers demanding very high degree of operational effectiveness. At the same time, the Armed Forces are under pressure to be extremely cautious and avoid collateral damage and loss of innocent lives or property.

Is the Act Illegal?

One of the most important tasks before the Government is to maintain proper balance between the interest of the individual and those of the democratic society. Individual freedom has to be balanced with the freedom of other individuals and with reasonable demands of the community and the general public. It is the duty of the state to harmonise the rights of the individual with the requirements of the community. The Central Government vide Article 355 of the Constitution of India is duty bound to protect every state not only against external aggression but also internal disturbances and to ensure that every state is governed in accordance with the provisions of the Indian Constitution.

The term 'Draconian', which implies exceedingly harsh or very severe, normally refers to a legal code or a set of government laws. Public sentiment and those swaying with it, be they NGOs, human rights activists and the like often term the AFSPA as illegal and unconstitutional. Nothing could be further from the truth.

The *vires* of the said Act in general and of Sections 3, 4 and 6 thereof in particular, came up for scrutiny before a Constitutional Bench of the Apex Court in a case titled 'Naga People's Movement of Human Rights Vs the Union of India'. The five-judge constitutional bench elaborately dealt with the challenge to the legality of deployment of the Armed Forces in aid to civil power. The Court unambiguously ruled that the AFSPA cannot be regarded as a colourable legislation or a fraud on the Constitution. The Court opined that the conferring of powers vide Section 4 of the AFSPA could not be held arbitrary or violative of Articles 14, 19 or 21 of the Constitution. In fact, having considered the role and circumstances under which the Armed Forces have to operate, the honourable Court extended the scope of powers vested vide sections 4 and 6 of AFSPA so as to include, by implication, the power to interrogate persons arrested. It also allowed the Armed Forces to retain the weapons seized during operations instead of handing over to the police authorities.

The mere fact that the provisions of the AFSPA have to be invoked with regard to a particular area *ex facie* establishes that the law and order situation in the said area had degenerated to such an extent that the State Government with the aid of the police at its disposal was unable to maintain peace and tranquility. A natural corollary to the above would be that if the Armed Forces, who are called upon to assist the State administration in restoring normalcy, have to succeed in their task, they enjoy at least similar powers, if not wider ones as the police does. A perusal of the various powers available to the police authorities under the provisions of the Criminal Penal Code vis-à-vis those available to the Armed Forces under the AFSPA would reveal that the police authorities still enjoy more encompassing and wider powers relating to arrest, search, seizure, summoning of witnesses and preventive detention than the powers enjoyed by the Armed Forces.

Demand to Repeal/Revoke AFSPA

The longstanding demand of separatists, their supporters and some political parties has been to repeal the AFPSA altogether. A partial revocation from certain areas of the state has also been proposed. Echoing public sentiment, its votaries repeatedly blast the Act as "Draconian" in nature and the Army's misuse of the Act to perpetrate human rights violations and excesses.

Comments

As mentioned initially, the Act has become symbolic of all the wretchedness, sufferings, curtailment of civil liberties and difficulties faced by the common public on a day to day basis. Hence the constant refrain for its revocation. However, the revocation is easier said than accomplished. This is because of the strong reservations of the central security establishment. In October 2010, the Chief of the Army Staff, in an interview to The Tribune [2] categorically stated that, "The AFSPA is an enabling provision and Act passed by the Parliament. It assists the Armed Forces in dealing with special situations." According to him, the Act provides protection to the soldiers who are operating under difficult and sensitive circumstances.

Opinion of the Defence Establishment. Revocation of Disturbed Area Act by the Jammu and Kashmir Government will not affect the applicability of AFSPA in the State as the two laws are not interlinked. The Defence Minister stated in Parliament that he was not in favour of revoking AFSPA due to the under mentioned reasons:[3]

- AFSPA is a must for effective performance of the forces in the Jammu and Kashmir State.
- AFSPA cannot and should not be revoked from any part of Jammu and Kashmir so long as the proxy war in the State abetted by Pakistan continues.
- Intelligence inputs received by various Army formations in Jammu and Kashmir appear to suggest that infiltration is on the rise after the State Government's move for a partial withdrawal of AFSPA.
- Revocation of the AFSPA Act from Jammu and Kashmir could be some time away as consensus will have to be evolved among all stakeholders on the crucial issue as positions were not "unified" at the moment at the Centre.

Opinion of the Political Establishment

Former Chief Minister Omar Abdullah voicing the general opinion of the political establishment in the State gave the following reasons in support of his call for the revocation/partial revocation of the Act:

- Removal of AFSPA is part of the aspiration of people of Jammu and Kashmir. It is a reflection of the sentiments of people who want to get rid of the laws that were imposed two decades back when the situation was abnormal.[4]
- Withdrawal of the AFSPA from certain areas of the State was in no way an effort to undermine the role of the Army. AFSPA can be withdrawn from some areas in the State with a rider that the Army could step in again if the situation so warranted.[5]
- The Government has constituted two committees, one each for

Jammu and Kashmir regions respectively, to look into the areas where from AFSPA could be withdrawn.[6]

- We have requested the Home Minister to identify the areas where the footprint of Army was minimal and then go for revocation of Disturbed Areas Act and subsequently the AFSPA withdrawn.[7]
- State Government was ready to amend the Ranbir Panel Code (RPC) to make it at par with Criminal Penal Code (CrPC) to provide legal protection and immunity to armed forces in Jammu and Kashmir at par with other States.[8]

Conclusion

Discussion on the AFSPA has been going on over the last two decades. The pitch is raised especially when a human rights violation is alleged to have taken place. The reality on the ground is that not only do the troops operate in a hostile terrain, they also work in an unfriendly population environment. Any violation or perceived violation attracts media attention and provides an opportunity for propaganda to factions with vested interests. On most occasions allegations have been found to be false and evidence fabricated but nevertheless, have to be answered, rebutted or contended with. Operating under such environment requires a protective law lest the forces get embroiled in legal battles and their effectiveness is reduced in operations for which they have been deployed in the first place.

In the opinion of the author, revocation of the AFSPA is more in the hands of the *Hurriyat*, the insurgents and their mentors in Pakistan than in the hands of the state or central government. The day the former forgoes the option of armed resistance, there would be no need for the imposition of AFSPA.

NOTES

1. Lt Gen Mukesh Sabharwal, *Operational Importance of AFSPA*, IDR Issue Vol. 27(2) Apr-Jun 2012.
2. Ibid Annual Report 2010-11, Ministry of Home Affairs.
3. Interview to the Daily Excelsior.
4. Ibid.
5. Government reply to a question posed in the State Assembly on 23 March 2010.
6. Interview to the Daily Excelsior.
7. Ibid.
8. Government reply to a question posed in the State Assembly on 23 March 2010

8

Human Rights

"The Kashmiri militants and their supporters know well the political appeal to Westerners of human rights issues and naturally they make the most of it. They can be no doubt, in other words, that reports of human rights abuses are often exaggerated."

—Robert Wirsing

The issue of human rights violations in the state of Jammu and Kashmir figures prominently in the reports of all human rights organizations and observers. There is scarcely any incident which goes unreported. This is because of the media spotlight on the State which ensures that nothing can be swept under the carpet. Human rights in Jammu and Kashmir has been a subject of many a debate in national and international fora. The central security forces have come in for a lot of criticism and going by the hype and hysteria on the streets and reported, at times exaggerated, in the media, one would think that the security forces have been unleashed by the government with the sole purpose of wiping out the entire Kashmiri race. This is far from the truth. There is no denying that there have been instances of violations of human rights in the State. Nor is it the intention of the writer to give a clean chit to the security forces. But giving the Devil his due, one has to emphasise that there is no institutionalized culture of torture, rape, loot and all the other misdemeanors that the security forces are accused of. Coming from a person in uniform (albeit retired), this statement may not sound convincing. It may be better to buttress this argument with the opening paragraphs on the human rights situation in India as quoted in Wikipedia[1].

"The situation of human rights in India is a complex one, as a result of the country's large size and tremendous diversity, its status as a developing country and a sovereign, secular, democratic republic, and its history as a former colonial territory. The Constitution of India provides for Fundamental rights, which include freedom of religion. Clauses also provide for Freedom of Speech, as well as separation of executive and judiciary and freedom of movement within the country and abroad.

"According to the United States Library of Congress, although human rights problems do exist in India, the country is generally not regarded as a human rights concern, unlike other countries in South Asia. Based on these considerations, the 2010 report of Freedom in the World by Freedom House gave India a political rights rating of 2, and a civil liberties rating of 3, earning it the highest possible rating of *free*".

Having leveled the playfield, somewhat, we can proceed to analyze the conditions of human rights in the State. The average Kashmiri yearns for peace. He is upset at his homeland having been converted into a battleground. The unfortunate truth is that in any zone of conflict, there are bound to be restrictions on civil liberties imposed by one or other side. In the initial period of insurgency, it was the writ of the terrorists which held sway. As the situation was brought under control, it was the writ of the security forces which ultimately prevailed. However, so long as the control vests with the security forces, it implies that the local police force is not yet ready, willing or capable of resuming control of the situation and there will be some measures of population control in place. The security forces are perfectly aware that they cannot afford to lose moral legitimacy of their task by permitting troops to indulge in actions like murder, torture and rape. They are not occupation troops nor would they like to behave as such. The average person in uniform is only concerned about serving with honour, doing what it takes to achieve the task at hand, while still managing to stay alive and returning home to his family after completing his tenure in the conflict zone. However, at times, there are some elements in the security forces who may be misguided into thinking that rules of armed conflict do not apply in the counter-insurgency scenario because the threat the terrorists represent justifies extraordinary means including torture.

The higher leadership is well aware of the dangers of troops running amok. Discipline is the bedrock of any uniformed force, and no leader worth his salt would permit his troops to indulge in any action which militates against the spirit of discipline. When incidents of violations of human rights occur, and there is definite proof of misdemeanor on part of any individual or group of individuals, strict action is taken against the transgressor. Where it appears that the security forces have glossed over a serious incident, is generally a matter of perception. For example, if there is an incident of firing in which a number of people lose their lives, it is an incident of cold blooded murder as far as the people who were fired upon are concerned. But the court of inquiry cannot be swayed by sentiment. Premeditated intent to kill has to be established and conditions leading up to the incident, frame of mind and other mitigating factors may result in a punishment which does not measure up to the expectations of the people who were fired upon.

Unfortunately, truth is the biggest casualty in conflict situations. The security forces tend to downplay the severity of an incident and under-report the extent of casualties. On the other hand, the propaganda machinery of the insurgents exaggerates the incident manifold, greatly inflates the number of casualties, and spares no effort to project the government in a poor light and gain maximum mileage and publicity out of the incident. Robert Wirsing has this to say:[2] "Scepticism in regard to some of the more extravagant claims in this regard is essential. The Kashmiri militants and their supporters know well the political appeal to Westerners of human rights issues and naturally they make the most of it. They can be no doubt, in other words, that reports of human rights abuses are often exaggerated."

Where the security forces lose out, is in the battle of publicity and propaganda. No government machinery can match the insurgent in spreading disinformation. In this context one can quote Galula[3], "The insurgent, having no responsibility, is free to use every trick; if necessary, he can lie, cheat, exaggerate. He is not obliged to prove, he is judged by what he says, not by what he does.... The counter-insurgent is tied to his responsibilities and to his past, and for him, facts speak louder than words. He is judged on what he does, not on what he says. If he lies, cheats, exaggerates, and does not prove, he may achieve some temporary success, but at the price of being discredited for good.... And he cannot cheat... for the legitimate opposition in his own camp would soon disclose his every psychological maneuver. For him, propaganda can be no more than a secondary weapon, valuable only if intended to inform and not to fool"

Analysis of the Human Rights Record of the Security Forces in the State

The figures for complaints registered with the NHRC as extracted from their annual reports[4] are shown and analyzed in the following paragraphs. The period of analysis pertains to the time when the insurgency was at its peak.

Position of Complaints

Year	Dismissed in limine	Disposed with directions	Taken cognizance of/ concluded	Pending	Total
93-94	2	-	-	8	10
94-95	25	8	11	73	117
95-96	35	9	10	93	147
96-97	44	6	6	185	241
97-98	99	23	-	106	228
98-99	356	35	8	93	492
01-02	29	55	14	137	235
02-03	9	49	22	107	187
03-04	96	23	24	129	272
04-05	109	27	47	500	683
05-06	103	25	132	410	670
06-07	109	71	22	103	305
07-08	128	59	71	198	456
08-09	133	35	138	89	395
09-10	132	22	46	98	298

Details of Custodial Deaths
[Comparative Study of Three Sample States]

Year	J&K	Bihar	Haryana
1993-94	1	4	1
1994-95	3	17	2
1995-96	15	75	9
1996-97	4	93	9
1997-98	2	117	10
1998-99	0	192	22
1999-2000	0	162	29
2000-01	1	139	24
2001-02	0	146	39
Total	26	945	145

Number of Deaths Allegedly in Fake Encounters
[Comparative Study with Andhra Pradesh]

Year	Jammu and Kashmir	Andhra Pradesh
1993-94	-	-
1994-95	-	-
1995-96	-	-
1996-97	-	-
1997-98	5	1
1998-99	-	3
1999-2000	2	22
2000-01	1	14
2001-02	3	4
Total	11	44

State-wise List of Cases Registered during 2003-2004[5]

(Total Cases—72990)

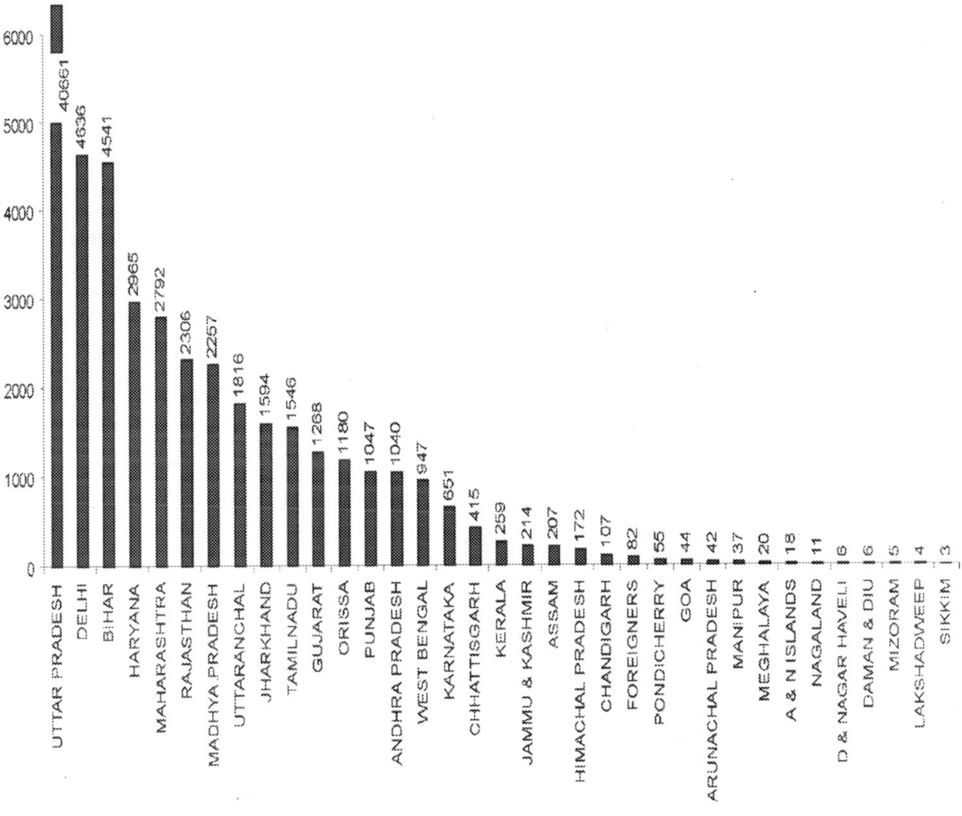

Source: Ministry of Home Affairs Annual Report 2004-05

Comments

The figures given in the tables on page 134 indicate that there have been 26 custodial deaths in the state of Jammu and Kashmir in the nine year period ranging from 01 April 1993 to 31 March 2002. (These figures will be questioned by some, but these are as reflected in the annual reports of the NHRC. The NHRC has been uncompromising in reflecting the figures of the other states of the Indian union, so there is no reason why they should dilute the figures in the case of Jammu and Kashmir). The figures work out to an average of about 3 custodial deaths per year. For a state embroiled in a serious counter-insurgency problem these figures contrast very favorably with, say, the states of Bihar and Haryana, both states which do not have any significant insurgency problem, but whose figures for the same period come to 945 and 145 with a yearly average of 105 and 16 respectively. The author has not even attempted to compare the State's statistics with those of Uttar Pradesh which is a wide aberration from the Indian norm.

Similarly, if we were to compare the number of complaints received from sources other than state government, including the media, in respect of deaths allegedly in fake encounters, we see that the statistics of the State compare very favorably with the state of Andhra Pradesh.

While the intention is not to diminish the severity of the problem in any way, the figures definitely reflect the Jammu and Kashmir Police in a positive light. The table on page 135 shows the state wise list of cases registered during the year 2003-04. For a state embroiled in the thick of a counter-insurgency situation, the state has scored very creditably on the human rights index especially when compared with more advanced states like Delhi, Maharashtra and Gujarat.

Report of the Working Group on Human Rights Violations in Jammu & Kashmir - 2000

A working group to inquire into human rights violations in Jammu and Kashmir comprising Dr. Kamal Mitra Chenoy, Associate Professor, School of International Studies, Jawaharlal Nehru University, New Delhi, as Convenor; Dr. Ambrose Pinto, S.J., Executive Director, Indian Social Institute, New Delhi, and Shri Zafar Iqbal Manhas, columnist and cultural activist, Srinagar, as members; was constituted under the auspices of the Kashmir Foundation for Peace and Developmental Studies, Srinagar in August 2000. The recommendations of the working group are given in the paragraphs below:[6]

The only real solution to human rights atrocities is the cessation of hostilities. But for this to occur, and last, a political solution is imperative. Failing that, some measures are possible that will reduce, but not wholly eliminate, human rights violations. Some of the most major are briefly listed below:

- Withdraw the Armed Forces [Special Powers] Act, Public Safety Act and other draconian laws from operation in the State. The armed forces have sufficient powers under other laws to function adequately.
- Amend the Acts under which the NHRC and SHRC function to enable them to inquire into allegations against the Army and paramilitary forces. The NHRC and SHRC must be provided with sufficient investigative staff to inquire into such complaints.
- All such NHRC and SHRC reports and recommendations should be binding on the concerned governments and forces, subject only to judicial review. These should be public documents.
- Since amendments to these Acts will not be retrospective, action taken by the Army and paramilitary forces on earlier complaints should be made public. An enabling law should be passed facilitating judicial review of these earlier decisions/actions.
- All incentive schemes that reward security forces and police for the killing of militants must be withdrawn. Under both International and Indian law, militants should be captured alive if possible. Financial rewards for killing tantamount to 'blood money' are repugnant to civilized values and societies.
- Peace committees must be set up in all localities in the insurgency affected areas. Counter insurgency forces must coordinate with these committees when carrying out their operations in these areas.
- Counter insurgency forces and the civil administration must coordinate to reduce harassment to civilians in the course of 'normal' everyday patrolling and checking. A coordination committee should be set up to examine complaints and take remedial action.
- All counter insurgency forces must be trained in human rights and gender sensitivity. They must be aware of the requirements of international humanitarian law. Consequently, ranks must be instructed that orders that violate these laws are illegal.
- Surrendered militants should be removed from counter insurgency operations. If absolutely necessary, they may be used as 'spotters' but should not be deployed in armed formations.
- Urgent measures should be taken to facilitate the return of the

Kashmiri Pandits. Until then the relief and rehabilitation packages officially made available to them should be drastically increased, with Central government assistance.

- International human rights agencies like Amnesty International, Human Rights Watch and others should be allowed to investigate alleged human rights violations in the State.
- Militants, as 'non-state actors,' should sign the Optional Protocols 1 and 2 of the Geneva Conventions.

Report on Human Rights Violations In Jammu & Kashmir - 2010

On 21st February 2010, the study group of the Independent People's Tribunal under the auspices of the Human Rights Law Network (HRLN) and the NGO ANHAD, submitted its recommendations on measures to improve the human rights situation in Jammu and Kashmir. The study group comprised Justice S. Suresh, former Judge Bombay High Court, Justice Malay Sengupta, former CGI Sikkim High Court, Justice A. Baruah, former Judge, Calcutta High Court, Professor Kamal Mittra Chenoy, Jawaharlal Nehru University, Dr. Nusrat Andrabi, former Principal, Government Women's College Srinagar, Professor Anuradha Chinoy, Jawaharlal Nehru University and Shujaat Bukhari, senior journalist based in Srinagar. The recommendations of the study group are given in the paragraphs below.[7]

- The controversial Armed Forces Special Powers Act should be withdrawn from J&K. Even the Public Safety Act and other anti-terror laws should correspond to the provisions of the International Covenant on Civil and Political Rights which India has ratified - It should be noted that India has been repeatedly criticized in the UN Human Rights Committee for the existence of the Armed Forces Special Powers Act, which violates crucially several articles of the ICCPR.
- The large concentration of military and paramilitary forces in the state of Jammu & Kashmir, is disproportionate to the civilian population and is also making civil administration ineffective in many matters. The Government of India should take immediate steps to minimize the number of these forces in order to bring relief to the civilian population.
- We recommend the establishment of a special judicial authority making an independent and thorough inquiry into all allegations of human rights violations, including disappearances, custodial killings, rape, torture, including torture of prisoners, fake encounters, and all other cases related to excesses by security forces.

- Every case of killing by police and security forces in situations like protests, demonstrations, riots, etc. should be followed by a judicial inquiry into the police/security forces firing/actions, followed by proper, time-bound administrative action. It is made clear that the police have no license to kill anyone in any situation, unless they can justify this action under Section 100 of the IPC, which has to be done in a judicial procedure.
- Provide proper rehabilitation to families of deceased, injured, and traumatized victims, especially the raped.
- Compensation as interim relief should be arranged promptly. Compensation should be adequate and purposeful. Compensation should be for both injuries to person as well as for damage to property, i.e. houses, etc.
- The State should immediately establish Fast Track Courts for the purpose of trying the large number of cases which are pending.
- Both state as well as central governments should take immediate steps to address the sufferings of detainees who are languishing in various jails and interrogation centres in and outside the state of Jammu and Kashmir and have been complaining of torture and inhuman treatment inside the jails.
- The State should provide witness protection since many of the witnesses are being threatened.

Comments

Comments on the recommendations of the working group and the study group on human rights violations in Jammu and Kashmir are given in the succeeding paragraphs:

- The Armed Forces Special Powers Act (AFSPA), the Public Safety Act, and the other "draconian" acts are in place to enable the central security forces to conduct their operations in an unhindered manner. These acts are invoked only when the situation is beyond the capabilities of the local police force. In other words, the services of the centre security forces are requisitioned only in an emergency. It has to be understood that when a security force is employed on tasks that are normally handled by police, they have to be vested with the same powers as enjoyed by the police. That is where the relevance of the AFSPA comes in. The AFSPA is essential for the armed forces because it enables them to conduct police operations. Without it, the requisitioned forces are toothless; they might as well not be requisitioned at all. When the AFSPA is in force, it is tantamount to the imposition of martial law. It also implies that the law and order situation is grave. If the armed forces have to be called in, it is implicit that they will come empowered with the AFSPA. Demands for withdrawal of the AFSPA are meaningless because it is tantamount to saying that the situation is normal and that the central security forces can revert to their barracks. What, however, is possible is to dilute the provisions of the Act. But that cannot be done at the level of the State or the Army HQ. This would require an act of Parliament. So these demands, while they serve the purpose of publicity by raising the issue at every public forum nationally and internationally, would be better realised if debated seriously in Parliament. The same is true for the Public Safety Act.

- The recommendation, to amend the Acts under which the NHRC and SHRC function to enable them to inquire into allegations against the Army and paramilitary forces, can be considered and, if found appropriate, incorporated into the amended AFSPA. What needs to be guarded against, is the fact that in most commissions there are entrenched lobbies with agendas of their own, which manage to influence the outcome of inquiries. They should also be made to sign the Official Secrets Act so that action can be taken against anyone found divulging information of restricted nature such as premature leaks of the outcome of inquiries to agencies not authorized to receive them.
- The point that all such NHRC and SHRC reports and recommendations should be binding on the concerned governments and forces, subject only to judicial review, is debatable. In a democracy the authority to accept or reject recommendations of the commission of inquiry, even a statutory body, rests with the elected government of the day. Ultimately, the issue is of governance. The Central or State governments may be faced with a number of situations where drastic actions may be called for. In nation-building, certain so-called "unethical" actions may have to be condoned or overlooked when viewed against the larger interest of the nation. All great countries have done so in the past, and will definitely do so in the future also. The writer in no way suggests that this should be the norm. Of course, in a democracy the last word in such matters should be that of the government, and definitely not with the armed forces. Where the government errs, recourse can always be taken to the courts of law.
- Culturally, the defense forces are introverted and suspicious of the motives of politicians and others when they transgress into what they perceive as their domain. However, the accusation that they

are secretive and sweep wrongdoings under the carpet is patently false. Every action is logged and recorded. Justice is swift and ruthless when compared with the timeframe how similar offenses are dealt with and punished in civil life. The findings may not be made public in the interests of maintenance of morale and public image. Asking for a judicial review on earlier decisions/actions is unfair and may not be correct in law as it would be tantamount to a punishing an individual twice for the same offense. There is definitely a case, however, for security personnel to be made more sensitive to human rights issues.

- The recommendation that all incentive schemes in the security forces and police that reward the killing of militants must be withdrawn, is agreed to. The notion, that financial rewards for killing tantamount to 'blood money' are repugnant to civilized values and societies, is laudable. However, even the most advanced of societies have put a price on the heads of wanted terrorists. An example of this is the $25,000,000 bounty on the head of Osama Bin Laden. In the context of the Indian Armed Forces, it must be pointed out that the prevailing ethos is to recognize bravery and outstanding leadership with gallantry awards and not with financial rewards.
- The points regarding peace committees, coordination amongst the counter-insurgency forces and the civil administration, training and sensitization of security forces in human rights are well taken. Permitting international human rights agencies like Amnesty International, Human Rights Watch and others to investigate alleged human rights violations in the State is acceptable provided it does not impinge on security of operations of an immediate nature and the composition of the investigation agency is acceptable to the State government.
- It is interesting that the Commission should recommend that militants sign the Optional Protocols 1 and 2 of the Geneva Conventions, as 'non-state actors', when India itself is not yet a signatory to the protocol. Vide Articles 43 and 44 of Protocol 1, military status is accorded to members of guerrilla forces. Additionally combatant and prisoner of war status is granted to members of dissident forces when under the command of a central authority. Such combatants cannot conceal their allegiance; they must be recognizable as combatants while preparing for or during an attack. None of these conditions is applicable to the terrorists who engage the Indian state machinery in sneak hit and run tactics

many times in the garb of army uniform. This suggestion cannot and should not be accepted so long as India does not sign the protocol and so long as the terrorists keep up the terror campaign.

The Government Point of View[8]

It is the stated policy of the government to ensure that all reported cases of alleged human rights violations are taken serious note of, investigations made promptly in a transparent manner and taken to their logical conclusion and suitable punitive action is taken against those found guilty. Between January 1994 to December 2009, out of 1206 complaints of human rights excesses received against the personnel of Army and Central Para Military Forces, 1180 have been investigated, 1147 of them found false, in 33 cases where the complaints were found genuine, penalties have been imposed on 74 personnel of the Army and Central Para Military Forces, while in 6 cases compensation has been awarded.

Action has also been taken by the State Government to further strengthen the State Human Rights Commission (SHRC) by the provision of an Investigating Wing headed by an Officer of the rank of Inspector General of Police. A high level committee has also been set up to examine the recommendations made by the SHRC, from time to time, and review the action taken thereon.

The Prime Minister, in his closing remarks in the first Round Table Conference on Jammu and Kashmir held on February 25, 2006, affirmed Government's commitment to respect the human rights of all people and emphasized that every effort will be made in dealing with terrorism and militancy so that no innocent person should suffer. Whenever there is any violation of human rights, there must be transparent mechanisms to fix responsibility and to punish those found guilty.

On May 24, 2006, the Prime Minister exhorted the security forces to respect human rights, present a humane image and to ensure minimum disruption of normal life while performing their day-to-day operational duties in Jammu and Kashmir. He reiterated the need to educate the security forces personnel to be more sensitive in their interaction with the local public without compromising on security related issues. He asked the forces to act in a manner so that collateral damage is avoided while combating militancy. He also made it clear that there would be zero tolerance for custodial deaths.

An Alternate View

It is common to read articles berating the security forces for violation of human rights and in human behaviour. It is rare to come across any criticism in writing on the human rights abuses perpetrated by the terrorists. Reproduced below are a couple of paragraphs from an essay on the subject.[9] The writer, Dr Shabir Choudhry, is a political analyst and Director of the Institute of Kashmir Affairs.

"I discussed and strongly opposed human rights abuses perpetrated by the para military forces in Kashmir in my last article; but fact remains that human rights abuses are not only committed by people in uniform. People roaming around in various parts of Jammu and Kashmir with guns in their hands are also responsible for human rights abuses. These *jihadi* warriors could be characterised in to (sic) Kashmiri *jihadis*, and non-Kashmir *jihadis*. Acts of violence committed by the local *jihadis* could be understood, as they feel enslaved by India; and feel all avenues of peaceful struggle were exhausted; however, non-Kashmiri *jihadi* warriors fall in to different category; and in view of many critics they are 'mercenaries' trained and armed by Pakistan to commit acts of violence in Jammu and Kashmir.

"Some *jihadi* warriors belonging to *Salafi* and *Wahabi* sects of Islam do not regard *Sunni Brailvi* and *Shias* as Muslims, and justify their killings and destruction of their places of worship. I know, many people will either find Indian, Israeli or American hand behind these tragic acts; but fact remains that culprits or those who actually commit these acts of religious terrorism are Muslims and claim to be performing a religious duty. Some of them even say they are 'purifying' Islam. So when looking at sources of human rights abuses one cannot ignore this aspect of terrorism and human rights abuses...most militants—*jihadis* or others—have very little formal education, no system of discipline or accountability; and after getting guns and some training to commit violence they feel unable to control newly acquired power and status and commit all sorts of acts".

Human Rights Violations in Jammu & Kashmir

Paragraphs 6.8 to 6.12 from the Annual Report 1993-94 of the NHRC Report on human rights violations in Jammu and Kashmir are reproduced below.[10]

The Commission is more than aware that, while the people of this country must be made aware of their rights through programmes of literacy, and vigorously supported in the defence of their rights by the Courts, the Commission, the media, non-governmental organizations and others, it is no less—and probably far more-important to retrain and reorient public servants and particularly members of the police and the security forces-both of the army and of paramilitary wings-so that they learn to respect such rights, and remain constantly mindful of them, despite the difficult and provocative circumstances in which they often have to function, particularly in areas facing insurgency and terrorism.

The Commission has therefore been giving the highest priority to encouraging the training and re-orientation of members of the police and armed forces. As regards the police, while all States have now made efforts to include human rights in the instruction of their cadres in their various institutes, the Commission recommends that the courses need to have a far higher standard and a greater degree of consistency. A meeting was called by the Commission of some Directors-General of Police, a group of whom were thereafter entrusted by the Commission to prepare model training syllabi for all levels of the police force.

The training and re-orientation of the military and paramilitary forces has been of no less concern to the Commission. Accordingly, this subject has been central to the discussions that the Commission has had with the Chief of Army Staff and the Director-General of the Border Security Force, among others. The Commission encouraged and welcomed the involvement of the International Committee of the Red Cross (ICRC) in courses conducted for officers of the Border Security force on International Humanitarian Law. Members of the Commission addressed the trainees in visits to the BSF Centre in Tekanpur.

As regards the Army, the Commission has noted the efforts being made to spread the message of human rights from the level of jawans to Commanding Officers. In many of the visits which the Commission has made to areas of army deployment, its attention has been drawn to the 'Ten Commandments' issued by the Chief of Army Staff to all serving personnel. Likewise, the Commission has been informed of the instructions issued by the Corps Commanders to their troops in regard to the conduct of armed forces personnel in situations involving civil populations. The Commission welcomes these instructions as evidence of a growing sensitivity amongst armed forces personnel to human rights matters. At the same time, it recommends that the training of both officers and men needs to be sustained at a high-level so that errors in conduct are avoided to the maximum possible extent. The Commission further recommends that where violations of human rights occur as a result of the conduct of armed forces personnel prompt and effective action be taken under the law to prosecute those accused of wrong-doing. This would be in the interests of all concerned-the victims, the armed forces themselves, and the country at large. The Commission has been gratified to learn that the upper-most echelons of the armed forces concur with the Commission in this approach. In consequence, as indicated earlier in this report, both the Army and the BSF have made available to the Commission data relevant to the prosecution of those accused of violating human rights. The example of the armed forces leadership needs to be followed at all levels, so that the reputation of the security forces of the country-whether police, military or paramilitary-remains above question in regard to its probity and commitment to justice.

As part of the overall sensitizing of the security forces to human rights matters, members of the Commission, its Secretary-General and Director-General (Investigation) have seized a number of opportunities to participate in discussions and courses relevant to such matters.

Indian Army and Human Rights

The human rights policy of the army is that of zero tolerance, transparency and strict punishment.[11] Chief of the Army Staff, Gen Deepak Kapoor reiterated this policy in the following words, "Upholding Human Rights is one of the cornerstones of our anti-terrorist operations and our record is worth emulating."[12]

- **Chief of Army Staff's Commandments**[13]
  1. No rape.
  2. No molestation.
  3. No torture resulting in death or maiming.
  4. No military disgrace loss of arms/mil post or surrender or imbibing of un-army like culture.
  5. No meddling in the civil administration i.e. land disputes or quarrels.
  6. Competence in platoon/company tactics with innovations.
  7. Willingly carry out civic action with innovations.
  8. Develop media interaction modules—Use them as a 'force multiplier' and not as 'force degrader'.
  9. Respect human rights.
  10. Only fear God, uphold Dharma (ethical mode of life-the path of righteousness) and enjoy serving the country.
- **Corps Commander Dos and Donts**[14]
  1. Display compassion and humanity towards local populace.

2. Do not look down upon local customs and traditions.
3. There are no insurgents here - only misguided countrymen.
4. Never molest women - they are our sisters and mothers.
5. Do not harm children - they are our heritage.
6. No reprisals under any circumstances.
7. Apprehendees to be treated with respect.
8. Honour democratic norms and rightly adhere to human rights.
9. Constantly seek contact with USs (sic).
10. Aggressiveness and spontaneous reaction is the key to success and survival.

Conclusion

Even prior to induction in the state of Jammu and Kashmir, the Indian Security Forces have had a long and proud history of experience in counter-insurgency operations. Over the years, there have been many allegations of violations of human rights by the security forces, but that is a factor one has always to take into account when employing on the security personnel to combat violence. When bullets are being exchanged, within that limited space it is like a war between two antagonists. Occasions may arise when an individual or a group of individuals, in uniform takes the concept of 'All is fair in love and war' to an unacceptable degree. But to suggest that human rights violations and torture are institutionalized and practiced on a widespread basis is to deliberately distort the truth and spread false propaganda.

Various countries have dismissed excesses by their troops as 'collateral damage' and other such terms, implying thereby that the excesses were unfortunate but unintentional and justified in the pursuit of the larger goal. No army, including the most modern from first world countries, can claim to have a 100 percent clean human rights record when employed in counter-insurgency operations over a length of time. All modern armies take human rights very seriously, and conduct regular training programs in sensitizing all ranks on this issue. So it is also with the Indian security forces. Prior to induction into a theater of insurgency, all ranks are put through an intense training capsule on the legal aspects and the dos and don'ts of human rights. Apart from the initial training, all ranks are also put through periodic courses to keep them continuously sensitized to the rights of the locals and the rules of personal conduct in the counter-insurgency environment.

NOTES

1. Wikipedia article on Human Rights in Jammu and Kashmir
2. Wirsing, Robert G. 1995, *India, Pakistan, and the Kashmir Dispute: On Regional Conflict and its Resolution* (MacMillan) ed. 1996, p 159
3. Galula David, *Counterinsurgency Warfare Theory and Practice*, Published by Frederick A. Praeger, New York, London, 1964, p 11
4. Annual Reports, National Human Rights Commission.
5. Annual Report Ministry of Home Affairs 2004-05.
6. Report of the Working Group on Human Rights Violations in Jammu & Kashmir – 2000
7. Report on Human Rights Violations in Jammu & Kashmir - 2010
8. Annual Report, Ministry of Home Affairs 2007-08
9. Shabbir Chaudhri, www.drshabirchoudhry.blogspot.com, 3 Dec. 10
10. NHRC Annual Report 1993-94 on Human Rights Violations in Jammu & Kashmir
11. Lt Gen Bammi, *War Against Insurgency and Terrorism in Kashmir*, p. 260.
12. IDSA National Security Lecture Series, *Strategic Digest*, August 2008, p. 1031.
13. Annual Report, Ministry of Home Affairs 2004-05.
14. Annual Report, Ministry of Home Affairs 2004-05, Annx III, Para 6.11.

9

Numerical Requirements of Forces

In 2004, Dr. John Llewellyn, the Global Chief Economist of the Lehman Brothers Global Weekly Economic Monitor, and John Dew, Senior Policy Advisor, presented a paper based on the study of the UK experience in Northern Ireland and other insurgencies across the globe over the past fifty years, that recommended the numerical requirements of troops to restore, and then maintain, order and stability in an environment of counter-insurgency. Although the recommendations have been made in the context of NATO, they are universally relevant to areas prone to insurgent problems across the world. This would explain why, apparently, there seems to be an excess of security forces in Jammu and Kashmir. The principal conclusions from this study, with additional comments in italics where relevant in the Indian context of Jammu and Kashmir, are as follows:[1]

1. **Interrelationship between Security Operations and Political Progress.** History shows that order and stability are necessary preconditions for political, administrative, and economic reform: but without a realistic prospect of such reform, the population will oppose the forces of order and stability.
2. **Numerical Requirements for Stability Operations.** When there is any significant domestic opposition restoring and maintaining order and stability typically requires a force ratio of 20 or more security personnel per thousand head of population. *In the context of Jammu and Kashmir, it has been an oft repeated criticism that the force ratio in the State is inordinately high. It must be appreciated that the police-to-population ratios mentioned earlier in the section on Police are*

only relevant to peaceful and violent societies. In a situation of insurgency the force levels are bound to increase manifold.

3. **The Requisite Pool of Troops.** Modern professional militaries find that they need to limit tours of duty to about 6 months in every 30. This is known the 'Rule of Five', whereby only a fraction of the potentially available troops can be deployed at any given time: the rest are preparing for deployment, recovering, or re-training. Professional militaries, where soldiers remain in service for years at a time, try to keep the interval between deployments at 24 months or more. Thus, to the extent that a 6-month tour of duty and a 24-month interval are achieved, troops are on an operational tour only 6 months in every thirty. This means that five troops are required for every soldier deployed in the theatre of operations. If a stabilization effort cannot adhere to this 'Rule of Five', then either the deployment time has to be extended beyond 6 months, or the interval between deployments reduced below 24 months, with a consequent loss of troop morale. A long-stay force of say, 100,000 would thus require a pool of around 500,000 soldiers. *The tour of duty for soldiers of the Indian armed forces employed in counter-insurgency operations is 24 months i.e. a four times longer duration than what has been recommended for NATO troops.*
4. **The Cost of Stability and Control Operations.** The cost of maintaining security personnel is extremely high and a considerable drain on the national exchequer in the long run. *This is valid for any country anywhere in the world. The cost of the logistics of maintaining a force for an inordinately long time can be crippling for any economy, no matter how strong. A comparison can be drawn from the case of the conflict in Northern Ireland. Montgomery Sapone states[2], "Despite the excellent training benefits it provided for British Army regiments, the conflict in Northern Ireland had become enormously expensive. Deployment of nineteen-thousand troops has cost over £1 billion per annum, compensation to victims of violence by the Northern Ireland Office cost £30-50 million per annum, and the Exchequer grant to Northern Ireland cost over £3 billion. In the Indian context, given the size of the geographical area, the terrain and the poor lines of communication, the figures can only rise higher.*
5. **Duration of operations**. There is apparently no quick route to peacekeeping, even less to nation-building. 5 years could be the minimum to bring about order and stability, and 10 years to establish a self-sustaining political and economic system. However, these figures are only suggestive: it is unwise to set a timetable.

6. **Political Change.** Military operations alone cannot succeed if used as an alternative to the search for political solutions, or to impose a political solution on a hostile population. *In Northern Ireland, successive British governments failed to end the violence until they presented a political solution that all parties,* ***including those who had supported or sympathised with the violence****, could accept as a credible basis for negotiation. Likewise, unless the proposed solution is fair and all-inclusive, the chances of lasting peace are slim.*
7. **Civil Administrative Reform.** Such reform can be crucial to the long-run viability of nation-building. Often requiring both the establishment of new institutions and education and training in running them, administrative reform can require a considerable input of experienced manpower. And building up the requisite capability in sufficient strength can take many years. *In our context, the administrative machinery is fully in place. What, however, is required is for the administration to develop a spine and for the police force to develop the capability to maintain law and order and to conduct its operations without the need for additional central police forces except in exceptional circumstances.*
8. **Economic Reform and Assistance.** Successful economic assistance often requires both aid and reform of economic policy and policy-making institutions. *No one can accuse the central government of not providing enough finances in the budgetary allocations for the state of Jammu and Kashmir. What needs to be ensured, however, is that the funds are actually expended for the purpose that they were released and that no funds are siphoned off midway.*
9. **Control and Coordination.** The achievement of order and stability, and thereafter the process of nation-building is extremely complex but the payoff will produce a complete transformation and greater regional reconciliation.
10. **Importance of a Complete Vision.** Achieving a self-reinforcing circle between peacekeeping and nation-building requires success across a wide range of issues, and hence a clear vision of the totality of the exercise. That vision may evolve over a period of time, but it needs to be clear to, and accepted by, the population. *In our context, the vision is clear i.e. Kashmir is an inseparable part of India. That issue is non-negotiable. Within this broad framework, degrees of autonomy and other measures can be discussed and a mutually acceptable solution arrived at.*
11. **Implications**. While order and stability are a necessary precursor of political, administrative, and economic reform, equally essential

is the belief that political, administrative and economic reform will be delivered consequent to achieving order and stability. People who do not believe that they are going to get the political reform that they desire will resist, often with considerable vigour. A number of fundamental changes will probably have to be made to the strategy, if there is to be a successful transition and sustained economic development. It would take a major commitment in terms of the provision of human and other resources, and would take many years. *This is very relevant in our context also. There is no better proof of good intentions than improved infrastructure and sustained economic development. The challenge is to enter the virtuous, and not the vicious, circle.*

RAND Report on 'How Terrorist Groups End'

The RAND Corporation conducted a study on how most terrorist groups ultimately end. The conclusions shed a considerable amount of light on the manner in which a democratic government should respond to the challenge posed by the terrorist threat. The conclusions of the study are enumerated below: [3]

1. All terrorist groups eventually end. But how do they end? Answers to this question have enormous implications for counter-terrorism efforts. Following the examination of 648 terrorist groups that existed between 1968 and 2006, the evidence indicates that most groups ended because:
   - They joined the political process or
   - The local police and intelligence agencies arrested or killed key members.
2. Military force has rarely been the primary reason for the end of terrorist groups, but at the same time hardly any terrorist group has achieved victory within the period of study.
3. This has significant implications in planning for the long-term counter-terrorism strategy. The ending of most terrorist groups requires a range of policy instruments, such as careful police and intelligence work, military force, political negotiations, and economic sanctions.
4. Policy makers need to understand where to prioritize their efforts with limited resources and attention. Evidence suggests that a transition to the political process is the most common way in which terrorist groups ended (43%).
5. The possibility of a political solution is inversely linked to the breadth of terrorist goals. Most terrorist groups that end because

of politics seek narrow policy goals. The narrower the goals of a terrorist organization, the more likely it can achieve them without violent action; and the more likely the government and terrorist group may be able to reach a negotiated settlement.

6. Against terrorist groups that cannot or will not make a transition to nonviolence, policing is likely to be the most effective strategy (40%). Police and intelligence services have better training and information to penetrate and disrupt terrorist organizations than do such institutions as the military. They are the primary arm of the government focused on internal security matters. Local police and intelligence agencies usually have a permanent presence in cities, towns, and villages; a better understanding of the threat environment in these areas; and better human intelligence information to penetrate and disrupt terrorist organizations than do such institutions as the military. They are the primary arm of the government focused on internal security matters. Local police and intelligence agencies usually have a permanent presence in cities, towns and villages and therefore a better understanding of the threat environment in these areas and better human intelligence.
7. Other reasons are less common.
   - In 10% of the cases, terrorist groups ended because their goals were achieved.
   - Military force led to the end of terrorist groups in 7% of the cases.

Results of quantitative analysis of terrorist groups that have ended since 1968 or are still active, yielded several other interesting findings:

1. When a terrorist group becomes involved in an insurgency, it does not end easily.
2. Religious terrorist groups take longer to eliminate than other groups. Since 1968, approximately 62% of all terrorist groups have ended while only 32% of religious terrorist groups have ended.
3. Religious groups rarely achieve their objectives. Since 1968, no religious group that has ended, achieved victory.
4. Size is a significant determinant of a group's fate. Victory is rare when groups are smaller than 1,000 members.
5. There is no statistical correlation between the duration of a terrorist group and ideological motivation, economic conditions, regime type, or the breadth of terrorist goals. But there appears to be some correlation between the size of a terrorist group and duration viz larger groups tend to last longer than smaller groups.
6. Terrorist groups from upper-income countries are much more likely

to be left-wing or nationalist and much less likely to be motivated by religion.

How Insurgencies Die Out

Another study conducted by the RAND Corporation in 2006, concerned the life cycle of counter insurgencies across the world. Some of the findings relevant to the problem in Jammu and Kashmir along with comments in italics and are given in the succeeding paragraphs: [4]

Characteristics of Typical Insurgencies

Modern insurgencies last approximately ten years, and the government's chances of winning may increase slightly over time. Quantitative analysis of the cases selected for the study shows that the median length of an insurgency is ten years. An insurgency that hits a clear tipping point at or just before ten years typically tails out gradually to end state at 16 years. This is shown below in the graph depicting the art of insurgent defeat. This finding squares with conventional wisdom, as well as existing conclusions published in a range of counter-insurgency literature. The statistical data also indicates that the longer an insurgency lasts, the more likely the government is to win. *This finding is definitely relevant in our case as the insurgency commenced in the early 1990s and tapered off in the mid 2000s. This is also depicted graphically below.*

Arc of Insurgent Defeat

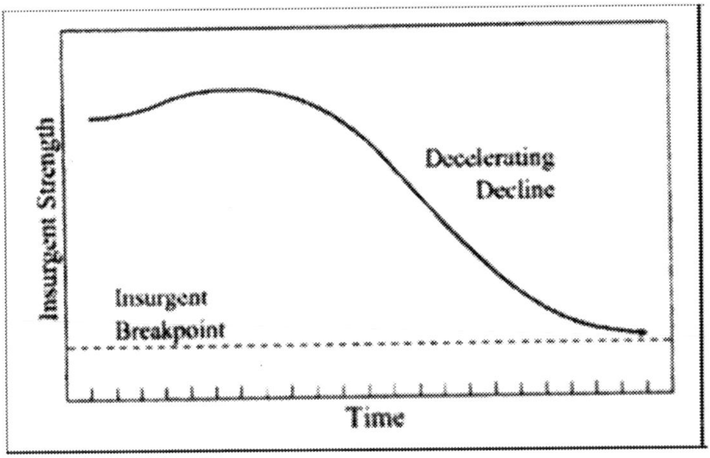

Source: RAND MG965-2.2 McCormick, Horton, and Harrison (2006).

Withdrawal of state sponsorship cripples an insurgency and typically leads to its defeat. State sponsorship is simply defined as either direct or indirect support provided to an insurgency by a nation-state. *With the overt and overt support from across the LOC provided by Pakistan, there is always hope for the insurgents to retreat to their secure bases in POK after a setback to recover, re-group and reorganize for the next round of violence against the state machinery.*

Anocracies (pseudo-democracies) do not often succeed against insurgencies and are rarely successful. Anocracies are democracies in name only. In an anocracy, the population gains little benefit from reform and the government is mostly interested in preserving and prolonging its power structure and is rarely serious about implementing policies which are aimed at improving governance and uplifting the population. *We would like to believe that we are a properly functional democracy and this point is not relevant to us. However, it must be borne in mind that unless concrete developmental and corrective action commences as soon as feasible, we can also suffer the same fate as an anocracy.*

Information and Reporting. Qualitative analysis of the cases under study substantiates conventional wisdom in that civilians' willingness to report on insurgent activity to the government usually reflects the success of government security and pacification programs. Conversely, a lack of reporting correlates with a lack of progress. A change in the frequency and quality of reporting in either direction may mark a shift in momentum, particularly at the tactical level. Change in the quality of intelligence is a key indicator for the government to assess the direction and progress of the counter-insurgency program, and accordingly initiate mid-course corrections that may be required.

Complex Insurgency Means a Complex and Protracted Ending. Insurgencies with more than two clear parties involved have longer, more violent and more complex endings. India, Pakistan and various insurgent groups with conflicting aims and interests are all claiming a stake in the outcome of the conflict. While not all parties must be satisfied to bring an end to the immediate conflict, the dissatisfaction of one or more parties will probably complicate the ending and may allow the insurgency to smolder and eventually reignite. *While it is next to impossible to expect the insurgent groups to be satisfied with the ultimate resolution of the conflict, it is imperative that the people of Jammu and Kashmir, in particular the Kashmiri speaking people of the Valley, be reconciled with the resolution. Once that is achieved the raison de etre of the conflict will cease to exist.*

Governments Outlast Insurgents. Insurgents cannot win by simply trying to outlast the government. In fact, in the long run, governments tend to win more often than not. Most insurgencies fail, since states, no matter how weak or feckless, are typically stronger, better organized, and more professional than non-state forces. Government victories are typically not signaled by a dramatic or sudden collapse of the armed opposition: "The insurgency that comes in like a lion . . . may go out like a lamb. Indeed by the time the end comes, many observers will have assumed it has already come and gone".[5] *This finding must not be taken as empirical and should not induce a sense of complacence in the government troops. On the contrary, the effort should always be to push for dialogue and resolution whenever it is sensed that the insurgent groups are weakening in their resolve and maybe amenable for talks.*

Governments Are Better Off Without Support. Governments benefit from direct support but tend to lose more frequently when provided indirect support; they do slightly better with no external support at all. Once support is given, it almost always creates a dependency on the external sponsor. *This finding is not relevant in our case, and we have consistently resisted any kind of help from another country because that help would always have come with some strings attached. We have always been insisting that the problem in Jammu and Kashmir is an internal matter and that it would be resolved internally.*

Terrorism Often Backfires. Broad terror campaigns by insurgents correlate with insurgent defeat, but selective terror attacks that do not kill innocent civilians correlate with a marked insurgent advantage. In other words, those insurgent groups that were able to restrict their use of terrorism by minimizing civilian casualties were more likely to win than those that did not. Qualitative analysis shows that the use of indiscriminate terror often is a sign of overconfidence or, conversely, of weakness. *This lesson was learnt by insurgent groups operating in the State, and in the latter part of the insurgency, they attempted to desist from mindless terror attacks and concentrated on selected targets of government and security personnel. In fact, they preferred to conduct terror attacks outside the Valley in Jammu Province or outside the State so that the backlash of the security forces would not affect their own constituency in the Valley.*

Weak Insurgents Can Win. Insurgents do not need to be militarily strong to win, and, in fact, military strength can backfire if the threat of insurgent military victory galvanizes government security forces. *By unleashing an all out insurgency in the State, the central security forces including the Indian Army were sucked into the conflict and ultimately the balance was tilted in favor of the Government forces. Had the insurgents restricted themselves to minor skirmishes with the Jammu and Kashmir Police, they may have been successful* *in launching a genuine non-violent mass movement, controlling which would have been far more difficult for the Indian establishment.*

Sanctuary is Vital to Insurgencies. Availability of sanctuary directly correlates with an improved likelihood of insurgent victory, but only if it is provided voluntarily. Insurgencies rarely survive or succeed without some kind of sanctuary. Internal sanctuary is also very valuable, perhaps as valuable as voluntary, external sanctuary. *The Jammu and Kashmir insurgency has had no dearth of sanctuaries across the Line of Control in POK. The Jammu province got embroiled in the insurgency primarily because the insurgents needed safe sanctuaries on the Pir Panjal Ranges. The Indian Security establishment has had to go to extraordinary lengths, like border sealing and fencing, to prevent the insurgents from the availing of the sanctuaries across the Line of Control.*

The findings of the study report mentioned in the previous paragraphs can at best be used as a references and guides. It would be foolhardy to take templates from one insurgency and apply them on another. Recognized counter-insurgency expert David Kilcullen sums up the various pitfalls thus:[6] There is no standard set of metrics, benchmarks, or operational techniques that apply to all insurgencies or remain valid for any single insurgency throughout its life cycle. And there are no fixed 'laws' of counter-insurgency.

Comments

Going by the conventional wisdom that an insurgency can be ended within 10 to 15 years, we can state that the security forces have been able to bring the situation under control within the standard time frame. However, no one can argue that the conflict is far from over. This is the period of consolidation for both sides. The side that utilizes this time profitably is bound to reap rich dividends in the longer run. The Government must utilize this time to implement reforms, improve administration and strengthen the social fabric of the State. The security forces must utilize this time to improve the intelligence structure, train, refit and re-equip the forces. The police must utilize this time to improve its relationship with the population while at the same time keeping an ear constantly on the ground and a finger on the pulse of the people. Determining the end of the insurgency is not a simple matter, because there is no clear-cut end to the conflict. Intermittent waves of violence will keep disrupting the peace, so the security forces and the administration cannot afford to let their guard down.

The insurgency in Jammu and Kashmir could not have lasted this long but for the constant and steadfast support from Pakistan. The value of this support cannot be underestimated. The significance of the support from various sources ie State (in this case, Pakistan) and other sympathetic Islamic countries, diaspora and other non-state sources is tabulated below.

Sources of Support

Form of Support	*State (Pakistan)*	*Diaspora*	*Other Non-state Actors*
Money	Significant	Significant	Minor
Safe haven	Significant	Minor	
Diplomatic backing	Significant	Limited	
Arms	Significant	Minor	Limited
Training	Significant	Minor	Minor
Intelligence	Limited	Minor	
Direct mil support	Significant		Minor
Inspiration	Limited	Minor	Minor

Source: Byman, Chalk, et al. (2001, p. 105).

A lesson needs to be drawn from the insurgency in Thailand which is now in its fourth decade and yet there seems to be no end in sight. As per Chalk[7], "...the hard military track was not accompanied by a softer, more nuanced policy line to win popular support. The Thai government made virtually no effort to address the poverty, under-development, and general alienation that fuels Malay-Muslim discontent. In its current incarnation, the insurgency appears to have morphed into a disassociated manifestation of popular discontent. Military action is little more than population control". We cannot afford to follow a similar path.

The Ending of the Insurgency

Going by the findings of the studies mentioned in the earlier paragraphs we can draw a few definitive observations as given in the succeeding paragraphs.

With a few exceptions, lasting insurgency endings are shaped not by military action but by social, economic, and political change. At their core, insurgencies are battles for the control of public support. Therefore, violence is useful to the insurgents only when it creates a level of instability that allows them to effect social change in their favor, and violence is useful to the government only when it helps stabilize the population long enough to effect lasting change in its favor. The government may defeat the insurgent military cadre, but, with few exceptions, insurgencies do not end until case-specific root causes are addressed. The kind of grassroots support necessary to build and sustain an insurgency is fed on social, economic, and political discontent. If a government successfully addresses root causes, it is possible to defeat an insurgency without defeating the insurgents themselves.

Government victories often cause the insurgency to splinter, leaving behind small elements of irredeemables that may or may not represent an immediate threat. Tracking these splinter groups can provide tremendous insight into the nature of the insurgency ending. When the government is winning and the insurgency is in its "tail" phase, often a small group of insurgents splinters away from the cadre or leadership group. In some cases, this splinter element is an irredeemable fringe unwilling to negotiate or enter into an amnesty program. In others, the splinter is formed from an irredeemable core leadership element. In both cases, the splinter groups are intent on continuing the struggle against the government in one form or another. They may try to sustain or reignite the insurgency immediately, or they may be willing to hibernate until they see an opportunity to reemerge. The Government should be able to tell a great deal about their long-term prospects by observing how the general populace perceives this splinter group. If the irredeemables are absorbed and protected by the indigenous population and are able to demonstrate continuing grassroots support, then the insurgency probably has not ended. If, however, an exhausted or government-leaning populace ostracizes these irredeemables, they become little more than an isolated terrorist cell. It is at this point, when the root causes of the insurgency have been addressed and all willing insurgents reconciled, that the end of the insurgency has been attained.

David Kilcullen emphasizes that there are no cookie-cutter approaches to counter-insurgency. Counter-insurgents must adapt tactics, operations, and strategy to fit specific circumstances and then be prepared to change them as often as necessary to win.[8]

How Terrorist Groups End

In the foregoing paragraphs, we have seen the conclusions of two different study reports on how insurgencies are brought under control and ultimately die out. Another study carried out by the RAND Corporation in 2008, has gone into mechanics of how terrorist groups end. The conclusions of this study report are given in the succeeding paragraphs.[9]

Terrorist groups usually end for two major reasons. They decide to adopt nonviolent tactics and join the political process or local law-enforcement agencies arrest or eliminate key members of the group. As depicted graphically in the pie-chart below, application of military force alone has rarely been the primary reason that terrorist groups end.

This suggests that, where terrorist groups cannot or will not make a transition to non-violence, policing is usually most effective in defeating terrorist groups. The ending of most terrorist groups requires a range of policy instruments, such as careful police and intelligence work, military force, political negotiations, and economic sanctions.

A transition to the political process is the most common way in which terrorist groups ended (43 percent). The possibility of a political solution is inversely linked to the breadth of terrorist goals. Most terrorist groups that end because of politics seek narrow policy goals. The narrower the goals of a terrorist organization, the more likely it can achieve them without violent action—and the more likely the government and terrorist group may be able to reach a negotiated settlement.

How Terrorist Groups End

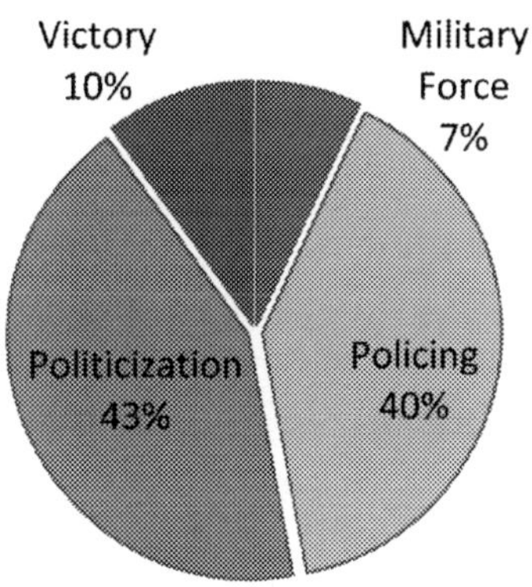

Source: RAND 741 - 2008.

Against terrorist groups that cannot or will not make a transition to nonviolence, policing is likely to be the most effective strategy (40 percent). Police and intelligence services have better training and information to penetrate and disrupt terrorist organizations than do such institutions as the military. They are the primary arm of the government focused on internal security matters. Local police and intelligence agencies usually have a permanent presence in cities, towns, and villages; a better understanding of the threat environment in these areas; and better human intelligence. This means that they are best able to understand and penetrate terrorist networks.

Against most terrorist groups military force is usually too blunt an instrument. Military tools may have increased in precision and lethality, especially with the growing use of precision standoff weapons and imagery to monitor terrorist movement. But even precision weapons have been of limited use against terrorist groups. The use of substantial military power against terrorist groups also runs a significant risk of turning the local population against the government by killing civilians.

Religious terrorist groups take longer to eliminate than other groups. But at the same time it is significant that religious groups rarely achieve their objectives. No religious group has achieved victory since 1968.

Most terrorist groups that have ended did so by pursuing their goals through politics. The possibility of a political solution is linked to a key variable: the breadth of terrorist goals. The narrower the goals, the more difficult it is for terrorists to achieve them, and the more willing they will be to seek nonviolent means. One path to politics includes an explicit *peace settlement*. It involves a bargaining process with the government in which terrorist groups reach an agreement to disband their militant wings and transition to a political party.

Use of Military Force

The use of military force is necessitated in defeating terrorist groups when the terrorist groups get involved in an insurgency and it is beyond the capability of the law enforcement agencies to get them under control. For the information of the lay reader, an insurgency may be defined as an internal conflict in which:

- A group or groups are attempting to overthrow the government or secede from it by resorting to arms.
- More than 1,000 persons have died over the course of the conflict.
- More than 100 persons have died on each side.

Conflict Resolution Cycle

Military force has rarely been the primary reason for the end of terrorist groups. Yet, there is no alternative available to the government other than military force which will compel the belligerents to come the negotiating table. Therefore, it can be said that though military force is essential to establish the writ of the law in the initial stages of the insurgency, military force has to give way to diplomatic measures in the concluding stages of the conflict. This is best understood by the Conflict Resolution Cycle depicted opposite:

Conflict Resolution Cycle

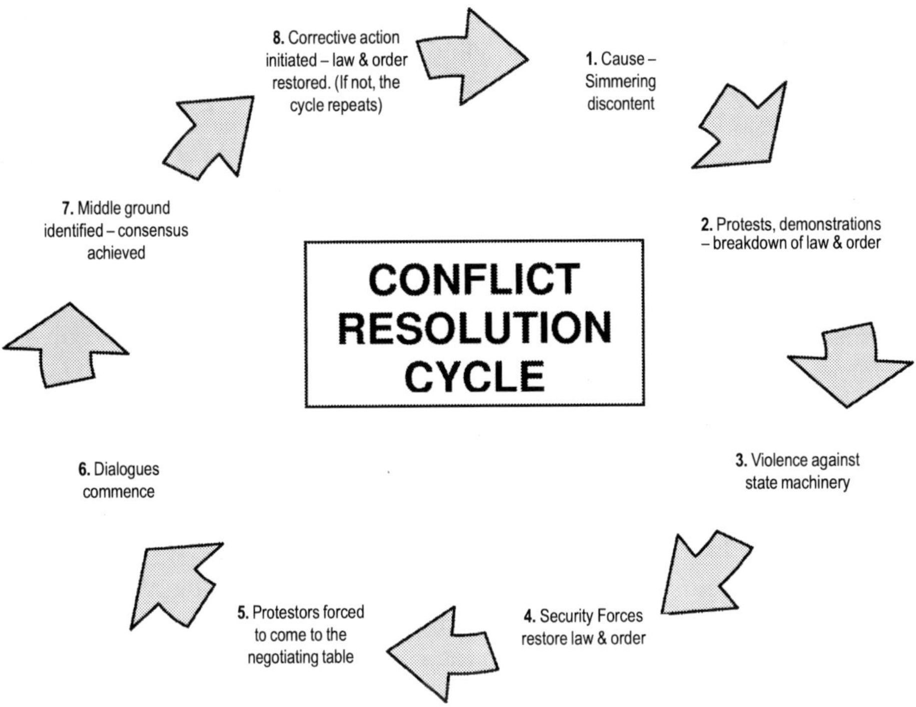

Source: Lecture by the author at the Centre for Advanced Strategic Studies, Pune

If one were to study an armed conflict commencing from the cause of the problem right up to its solution, we would find that the timeline of the conflict can be roughly divided into 8 Stages, with Stage 1 being the simmering discontent and popular dis-affectation which may be due to various reasons and Stage 8 being the resolution of the conflict, restoration of law and order and the implementation of the provisions of the peace accord. As can be seen the use of the military machinery more or less ends at Stage 4. Thereafter they remain as a threat-in-being to deter the militant/terrorist groups from taking to arms again. Stages 5 to 8 are purely the domain of the administration and the politician. By the end of Stage 8, the situation should be close to a resolution. However, this is not always the case as talks frequently break down. In that case, the cycle repeats itself in either an expanding spiral or a contracting one. The nature of spiral will dictate the time taken for resolution of the problem.

The Logic of Military Force

Herein lies a paradox; in the initial stages of the conflict, the state is heavily dependent on the use of military force without which the militant/terrorist cannot be brought to the negotiating table. Once he is at the table, the military has to take a back seat, yield space to the negotiators and more often than not be an unwilling and dismayed witness to the frittering away of hard-won tactical advantages.

Under most conditions, there are limits to the use of military force against terrorist groups. Most groups are small. Military forces may be able to penetrate and garrison an area that terrorist groups frequent and, if well sustained, may temporarily reduce terrorist activity. But once the situation in an area becomes untenable for terrorists, they will simply transfer their activity to another area, and the problem remains unresolved. Terrorists groups generally fight wars of the weak. Most do not put large, organized forces into the field unless they are sure that they will be no immediate retaliation. There are limits to how military force can be used. As David Galula explains,[10] "Conventional operations by themselves have at best no more effect than a fly swatter. Some guerrillas are bound to be caught, but new recruits will replace them as fast as they are lost."

There are many other reasons for which one has to be careful not to prolong the military involvement in the resolution of the conflict by force. Some of these are enumerated in the succeeding paragraphs.

Jones and Libicki state that military force usually has the opposite effect from what is intended: It is often overused, alienates the local population by its heavy-handed nature, and provides a window of opportunity for terrorist-group recruitment.[11] This terrorist strategy is often referred to as *provocation*. Terrorist groups seek to goad the target government into a military response that harms civilians within the terrorist organization's home territory. The aim is to convince the population that the military is so evil that the terrorists' radical goals are justified.[12]

Terrorist groups do not put large, organized forces into the field. This means that military forces can rarely engage terrorist groups using what most armies are trained in: conventional tactics, techniques, and procedures. Most soldiers are not trained to understand, penetrate, and destroy terrorist organizations.

Militaries tended to be most effective when used against terrorist groups engaged in an insurgency in which the groups were large, well armed, and well organized. Insurgent groups have been among the most capable and lethal terrorist groups, and military force has usually been a necessary component in such cases. Against most terrorist groups, however, military force is usually too blunt an instrument.

Military tools may have increased in precision and lethality, especially with the growing use of precision standoff weapons and imagery to monitor terrorist movement. But even precision weapons have been of limited use against terrorist groups. The use of substantial military power against terrorist groups also runs a significant risk of killing innocent civilians in collateral damage and turning the local population against the government.

Winning the media war to label terrorists as criminals is especially important and virtually impossible to do in the face of a strategy based on military force. Security forces need to be especially careful to abide by both national laws and, depending on the situation, international laws of land warfare. Further, they must also understand and abide by local customs. Security forces cannot conduct operations in a vacuum. When they cause damage, they must be prepared to pay compensation and follow up with civil aid.

The Cornwallis Group, a UK think tank of operations and strategic and analysts, conducted a study, "Analysis of Societal Conflict and Counter-insurgency The British Army's Effectiveness in the Irish Campaign and the Lessons for Modern Counter-insurgency Operations, With Special Reference To C3I Aspects". The study group identified lessons from the Irish Campaign, which are relevant in our context also. The principal lessons identified were as follows:[13]

1. The need to have a unified and coherent policy.
2. The need to have a unified intelligence system, particularly between civil and military authorities.
3. The need to target the most radical elements and the use of less coercive methods against moderates.
4. The avoidance of tit-for-tat violence and terror measures.
5. The need to consider effects on the wider stage i.e. propaganda.
6. Rapid and secure communications.
7. The need to deal promptly with security breaches and to protect sources, i.e. an active counter-intelligence and security capability.
8. Do not seek quick-fix solutions.
9. Do not under-estimate the enemy

Policing vs Military Force

Some argue that terrorist groups can be defeated primarily by *military force*. MIT political scientist Barry Posen argues, "Offensive action and offensive military capabilities are necessary components of a successful counter-terror strategy."[14]

Others contend that groups break up primarily because police defeat them. Policing involves the use of police and intelligence units to collect information on terrorist groups, penetrate cells, and arrest key members. A law-enforcement approach may also include developing anti-terrorism legislation. This can involve criminalizing activities that are necessary for terrorist groups to function, such as raising money or recruiting openly.

Working with local police and intelligence agencies is critical. They generally have better training and information to penetrate and disrupt terrorist organizations. They are the primary arm of the government focused on internal security matters. The military can strengthen the police forces by providing arms and other equipment and by training and mentoring the police forces. This strategy requires working "by, with, and through" local police forces.

Policing

The primary finding of this analysis was that policing and politics were far more likely to bring terrorist groups to an end than was military force. For terrorist groups that cannot or will not abandon terrorism, policing is likely to be the most effective strategy to destroy terrorist groups. The logic is straightforward: Police generally have better training and intelligence to penetrate and disrupt terrorist organizations. They are the primary arm of the government focused on internal security matters. This enables them to be best suited to understand and penetrate terrorist networks. However, the causal process is not entirely clear. How does policing work in practice? And how, specifically, do police infiltrate and destroy terrorist groups?

The mission of the police and other security forces should be to eliminate the terrorist organization—the command structure, terrorists, logistical support, and financial and political support—from the midst of the population. A police approach may also include enforcing strong anti-terrorism legislation. Therefore, a state's primary mechanism for dealing with a crime is through its criminal-justice system.

Policing and intelligence should be the backbone of our efforts. Police and intelligence services are best placed to implement these activities. This strategy should make police and intelligence efforts the backbone of our counter-terrorism policy and move away from its mantra of fighting a war on terrorism. This requires a paradigmatic shift. It should also include rebalancing our resources and attention on police and intelligence work. A police approach can include a range of steps. These are enumerated in the succeeding paragraphs.

Intelligence Collection and Analysis. Intelligence is the principal source of information on terrorists. The police and intelligence agencies have a variety of ways to identify terrorists, including signal intelligence (such as monitoring phone calls) and human intelligence (such as using informants to penetrate terrorist cells). Human intelligence can provide some of the most useful actionable intelligence. But it requires painstaking work and patience in recruiting informants who are already in terrorist organizations or placing informants in terrorist organizations. Intelligence collection and analysis can also be reinforced by countering the ideology and messages of terrorist groups through what is often referred to as *information operations*: the use of a variety of strategies and tools to counter, influence, or disrupt the message and operation of terrorist groups. In *Small Wars*, British Colonel C.E. Callwell wrote that security forces often work somewhat "in the dark" against terrorist organizations and that "what is known technically as 'intelligence' is defective, and unavoidably so."[15]

Arrest of Key Leaders and their Support Network. In democratic countries, this involves capturing key members and presenting the evidence in court. Terrorism involves the commission of violent crimes, such as murder and assault. Consequently, the investigation, trial, and punishment of perpetrators should be a matter for the wider criminal-justice system—including the police. The barriers can be significant. Finding sufficient evidence that can be presented in court but that does not reveal sensitive information about sources and methods can be challenging. This is especially true if a terrorist has not yet perpetrated an attack. In many cases, it may be easier and more effective to arrest and punish terrorists for other offenses, such as drug trafficking that may be ancillary to their terrorist activity.

In sum, a policing approach involves collecting intelligence on terrorists and terrorist groups (including their broader network), capturing key leaders, and passing legislation to prevent groups from operating and raising money. Friends and relatives of identified terrorists need to be pursued and investigated wherever they reside. Especially important are those who were friends of a terrorist just before he or she started *jihad*, such as traveling to Pakistan for training. These friends may have helped transform him or her from an alienated Muslim into a dedicated terrorist. Arresting key individuals would degrade the network into isolated units or cliques. They would be less capable of mounting complex, large-scale operations, because they would lack expertise, logistical support, and financial support. Isolation would reduce terrorism to simple criminality.

Monitoring of Communications. With good intelligence, law-enforcement authorities should be able to identify terrorist communication hubs. This includes intercepting and monitoring terrorist communication through telephone, landline phone, email, social media, and internet cafes. It also involves identifying, monitoring and tracking couriers being used by the terrorist organisations. The mission should be to penetrate and seize terrorists and other criminals—their command structure, members, logistical support, and financial and political support—from the midst of the population. Local police and intelligence know the language, people, culture, and terrain better than the central security forces drawn from all parts of the country.

Human intelligence is preferable to signal intelligence, since there are limitations to using technological means to monitor the activities of the terrorist organizations. All organizations are aware of phone taps, so they would be wary of discussing plans openly over cell phones or land lines.

Civil Defense Forces (CDF)

These programs—whether termed *militia, home guard,* or *self-defense forces*—figured prominently in some of the most successful and oft-cited counter-insurgency operations. In these campaigns, a CDF helped establish physical security by supplementing government forces while also fostering a perception of security and connectivity with the government. McCuen[16] places high value on CDFs: An important part—possibly the most important part—of counter-organization of the population is the organization of its self-defense against intimidation and extortion by way of taxation by the terrorists. Unless the people themselves have the means and commitment to resist, their desire for personal security is likely to overpower their loyalty to the government or neutrality. Even in the early phase of the insurgency, organization of local auxiliary police and militia units should be a first priority task of the governing authorities. O'Neill[17] points out that not only are civil militias a viable counter-insurgency tactic but they can serve to buffer the local governments. "In order to free regular military forces for counter-guerrilla operations and to provide security for government officials . . . local self-defense forces may be established. Where they are not, civilian officials who are in charge of social and economic programs can be intimidated or eliminated by insurgent violence". He goes on to point out that implementing a CDF program can be tricky. To be effective, it should complement local governance programs but must also be perceived as a legitimate alternative to insurgent presence: When local militias are established to prevent insurgent intimidation, their effectiveness will be partly contingent on whether they constitute a disciplined force perceived to be a servant of the people, or are instead ill-disciplined units guilty of excesses against the people.[18] The unpopularity of the *Ikhwanis* is a case in point.

Supported by the regular military forces dispersed throughout the country, these militia units should be hand-picked from among the people, staffed with local reservists and, if possible, commanded by small cadres of regulars. The governing authorities should make membership in the militia desirable. They can do this both by paying for duty periods and by social activities and various privileges.... In this manner, important members of the local community can be committed to the government. At the same time, the militia affords the population and its leaders a means of resisting revolutionary intimidation.

CDFs are often credited with providing excellent local intelligence to police and military units, gathering information that would otherwise be unobtainable through more-formal intelligence-collection means.[19] When the Government implements a successful CDF program, police and police intelligence (special branch) officers leverage their relationships with local leaders and militia commanders to build and expand their human-intelligence networks. CDFs generally proved to be both a force multiplier (in that they gave local advantage to the counter-insurgents over the insurgents) and an economy-of-force measure (in that they amplified counter-insurgent force levels, expanding the reach of the government in the absence of sufficient regular security forces). In some cases, the CDFs were successful in encouraging defections, as locally recruited insurgents observed stabilization and, eventually, some level of normalization in their home territories.

Qualitative analysis of the data set seems to show that volunteer (unpaid), part-time forces are generally more effective and longer lasting than paid, full-time forces, but this is not always true. While unpaid part-timers are often conscientious in their duties, they rarely succeed without the motivation of indiscriminate insurgent terror or locally applied government reform programs. Paid full-time militias can be thrown together quickly, giving the counter-insurgent a chance to establish immediate security in a specific area while taking young males off the streets. However, since the paid militia members are primarily motivated by money, they also are more vulnerable to infiltration, bribery, desertion, and defection. We cannot prescribe one or the other for any specific condition.

System of Government

Conventional wisdom suggests that unless the root cause of an insurgency is addressed, a satisfactory resolution of the conflict will not be forthcoming. The conflict between the insurgent and the Government is essentially a struggle for the hearts and minds of the population. The Government must provide the population security, a stable economy, and (legitimate) basic rights if the counter-insurgency is to succeed. Galula[20] believes that even a half-hearted effort is worthwhile: Knowing that his program will have no or little immediate appeal, the counter-insurgent has to somehow find a set of reforms, even if secondary, even if minor. He has to gamble that reason, in the long run, will prevail over passion. This can only happen in a democratic set up, because an anocratic government would be naturally hesitant to take on Galula's "gamble".

Basic Rights

Any democracy worth its name is duty bound to provide its citizens some basic rights which are enshrined in its constitution. Some of these rights directly impact on the efficient conduct of counter-insurgency operations. At the same time, denial of these rights over a protracted period depicts the government in a highly negative light. So it is in the interests of the government to provide the kind of environment wherein the citizen is able to enjoy basic freedom even in the midst of an operationally active situation. Some of the problems which ensue are as under:

- Freedom of the press demonstrates recognition of basic rights, it also allows the press to condemn government reforms as half-measures, criticize military tactics and leadership, and call for further, and further damaging, transformation.
- Freedom of speech allows supporters of the insurgency to stage mass rallies against the government, which might then develop into a general revolt.
- Freedom from random search by an aggressive security service.
- Speedy trials deny the use of emergency-power detentions.

When governments do attempt to grant various rights, they often do so in half-measures and only under tremendous pressure. In this way, it appears that they are conceding to insurgent demands, a sign of weakness that simply reinforces the impression that the insurgency is winning. Unrelenting insurgent propagandists jump at the chance to embarrass the government, which, in its weakened state, may offer added reforms. It quickly finds itself being dragged down by its own inconsistencies.

To succeed, the Government should attempt to establish and preserve security, minimize or eliminate public opposition to its policies through genuine and lasting reform, ensure the availability of essential services and employment, and either destroy the insurgents or co-opt them in a way that does not risk the regime's authority or legitimacy.

Public support can be won only if reforms are both legitimate and effective. It is not enough for the government to mean well—or pretend to mean well—it must also follow through consistently over a period of time. The government must actually transform into at least a rudimentary representative government. As McCuen puts it,[21] "...persuasion requires concrete evidence of action or implementation at the local level. Although the government power will encounter opposition within its own ranks to such actions as land reform, reduction of interest, and removing of disliked officials, these should be accomplished to the extent necessary to win popular support.

Civilians suffering through an insurgency will be slow to trust either side and will be very cautious in throwing their support behind the government. Support also may depend on the establishment of basic services, such as adequate food, clean water, electricity, access to medical facilities and employment. It seems obvious that both services and basic rights should be addressed simultaneously.

Total Elimination or Co-option

Barring independent collapse, defeating an insurgent military cadre requires either total elimination of its leadership and infrastructure or co-option. Co-option has proven to be the better of the two options. Annihilation of an insurgent cadre typically requires massive expenditures in money, broad use of force that commonly leads to civilian casualties, and (if it has passed the proto-insurgency phase) time. The counter-insurgent would be better off balancing security with reconstruction and reconciliation programs and avoiding civilian casualties in an effort to win hearts and minds; time is never a guaranteed commodity. Co-opted insurgents lend legitimacy to the political process and often contribute positively to the development of genuine reform

Unleashing a range of repressive and autocratic policies, ignoring democratic and human rights, is a course not available to true democracies, like India. In fact, Merom[22] states that democracies are incapable of the absolute repression sometimes necessary for survival.

When to Implement Reforms

Galula[23] warns against attempting reform during the pacification phase of a counter-insurgency operation: Implementing political reforms—if they have been conceived and announced by the government—would be premature at this stage. The time will be right when the insurgent political cells have been destroyed and when local leaders have emerged. As with all things counter-insurgency, strategy and tactics are situation-dependent. *If it does not come at the expense of security*, phased reform can and should be instituted contiguously with other measures in specific geographic areas. Asynchronous political reform in a targeted area could come in the form of local elections, reduced emergency powers, or other reforms enacted by local, rather than national governments.

Why the Insurgents get the Upper Hand

Governments give way to insurgencies under the weight of their own corruption, weakness, incompetence, or the general failure to address simple tenets of security and good governance. Based on both our quantitative and qualitative findings, it seems that governments defeat themselves more often than they are defeated by a dominant insurgency:

- Governments ignore the insurgency until it develops into a credible threat.
- Governments fail to address root causes.
- Governments address root causes half-heartedly or too late, stoking discontent.
- Governments fail to identify major shifts in strategic momentum.
- Governments fail to extend credible control into rural areas.

No matter how one applies individual quantitative lessons, favorably ending an insurgency remains a matter of conducting a well-timed, aggressive, fully resourced, population-centric campaign designed to address the root causes of the conflict. There are no "counter-insurgency shortcuts" or generalized exceptions to these onerous obligations: Half measures and inconsistent application of basic counter-insurgency tenets presage defeat or continuing violence.

Political Solutions

Two quotes suggest the solution to an insurgency in the simplest of terms. Samuel Huntington: "Governments that fail to meet the basic welfare and economic needs of their peoples and suppress their liberties generate violent opposition to themselves"[24] and Mousseau: "Terrorist groups tend to last longer in poor countries...one way to end terrorism is to improve the economic condition of countries where terrorism is most prevalent".[25] Both these experts convey the basic truth that terrorism thrives in deprived communities. Remove the deprivation and you remove the reason for the unrest.

Most terrorist groups that have ended, did so by pursuing their goals through politics. The possibility of a political solution is linked to a key variable: the breadth of terrorist goals. The narrower the goals, the more difficult it is for terrorists to achieve them, and the more willing they will be to seek nonviolent means. One path to politics includes an explicit *peace settlement*. It involves a bargaining process with the government in which terrorist groups reach an agreement to disband their militant wings and transition to a political party.

"If," Paul Pillar wrote, "the stakes are indivisible, so that neither side can get most of what it wants without depriving the other of most of what it wants, negotiations are less apt to be successful."[26] Terrorism may persist in a country precisely because the goals that the government and the terrorist group are pursuing are so far apart, "with nothing in between to contribute to the give and take of negotiation and bargaining."

Terrorists fighting for broad goals, such as social revolution or empire, are less likely to reach a negotiated settlement than are groups fighting for limited aims, such as policy change or territorial change. Where a terrorist group's goals are minimal, there may be a middle ground from which to draw a compromise settlement.

Legal and other Measures

A major step is the development and passage of legal measures. This involves not just that letting terrorism as an unlawful activity but also criminalizing activities that are necessary for terrorist groups to function, such as raising money or recruiting members. In democratic states, this inevitably leads to tension between civil liberties and security. As one scholar noted, "a democratic nation wants life, liberty, and unity as the products of its policies for dealing with terrorism, not just physical security.

Since terrorist groups need to move money to multiple cells to help sustain their operations, attacking their finances or following financial leads once terrorists are captured has provided effective results. But there are challenges. These informal *hawala* networks remain largely outside government control, and monitoring them presents a significant challenge to smashing terrorist financial exchanges.

Countering Ideology

Counter-terrorism is just as much about hearts and minds as it is about policing and intelligence. It requires taking calculated actions that do not alienate the masses. And it also requires effectively countering the ideology and messages of terrorist groups through information operations. This includes the use of a variety of strategies and tools to counter the appeal and influence of the separatist groups. The local government is always better placed to conduct information operations than the central government.

Mosques have historically served as focal points for major political upheavals in the Muslim world. Intelligence officials need to monitor religious leaders and activities within the mosques. It is critical to understand who holds power, whom the local population trusts, and where locals get their information—and then to target these forums. This means providing assistance to credible indigenous groups, such as Muslim clerics or tribal elders, who can effectively counter *jehadi* propaganda. These groups do not necessarily have to be supportive of India, but they do need to oppose insurgents and have credible influence among the population. Much of this funding may have to be indirect and covert to protect their credibility.

Assistance could be directed to indigenous media, political parties, student and youth organizations, labor unions, and religious figures and organizations that meet at least two criteria: They have a notable support base in the local population, and they oppose insurgent groups and insurgent ideology.

NOTES

1. Dr John Llewellyn, John Dew, *"Prospects For Iraq: Some Lessons From History,"* Unpublished Report, Lehman Brothers Global Economics 7 June 2004.
2. Sapone, Montgomery, *"Ceasefire: The Impact of Republican Political Culture on the Ceasefire Process in Northern Ireland,"* Peace and Conflict Studies, Vol. 7, No. 1, May 2000.
3. Seth G. Jones, Martin C. Libicki, *"How Terrorist Groups End,"* RAND Corporation 2008.
4. Ben Connable and Martin C. Libicki, *"How Insurgencies End,"* RAND Corporation 2010.
5. McCormick, Gordon H, Steven B. Horton, and Lauren A. Harrison, *"Things Fall Apart: The Endgame Dynamics of Internal Wars,"* paper presented to the RAND Corporation Insurgency Board, August 29, 2006, p. 6.
6. Kilcullen, David, *"The Accidental Guerrilla: Fighting Small Wars in the Midst of a Big One,"* Oxford, UK: Oxford University Press, 2009, p. 183.
7. Chalk, Peter, *"The Malay-Muslim Insurgency in Southern Thailand—Understanding the Conflict's Evolving Dynamic:* RAND Counterinsurgency Study—Paper 5, RAND Corporation, OP-198-OSD, 2008.
8. Kilcullen, David, *"Countering Global Insurgency: A Strategy for the War on Terrorism"*, Canberra and Washington, D.C., 2004.
9. Seth G. Jones, Martin C. Libicki, 2008.
10. David Galula, *"Counterinsurgency Warfare Theory And Practice,"* published by Frederick A. Praeger, New York, London 1964.

11. Seth G. Jones, Martin C. Libicki, 2008, p xvii.
12. Lawrence Wright, "*The Looming Tower: Al-Qaeda and the Road to 9/11*," New York: Knopf, 2006, p. 217 as quoted ibid.
13. Gordon Pattison, "*Analysis of Societal Conflict and Counter-Insurgency*," The Cornwallis Group XIV: 2010.
14 Barry Posen, "*The Struggle Against Terrorism: Grand Strategy, Strategy, and Tactics*," International Security, Vol. 26, No. 3, Winter 2001–2002, p. 39–55, p. 47 as quoted in RAND MG-741.
15. C. E. Callwell, "*Small Wars: Their Principles and Practices*," 3rd ed., Lincoln, Neb.: University of Nebraska Press, 1996, p. 43 as quoted ibid.
16. McCuen, John J., "*The Art of Counter-Revolutionary War: The Strategy of Counter-Insurgency*," London: Faber, 1966 p. 112, as quoted in RAND MG 965.
17. O'Neill, Bard E, "*Insurgency and Terrorism: Inside Modern Revolutionary Warfare*," Washington, D.C.: Brassey's (US), 1990, p. 130 as quoted ibid.
18. Ibid , p. 130.
19. McCuen, John J, 1966, p. 112.
20. David Galula, 1964 p. 75.
21. McCuen John J, 1966, p. 59.
22. Merom, Gil, "*How Democracies Lose Small Wars: State, Society, and the Failures of France in Algeria, Israel in Lebanon, and the United States in Vietnam*," New York: Cambridge University Press, 2003. p. 15 as quoted in RAND MG 965.
23. David Galula, 1964 p. 120.
24. Huntington, Samuel P, "*The Age of Muslim Wars*," *Newsweek*, December 17,2001, p. 48, as quoted in RAND MG 965.
25. Mousseau, Michael, "*Market Civilization and Its Clash with Terror*," International Security, Vol. 27, No. 3, Winter 2002–2003, pp. 5–29. (2002–2003, pp. 24–26).
26. Paul Pillar, *Terrorism and U.S. Foreign Policy*, Washington, D.C.: Brookings Institution Press, 2001, p. 21 as quoted in RAND 741.

10

Towards Police Reforms

"...instead of improving the police functioning and approach, what we have seen is a journey from bad to worse in these seven years".

—Hon'ble Supreme Court of India

Police-to-Population Ratio

The ideal police to population ratio as per standard UN norms is 2 to 2.5 per 1000 citizens. Most developed countries strive for this norm, but there are variations depending upon various factors such as an inherently violent society, urbanized areas and a prevalent insurgency. In intrinsically peaceful countries, such as the US and Canada, Western Europe, Japan, Australia, and others, the force ratio is typically between 2 and 4 per thousand of population. The same is depicted in the chart below[1]. As can be seen, India figures in the list of peaceful societies.

Benchmark Force Ratios—Peaceful Societies
(Policemen per 1000 head of population)

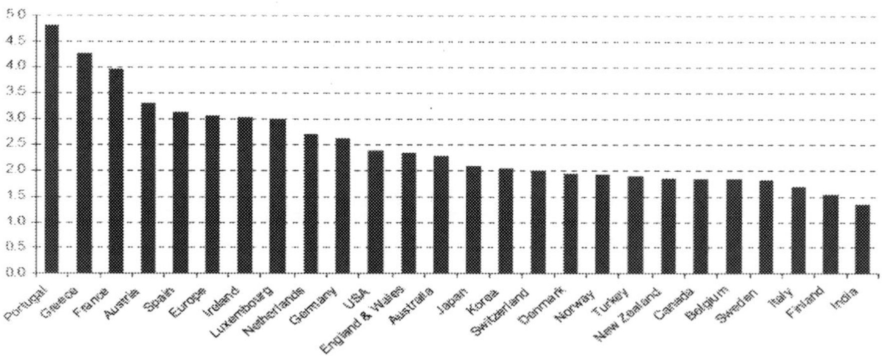

Source: UK Home Office Online Report September 2002

The police to population figures for some developing countries are given below:

Philippines	1 : 1000@
Malaysia	3.6 : 1000%
Pakistan	2.10 : 1000*
Sindh, Pakistan	2.63 : 1000#
India	1.33 : 1000^

Sources: @ Philippines Police Annual Report
% Centre for Public Policy Studies Malaysia
* Institute for Social Planning and Understanding, Detroit
# Official Website of the Ministry of Home Affairs, Govt of Sindh
^ BPR&D Report 2009.

The 24th November 2008 issue of the *Dawn* newspaper of Pakistan carried figures comparing police population ratios in major cities of Pakistan with the cities of Delhi and London in India and the UK respectively. The same are reflected below: [2]

Comparative Police / Population Ratio (Major Cities of UK, India and Pakistan)

City	*Population*	*Police Strength*	*Ratio*
London	7,387,868	47,874	6.45: 1000
New Delhi	14,000,000	58,000	4.15: 1000
Mumbai	19,000,000	53,000	2.80: 1000
Lahore	9,000,000	30,946	3.48: 1000
Karachi	18,000,000	31,861	1.75: 1000

Source: Dawn, 24 Nov 2008; Official Website of the Ministry of Home Affairs, Govt of Sindh.

Three important deductions can be drawn from the tables in the preceding paragraphs; first, peaceful societies can afford to have a police to population ratio less than the prescribed norm; second, urban areas need a higher ratio because of the need to control a higher density of population; and third, inherently violent societies need a higher police to public ratio. This can also explain why the city of Karachi has the highest incidents of violence in Pakistan, and probably in the entire subcontinent, since the police to population ratio in the city is woefully inadequate, even when compared with the Pakistani national average.

Police-Population Ratio in India

The sanctioned and actual total police per one lakh population (police-population ratio) at all-India level is 145.25 and 117.09, respectively as on 1.1.2007.[3]

State-wise Strength of Police in India as on December 31, 2010

State/UT	*Area (In Sqr. Kms.)*	*Actual Police Strength*			*No of Policemen Per 1000 Population*
		Civil	*Armed*	*Total*	
Andhra Pradesh	275045	95370	14534	109904	1.31
Aruncahl Pradesh	83743	3506	3939	7445	6.03
Assam	78438	28694	25375	54069	1.75
Bihar	94163	49915	11941	61856	0.64
Chhattisgarh	135191	26046	15779	41825	1.70
Goa	3702	4038	661	4699	2.70
Gujarat	196024	48648	15936	64584	1.11
Haryana	44212	42961	4535	47496	1.93
Himachal Pradesh	55673	9671	3904	13575	2.03
J&K	101387	47859	29153	77012	5.76
Jharkhand	79714	33806	12807	46613	1.51
Karnataka	191791	63689	7908	71597	1.22
Kerala	38863	37368	3182	40550	1.16
Madhya Pradesh*	308245	52765	23390	76155	1.06
Maharashtra	307713	165740	14215	179955	1.64
Manipur	22327	10249	13274	23523	8.71
Meghalaya	22429	5898	4349	10247	3.93
Mizoram	21081	3562	7171	10733	1.07
Nagaland	16579	5637	4366	10003	4.45
Orissa	155707	28965	14480	43445	1.06
Punjab	50362	47992	18678	66670	2.44
Rajasthan	342239	59608	11962	71570	1.07
Sikkim	7096	1645	2159	3804	6.24
Tamil Nadu	130058	72886	13869	86755	1.28
Tripura	10486	10671	13588	24259	6.72
Uttar Pradesh	240928	111234	30898	142132	7.10
Uttarakhand	53483	13884	4160	18044	1.84
West Bengal	88752	63906	22191	86097	0.95
Total (States)	3155431	1146213	348404	1494617	1.28
A&N Islands	8249	2933	806	3739	8.86
Chandigarh	114	4424	635	5059	4.50
Delhi	1483	67268	6594	73862	4.03
Lakshadweep	32	332	0	332	4.61
Total (UTs)	10973	77106	8588	85694	3.97
Total (All India)	**3166404**	**1223319**	**356992**	**1580311**	**1.33**

Source: BPR&D Report, 2009.

Strength of Police in J&K

The police figures for the state of J&K are tabulated below.

Year	*Actual Police Strength*			*Number of policemen*	
	Civil	*Armed*	*Total*	*Per 100 Sq Km*	*Per 1000 of population*
2006	39103	20106	59209	58.4	5.05
2007	38920	22791	61711	60.9	5.10
2008	39035	24733	63768	62.9	5.10
2009	—Incorrect data furnished—				
2010	47859	29153	77012	76.0	5.76

Source: National Crime Records Bureau, Government of India.

Police Reforms

The need for reform of police in India has been long recognised. There has been almost 30 years of debate and discussion by government created committees and commissions on the way forward for police reform, but India remains saddled with an outdated and old-fashioned law, while report after report gathers dust on government shelves without implementation. Many committees on police reforms have recommended major reforms in the police system coupled with systemic accountability. The major commissions/committees which were formed to produce a Model Police Act or to suggest recommendations to the existing Act were as under:

- National Police Commission (1977-81)
- Ribeiro Committee (1998-99)
- Padmanabhaiah Committee (2000)
- Soli Sorabjee Committee (2005)

In 1996, Prakash Singh, a former Director General of Police, launched a Public Interest Litigation (PIL) in the Supreme Court of India seeking the court's intervention in the implementation of the long-needed police reforms. The court noticed a marked reluctance on part of the states to implement any meaningful reforms with the following scathing comments, *"....instead of improving the police functioning and approach, what we have seen is a journey from bad to worse in these seven years"*. In September 2006, after the Supreme Court issued seven binding directives for all states that it felt were necessary to professionalise the Indian police force. These directives were as under:

Directive 1. Constitute a State Security Commission [SSC] to:

(a) Ensure that the state government does not exercise unwarranted influence or pressure on the police.
(b) Lay down broad policy guidelines.
(c) Evaluate the performance of the state police.

Directive 2. Ensure that the DGP is appointed through a merit based transparent process and secure a minimum tenure of two years.

Directive 3. Ensure that the Inspector General of Police and other police officers on operational duties [including Superintendents of Police in charge of a district and the Station House Officers in charge of a police station] are also provided a minimum tenure of two years.

Directive 4. Separate the investigation and law and order functions of the police.

Directive 5. Set up a Police Establishment Board [PEB] to decide transfers, postings, promotions and other service related matters of police officers of and below the rank of Superintendent of Police and make recommendations on postings and transfers above the rank of Superintendent of Police.

Directive 6. Set up a Police Complaints Authority [PCA] at state level to inquire into public complaints against police officers of and above the rank of Deputy Superintendent of Police in cases of serious misconduct, including custodial death, grievous hurt, or rape in police custody and at district levels to inquire into public complaints against the police personnel below the rank of Deputy Superintendent of Police in cases of serious misconduct.

Directive 7. Set up a National Security Commission [NSC] at the union level to prepare a panel for selection and placement of Chiefs of the Central Police Organizations [CPO] with a minimum tenure of two years.

Despite the criticism of the Supreme Court, the political class seems unwilling to relax its stranglehold over the police. All states have made only half hearted attempts to comply with the directives of the Supreme Court.

The graph shown opposite depicts the percentage of non-compliance by states with the SC order.

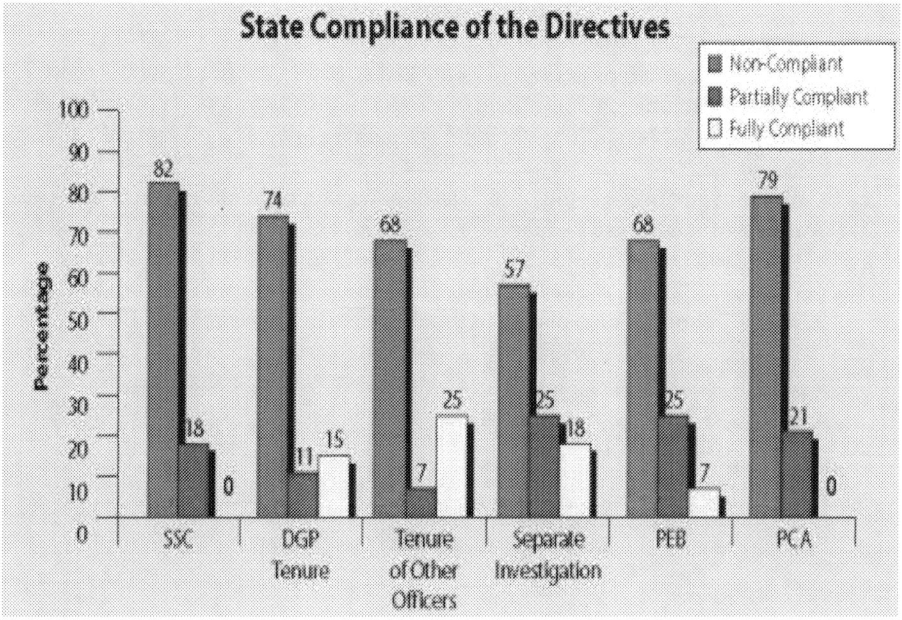

Comments

All the studies, recommendations and model acts on the subject of police reforms are gathering dust, because their implementation would be at the cost of the politicians losing partial control over the activities of the police force under their command. That said, it stands to logic that unless the Police Act is rewritten and the force is modernized and brought in line with present day requirements, efficient and accountable performance of the police will remain a wishful dream.

In the context of frontline states like Jammu and Kashmir, where there is an urgent and long standing demand for demilitarisation, it is essential that some urgent reforms need to be initiated if we expect the Jammu and Kashmir police to be able to function on a permanent basis in an environment which is fraught with the dangers of insurgency erupting once again. The modernisation, training and the reforms of the police force can commence immediately independent of reforms at the national level which can follow subsequently.

NOTES

1. "Police Service Strength England and Wales", Home Office Online Report 23/03, (30 September 2002), taken from House of Commons Hansard Written Answers (28 March 2003) *http://www.johnmannmp.co.uk/Commons/2003-03-28%2001.html.*
2. 24th November 2008 issue of the *Dawn* newspaper of Pakistan and the Official Website of the Ministry of Home Affairs, Govt of Sindh
3. Reply given in the Rajya Sabha by the Union Minister of State for Home Affairs on 15 July 2009, to a question regarding the police-population ratio in India, quoting information furnished by Bureau of Police Research and Development BPR&D

11

The Case for Demilitarisation

Demilitarisation hinges on the assumption that conditions in Jammu & Kashmir will revert to normal one day, sooner than later. This assumption is not far-fetched since the average man in the streets of Srinagar is as interested in living a normal life, as anyone else in the country. The realisation has set in that the terrorists/separatists can never achieve their aim despite the full backing, covert and overt, of Pakistan. The security forces are also clear in their understanding that the problem is political and therefore its resolution has to be by negotiations rather than enforcing a military solution. In fact the latter is highly undesirable as prolonging the armed conflict is detrimental to the interests of either side. The people of Jammu & Kashmir have to resolve their own problems but in the present circumstances this cannot be achieved without the complete involvement of India and within the provisions of the Constitution of India.

The term demilitarisation has different connotations for different people. If viewed purely in the context of the Indian Army, then it is a non-starter because the primary reason for the presence of the Indian Army in the state of Jammu and Kashmir is not counter-insurgency but ensuring the territorial integrity of the country. If, however, the term is used in the context of the central police forces, other central law enforcement agencies and to a certain extent the Indian Army, then there is a definite scope for de-induction, raising of an alternate force, re-training and re-equipping the police forces in enforcing law and order in roles and scenarios other than only counter-insurgency.

Impact of Demilitarisation

The impact of demilitarisation will need to be examined from various angles. Reduction in troop levels should be seen as the natural consequence of improvement in the ground situation and not as a sign of weakness of the security forces. Care has to be taken to ensure that there is no power vacuum created as a result of demilitarisation. We can ill-afford to have a state of anarchy once the civil administration takes over. The dimensions terrorism may assume, once the exit policy is implemented, need to be assessed in detail.

Lessons from Punjab

Lessons can be drawn from the experience of the counter-insurgency conducted in Punjab in the 1980s and 1990s. The state faced the same cycle of assassinations, bombings, and kidnappings directed at Indian officials and facilities, other Sikhs, and Hindus over nearly a decade, in pursuit of the independent Sikh state of Khalistan, aided and abetted from across the international border in Pakistan, which provided safe havens for the Sikh terrorists. In the initial years, the Indian Army had to be requisitioned to get the situation under control. Once the situation was brought under control and it became clear that the Army was no longer required, it was decided to let the police take charge of restoring normalcy to the state.

At that juncture, the security forces were deployed at a total force ratio (troops, paramilitaries, and police) of around 12 per thousand of population[1]. With the elimination of most of the militant leaders, the backbone of the insurgency was broken and the situation rapidly reverted to normal post 1992. The overwhelming majority of Sikhs in Punjab have since totally rejected terrorist violence and participate fully in Indian democratic politics.

Demilitarisation in Kashmir

Kashmir is at a similar crossroads. The backbone of the insurgents has been broken. The Indian security forces have achieved their objective. They are no longer actively required for the maintenance of law and order in the state. Continuing in this role can only be detrimental to its efficiency as an effective fighting force meant to combat external aggression. They should now only be required to look towards threats emanating from across the border or the line of control and leave the handling of the internal security to the local police force. That is not to say that they have totally outlived their utility. Far from it; they are required to pass on their knowledge, expertise and experience to the armed police who are rookies in the matter of conducting a counter-insurgency campaign. Luckily for the State, removal of the army and other central police forces from the scene is unlikely to weaken the counter-insurgency grid considerably because of the presence of the Rashtriya Rifles troops. What is to become of them in the long run, is a subject we shall consider in another chapter.

THE MECHANICS OF DEMILITARISATION

"Ultimate demilitarisation, in its true sense, can only take place once the Indo-Pakistan-China conflict is resolved".

The State Plan

After the period of 2007-08, the state government commenced to give a serious thought to the process of demilitarisation. To assuage the alienation of the population, it was decided to replace the CRPF by the state police. This was in keeping with the recommendation to the government that once the security situation showed signs of improvement, law and order being a state subject, be handed over completely to the state police. The deployment of the police and paramilitary forces had to be re-worked as per the present situation which is more a law and order problem and less of a terrorist problem. In July 2009, Chief Minister Omar Abdullah demanded that the plan for the first phase of withdrawal of the CRPF from the Kashmir Valley be submitted to his office within 10 days.[2] He admitted that the de-induction of the CRPF would be a prolonged process as the State did not have adequate Police forces to replace the CRPF immediately. The other regular paramilitary forces would continue to assist the State Police in counter-insurgency operations and other duties until the Jammu and Kashmir Police recruited more personnel, trained and deployed them for duties.

In the changed scenario, the police was expected to be better equipped and trained to deal with law and order situation. This also required a change in mindset of the force. Expecting the state police to replace the CRPF overnight would not be possible as they were over 70 battalions to be replaced, which was not within their capabilities. Besides no action was sought to be taken which might be detrimental to the State's security. So it was decided to take concrete steps in terms of augmenting the numbers of that the Jammu and Kashmir Police by raising additional battalions, upgrading their equipment and improving their levels of training.

The special armed units of the state police being raised are known as the Indian Reserve Police [IRP]. The basic premise in this proposal is that prior to taking over the security matrix of the state, these units would be adequately trained and equipped to handle insurgency situations.

However, the transition will take time as the process of raising and training the IRP battalions is likely to be a protracted one. The Chief Minister categorically stated that unless the state has adequate numbers, the CRPF cannot be replaced. Director General of Police (DGP) Kuldeep Khoda also confirmed that though the CRPF would definitely be replaced by the IRP, it was likely to take time, as apart from the physical raising of the battalions, the police personnel would first have to undergo intensive training.

However, contrary to the popular demand in the streets, nobody in government and police circles is willing to discount the requirement of the CRPF altogether. Some CRPF battalions would always be required for the Amarnath Yatra and others locations like elections in assisting J&K Police in the maintenance of law and order. "For law and order in Srinagar, we would always require the CRPF. See, we are not in a position to control 20 processions or protests at a time" a senior police officer confessed[3].

In March 2009, DGP Kuldeep Khoda said that the priority of the Jammu and Kashmir Police would be to lay stress on strengthening its infrastructure facilities across the State to meet the requirements of its increasing manpower. He also said that it was imperative that the Police adapt to new challenges posed by the changed security scenario. Taking serious note of its anti-terrorism role in the absence of the central security forces, the Jammu and Kashmir Police commenced providing basic commando training to a selected group of over 900 constables at the Commando Training Centre at Lethpore in Kashmir Valley.[4]

The Chief Minister acknowledged the liberal financial assistance from the Government of India in upgrading the state police infrastructure. These funds were used to create additional police posts of different categories, information technology upgrade, modernize and enhance the communication network and the upgrade, refit and renovation of police hospitals at Jammu and Srinagar have been upgraded and fitted with better medical equipment. All this has vastly improved the efficiency and effectiveness of the state police department, thus placing it in a better position to take on the additional responsibility of the de-induction of bulk of the central forces.[5]

The State Government Plan for Reduction of the CRPF

In April 2012, the state government announced a series of steps for the withdrawal of CRPF with a view to minimize its footprint and to reassure the population that the government on serious in its commitment of normalizing the situation and making the uniformed forces less conspicuous on the roads. The salient features of the plan were as follows:[6]

- Of the 52 CRPF battalions presently operating in Kashmir valley, several battalions are likely to be moved out at the end of the summer of 2012.
- CRPF would be replaced by Indian Reserve Police (IRP) of J&K Police. A proposal for the immediate raising of five more IRP battalions pending final approval from Union Home Ministry.
- The process of removal of most bunkers from Srinagar city would commence with immediate effect. Some bunkers at strategic locations will remain. In addition, 10 specially designed bullet-proof mobile bunkers have been added to the CRPF inventory.
- An estimated 50 additional police battalions would be required to be raised before the phased removal of paramilitary personnel from Jammu and Kashmir can be said to be complete.

Comments

It is evident that at the higher levels the actual nuts and bolts of the process of demilitarization has not been considered with the due deliberation and seriousness which it warrants. Replacing the CRPF by an equal number of police battalions is pointless when the intention is to reduce the number of uniformed personnel on the streets without compromising on efficiency and effectiveness. There has to be a visible decrease and that can only be achieved by replacing quantity by quality. How much and by whom is not something that can be arrived at by an off-the-cuff political statement.

What appears to emerge as the logical way to go about the process of demilitarisation is that an elite police force comprising specially selected, motivated and trained personnel with a handsome compensation package is raised to be the first line of forces to react to any armed incident. This force backed by a highly vigilant and proactive intelligence network would be able to meet most of the challenges thrown at them by the insurgents. Any incident beyond their capability can then be taken on by the Rashtriya Rifles.

NOTES

1. Mathur Anant, *Secrets of COIN Success: Lessons from the Punjab Campaign Faultlines*: Volume 20, January 2011
2. Interview to Kashmir Life
3. Interview of a senior police officer
4. Interview of the Director General of Police, J&K Police in March 2009
5. http://zeenews.india.com/news/jammu-and-kashmir/indian-reserve-police-battalions-raised-in-jandk_611456.html 15 Mar 2010
6. Shabir Ibn Yusuf, htttp://www.greaterkashmir.com news/2012/Apr/ 26/some-crpf-battalions-to-leave-srinagar-this-fall-71.asp

12

Economic Development of J&K

"Terrorist groups tend to last longer in poor countries...one way to end terrorism is to improve the economic condition."

—Mousseau

In the preceding chapters, we have seen as to how the resolution of the problem of insurgency and the process of normalization is intrinsically linked to development and improvement of infrastructure. In this section we shall see the quantum of financial and other assistance provided by the Centre to the Jammu and Kashmir government for the purposes of reconstruction, rehabilitation of displaced persons, development and generation of employment opportunities. It will not be wrong to state that, per capita, the state of Jammu and Kashmir has received the maximum central assistance as compared to that provided to any other state. However, how efficiently the funds have been utilized, whether they have been actually utilized for the purpose for which they were released and whether they have been siphoned off to line private pockets is another matter altogether. But one cannot fault the Centre for not having released adequate funds. The only regret is that it took an insurgency to shake the Centre into looking carefully as to the earnestness and honesty with which the projects were implemented and to the need to pay greater attention to the rural and border areas.

Central Assistance to J&K

Having brought down the violence to manageable levels by the turn of the century, it was abundantly clear that the restoration of peace and harmony and maintenance of internal security and public order in the state are intrinsically linked to economic development and prosperity. The

Central Government, therefore, worked out an attractive economic package for the development of infrastructure and the economy of the state with emphasis on the following:[1]

- Good infrastructure.
- Promotion of trade and industry to include:
  - Tourism.
  - Cottage industries and handicrafts.
- Adequate employment opportunities especially for the youth.

The focus was planned and balanced regional development for strengthening the physical, economic and social infrastructure, thereby improving the productive potential of J&K State. As a special dispensation, the Centre has been providing continuous financial support to the State government over and above the normal central plan assistance not only to fund the State Plan but also to cover its non-plan gap.

Central Economic Packages

Prime Minister's Package - May 2002.[2] On 23 May 2002, the Prime Minister, announced a package for over Rs 6000 cr aimed at expanding the existing infrastructure, provision of basic services, providing an impetus to employment and income generation and providing relief and rehabilitation for the dislocated and the families of the victims of militancy.

Prime Minister's Package April 2003[3]

On 19 April 2003, the Prime Minister announced the constitution of a special task force under the chairmanship of the Cabinet Secretary to prepare a comprehensive plan to tackle the problem of unemployment in the State of J&K and thereby reduce the sense of alienation among the people of J&K.

To achieve the objective of creation of one lakh employment opportunities in J&K, it was decided to make use of all existing schemes, modify some existing schemes and where acquired get new schemes approved, as identified by the task force approved. The Task Force identified and classified the potential employment opportunities worth approximately Rs 3000 cr under the following three categories:-

(i) Self-employment - 38.17%
(ii) Wage employment - 45.18%
(iii) Regular salaried employment - 16.65%

Prime Minister's Package August 2003.[4] On 29 August 2003, the Prime Minister released additional grants of over Rs 450 cr for the development of the State.

Prime Minister's Reconstruction Plan, November 2004.[5] On 17-18 November 2004, the Prime Minister announced a reconstruction plan for J&K involving an outlay of approximately Rs 24,000 cr as under:

Expanding economic infrastructure

- Power. (Rs 15,052 cr, besides amount required for rural electrification)
- Roads. (Rs 998 cr)
- Assistance for External Borrowings for Infrastructure (30% of Rs 1,970 cr =591 cr)

Expanding provision of basic services

- Education (Rs 142 cr)
- Health (Rs 120 cr)
- Physical Infrastructure for Civic Amenities (Rs 4,884 cr)

Thrust to employment and income generation

- Tourism (Rs 517 cr)
- Agriculture & Food Processing (Rs 101 cr)
- Other Industrial Promotion Related Measures (Rs 78 cr, besides compensation to industries)
- Other Employment Measures (Rs 163 cr)
- Relief and Rehabilitation for families of victims of militancy and assistance to the dislocated and the families (Rs 75 cr)

Prime Minister's Package for Ladakh Province June 2005.[6] On 11 June 2005, the Prime Minister announced additional measures for the development of the Ladakh province.

Prime Minister's Package, April 2008.[7] In April 2008, the Prime Minister announced the release of an additional 100 cr to the State Government from Security Related Expenditure (Relief & Rehabilitation) as relief measures for victims of militancy related violence.

Central Package 2011.[8] The Centre approved Rs 1,000 crore special package for imparting training to 8,000 youth annually in the State with the help of the corporate sector. Approximately 40,000 graduates, post-graduates and professional degree holders from the State would benefit over the next five years.

Monitoring of Development Schemes in J&K[9]

In order to effectively coordinate and accelerate efficient implementation of various development packages in J&K, a Standing Committee, headed by the Cabinet Secretary/Home Secretary, on development programmes in J&K was constituted with representation from the concerned Central Ministries, the Planning Commission and the State Government.

A Working Group under the Chairmanship of Special Secretary, Department of J&K Affairs was also constituted to assist the Standing Committee. Six sub-groups of the Working Group under the Chairmanship of Special Secretary, Department of J&K Affairs have been constituted to monitor the progress of implementation of Centrally Sponsored Schemes/ Centrally Financed Projects being implemented by various Central Ministries/Departments including those of Railways and Roads in the State of J&K and to facilitate more focused discussion and in-depth examination of issues requiring coordination.

Each Sub-group comprises representatives of concerned Central Ministries and State Government Departments as well as Planning Commission and Department of Jammu & Kashmir Affairs/MHA. While the responsibility of implementing a particular Central/Centrally Sponsored Scheme/Project continues to be that of the concerned Central Ministry/State Government, the Department of J&K Affairs, MHA facilitates and coordinates the implementation of development schemes and projects in the State.

Creation of Employment and Self-employment Opportunities in J&K[10]

The major sectors, in which the employment/self-employment opportunities are being created are as under:

(i) Roads, highways and railways
(ii) Textiles including handicrafts, carpet and silk
(iii) Agriculture (including horticulture, animal husbandry and food processing)
(iv) Education
(v) Tourism
(vi) Small and medium industrial units
(vii) IT and telecommunications
(viii) Existing Central/Centrally sponsored schemes
(ix) Banking support for self-employment activities

Border Area Development Program (BADP) in J&K[11]

During his May 2002 visit the Prime Minister released BADP Funds worth Rs 500 cr for next 5 years at Rs 100 cr per year instead of the State's normal share of Rs 34 cr per year to be implemented in 44 border blocks, 42 opposite Pakistan/POK and 2 in district Leh bordering China. 15% of the total amount per year has been approved for construction of roads in Border areas. The major initiatives undertaken by BADP include solar street lighting, purchase of medical diagnostic equipments, construction of link roads, rural sanitation, schools and medical facilities.

Border Area Migrants. About 30,771 families comprising 1,53,131 persons had been forced to migrate from the border areas/LoC of the Districts Rajouri, Poonch, Jammu and Kathua. The figure includes 6040 families (22000 persons) who had migrated from Akhnoor tehsil in the wake of Kargil conflict in 1999. The State Government formulated a relief package to these Border Migrants, which was enhanced after PM's announcement on 23 May 2002.

Relief for the Migrants from the Kashmir Valley

In 1996, the then Prime Minister announced a special package of Rs 6.60 cr for improvement of facilities in Jammu camps. The amount was utilized on the construction of one-room tenements, Sulabh type toilet complexes, drainage scheme and school buildings. Subsequently, a further sum of approximately Rs 23.5 cr was progressively released by the Government of India for improvement of the living conditions in Jammu camps.

Summary of Central Assistance

The estimated cost of all the schemes included in the Prime Minister's Reconstruction Plan for Jammu and Kashmir stood at Rs 28,004 cr up to 31 March 2012, whereas the expenditure incurred was just Rs 8,731 cr on central sector projects and Rs 3,967 cr on state sector projects, amounting to less than half of the released finance.[12]

With the change in governments, both at the Centre and at the State in 2014-15, a fresh impetus has been accorded to the centrally assisted schemes. The latest figure announced in early July 2015 stands at 70,000 cr with the likelihood of being increased to 100,000 cr.

Action Plan for Return of Migrants[13]

The National Conference Government had in October 1999 approved an Action Plan to facilitate the return of the Kashmiri Hindu migrants. To begin with, the State Government identified 166 houses forming 15 clusters in Srinagar and Badgam Districts, which were considered safe for the return of the owners of these houses. The list of these clusters was published in the newspapers and steps were taken to identify the families and find their willingness to return to their homes. About 50 families who were registered with the Relief Organisation, Jammu were contacted personally to give their consent for return to the Valley on the basis of the package announced by the Government. Interaction meetings with some of these families were also held, but none of the families agreed to return to the Valley.

The State Government had identified the shrines in Mattan and Kheer Bhavani where Kashmiri Hindu Migrants displaced from these places could be settled temporarily by developing two model clusters (containing temporary shelters), until such time they can repair their existing residential houses. The Ministry of Finance provided a grant of Rs 10 crore to the State Government for the reconstruction/renovation of houses and shrines at Kheer Bhavani and Mattan. Government of J&K has also proposed construction of flats at Budgam and Anantnag for the rehabilitation of Kashmiri Migrants. The Central Government had also approved construction of 200 flats at Budgam on an experimental basis and released a sum of Rs 4 cr as advance in March 2004.

The proposal to construct a separate township for those who are willing to return is being opposed tooth and nail, primarily by the Hurriyat. They want the Kashmiri Hindus to return to their original houses, knowing fully well that is an impossibility. Apart from the fact that a large number of Hindus have nowhere to go to having sold their properties in distress to enable them to survive wherever they had taken shelter, expecting them to feel secure in the same house from where they had fled fearing for their lives, is absurd. The trust deficit which set in during the fateful years of 1989-90 will take quite a while to diminish.

NOTES

1. Extracted from the Ministry of Home Affairs, Annual Report 2003-04.
2. Ibid, 2002-03, Prime Ministers Package, 2002.
3. Ibid, 2003-04, Prime Ministers Package, April 2003.
4. Ibid, 2003-04, Prime Minister's Package, August 2003.
5. Ibid, 2004-05, Prime Ministers Package, November 2004.
6. Ibid, 2005-06, Prime Ministers Package for Ladakh, June 2005.
7. Ibid, 2008-09, Prime Ministers Package, April 2008.
8. Ibid, 2008-09, Summary of Central Assistance.
9. Ibid, 2008-09, Monitoring of Central Development Schemes.
10. Ibid, 2009-10, Important Infrastructure Schemes.
11. Ministry of Home Affairs, Annual Report 2003-04.
12. BADP [Extracted from the Ministry of Home Affairs, Annual Report 2003-04].
13. J&K Government Plan for the return of Kashmiri migrants, 2006.

13

Pacts, Agreements and Dialogue

"If the stakes are indivisible, so that neither side can get most of what it wants without depriving the other of most of what it wants, negotiations are less apt to be successful."

—Paul Pillar

Since the accession of the State to the Indian Union, there have been a number of bilateral treaties between India and Pakistan. After the onset of insurgency in the nineties, it took a decade and more to create conditions conducive for talks with the belligerents represented by the Hurriyat. It was quite an achievement of the State to have convinced the separatists that talks and dialogue was the only option available to them to get their side of the view presented at the table.

Since the initial talks in 2004, there have been a number of rounds of discussion with every possible section of society that was willing to talk. This process was taken further by the interlocutors who had been nominated by the Centre to assess the latest factual position on ground, interact with the maximum possible cross section of society and recommend steps which would ultimately lead to a satisfactory resolution of the problem which would be acceptable to all, or at least most, stakeholders.

Important treaties/dialogues which have a bearing on the current study are given in the succeeding paragraphs.

Instrument of Accession[1]

Jammu and Kashmir (J&K) became an integral part of the Indian Union on Oct. 26, 1947 when the then ruler of the State, Raja Hari Singh, unconditionally signed the Instrument of Accession in accordance with the legal framework in terms of which the Princely States of British India could accede either to India or to Pakistan. The Instrument of Accession was common for all princely states of British India including J&K. The prescribed legal framework did not envisage ratification of such accession by the people of the princely state. Text of the Instrument of Accession is attached as Annexure 2 to this study.

India, since its independence, has been a vibrant, secular democracy providing to the people of all its states, including J&K, free and equal participation in political life and governance. Pakistan's refusal to accept the State's accession to India led it to launch an armed aggression in 1947 resulting in the forcible occupation of a part of the State that still remains under its illegal control. Pakistan's non-acceptance of the reality and its ambition to wrest Jammu and Kashmir from India by force led to wars between the two countries in 1965 and 1971.

Since the onset of terrorism in J&K in 1989-90, the people of J&K have voted in Parliamentary elections in 1996, 1998 and 2004, elections to the State Assembly in 1996 and 2002 and in *Panchayat* Elections in 2000 despite terrorist's threats and calls for boycott of elections. The UN Resolutions calling for the will of the people to be ascertained are no longer tenable because Pakistan has not fulfilled the precondition of withdrawal from the territory occupied by it through aggression. On the contrary, Pakistan has completely altered the demography of the Northern Areas by settling large numbers of Punjabis and Pashtuns there. The UN Resolution had called for a ceasefire and withdrawal of all Pakistani regulars and irregulars from the territory of the erstwhile Princely State of J&K, to be followed (once United Nations Commission on India and Pakistan had certified full Pakistani withdrawal) by a reduction of Indian forces to a level sufficient to maintain law and order and public order. Only on full compliance of the above conditions, was the choice of the people to be ascertained. Not only that, Pakistan still continues to occupy the territory illegally captured (and has even ceded a part of it to China), and has attempted to alter the status quo by force in the wars of 1965 and 1971. By a subsequent (Shimla) agreement of 1972, India and Pakistan agreed that the issue of J&K, along with other issues, would be addressed bilaterally. As such, Pakistan has no right to invoke the Resolutions.

U.N. Sponsored Cease Fire of 1st January 1949[2]

Text of the U.N. sponsored Cease-Fire Agreement is attached as Annexure 3 to this study. Main provisions of the Agreement are as under:

- Immediate ceasefire under supervision of the UN Observer Group (UNMOGIP).
- Pullback of the Pakistani troops and tribals to the original borders.
- Withdrawal of excessive Indian troops from Jammu and Kashmir.
- Plebiscite in Jammu and Kashmir under the aegis of the UN to decide on its future.

Indus Waters Treaty 1960[3]

At the time of independence, several disputes arose between India and Pakistan on the sharing of water. All the head works were in India, but the canals irrigated Pakistan. It was a very complicated arrangement. At that time Kashmir was already a flashpoint and the main fear was that war might erupt in Kashmir over the water's issue finish hence the Indus Waters treaty of 1960 came about. The World Bank and the Americans were deeply involved. Despite all the muscle flexing that we see every now and then, the treaty has endured and it has helped to keep the peace. Many experts consider that the treaty is more than fair to Pakistan, however Pakistan feels that its interests have not been adequately catered for. That argument does not cut much ice because Pakistan has the unrestricted supply of the three major rivers ie the Indus, the Jhelum and the Chenab. If anything, the treaty has not been fair to the State of Jammu and Kashmir as it has not taken into account for the future requirements of the State. Relevant extracts of the Treaty are attached as Annexure 4.

In an article titled, "Geo-political Significance of Kashmir: An overview of Indo-Pak Relations", co-authors, Naseer Ahmed Kalis and Shaheen Showkat Dar have this to say: "(sic) The Indus Waters Treaty has favoured Pakistan. This division provided Pakistan with 56% of the catchment area and only 31% to India. In Pakistan over 80% of the crop land is irrigated. The country has the world's largest contiguous irrigation network. The river of Indus basin provide 60% of the water utilized for irrigation while ground account for the rest. Indus Waters Treaty has benefited Pakistan. Pakistanis feel that in a major conflict, India could shut off the waters from the rivers. It is interesting to note that during the 1965, 1971 wars, limited wars of 1985 and 1999; India did not shut off water as it very easily could do."[4]

DIALOGUE PROCESS

Government Policy on Jammu & Kashmir

It has been the stated policy of India that the resolution of all problems lies in peaceful means only and, accordingly, the Government has kept its door open and has, from time to time, extended the offer of dialogue to different organizations/sections of people. The Central Government, conjointly with the State Government of J&K, is pursuing a multi-pronged strategy to bring peace and normalcy in the State of Jammu & Kashmir. These measures are also complemented by efforts in the diplomatic and media spheres. Four major prongs of the strategy are:[5]

- Pro-active tackling of cross border terrorism by security forces
- Accelerating economic development and redressal of public grievances within the State
- Being open to initiating the dialogue process with all groups in J&K and especially those who eschew the path of violence and express a desire for such talks
- Deepening of political processes through elections at all levels and encouraging political debate within J&K.

Dialogues with Pakistan[6]

Post 1989, there have been a number of dialogues/meetings at the level of Secretary, Foreign Minister and Head of Government. Though some progress was made, the talks have generally been inconclusive. The gains of one meeting were squandered away at the very next. Most of the talks were doomed to failure because of the fact that Pakistan did not cease providing moral and material support to the terrorists operating in Jammu and Kashmir. The salient points discussed during the dialogs are given in the subsequent paragraphs.

- **1996.** Indian and Pakistani diplomats met in Islamabad in June and announced an eight-point agenda for peace talks, including Kashmir. It was agreed to set up a mechanism to tackle Kashmir.
- **1998.** Indian Prime Minister Atal Behari Vajpayee and his Pakistani counterpart Nawaz Sharif met in New York in September and announced an agreement to resume peace talks, beginning with diplomats discussing peace, security and Kashmir in Islamabad.
- **1999.** Indian and Pakistan Prime Ministers met in Lahore in February and signed a Joint Declaration expressing resolve to settle all contentious issues between the two countries, including Kashmir, through bilateral dialogue.

- **1999.** Talks between the Foreign Ministers of Pakistan and India held in June at New Delhi failed to resolve the Kargil crisis.
- **2005.** During their talks in April at New Delhi, Prime Minister, Dr. Manmohan Singh, and the Pakistan President, Gen Pervez Musharraf, committed themselves to increasing the frequency of the Srinagar-Muzaffarabad bus service and commencing the Munabao-Khokhrapar railway link by the end of December 2005. While the Prime Minister described the talks as "very positive, fruitful and forward-looking", Gen Musharraf said progress had been made in the discussions during which all issues, including Jammu and Kashmir, came up.

  India and Pakistan while underlining that the peace process between the two countries was "now irreversible," agreed to open trade across the Line of Control (LoC) by allowing trucks between Srinagar and Muzaffarabad, open the trans-LoC Poonch-Rawalakot route and take steps for the meeting of divided families along the LoC. Condemning the attempts to disrupt the Srinagar-Muzaffarabad bus service, the Prime Minister, Dr. Manmohan Singh, and the Pakistan President, Gen. Pervez Musharraf, pledged in a joint statement that they "would not allow terrorism to impede the peace process."

  Gen. Musharraf also met leaders of the All Parties Hurriyat Conference at the Pakistan House in New Delhi on April 17. Both factions of the APHC, led by Mirwaiz Umer Farooq and Syed Ali Shah Geelani, met the President separately and reportedly apprised him of their views on the situation in J&K.

Dialogues with the *Hurriyat*

On 15 August 2002, the Prime Minister made an announcement that his Government is committed to have free and fair elections in J&K and that talks would be held with elected representatives after the elections. Accordingly, following the elections in October, 2002 and installation of a popular Government in J&K, Mr NN Vohra, former Union Home Secretary and former Principal Secretary to Prime Minister was tasked in April 2003 to initiate and carry forward the dialogue.

Mr Vohra interacted with the Chief Minister, Dy. Chief Minister, Leader of the Opposition in each House, Speakers of the legislative assembly, prominent and influential politicians and eminent citizens and met with persons representing a cross-section of organizations, political affiliations, NGOs, religious and community interests and sub-regional groups. Having ascertained the factual position on ground, he submitted his recommendations to the Prime Minister.

Acknowledging the interest shown by the All Party Hurriyat Conference (APHC) to have talks at the political level, the Cabinet Committee on Security, in its meeting held on 22 October 2003, offered to have a meeting with the *Hurriyat* leadership at the level of Deputy Prime Minister. The Hurriyat faction led by Maulana Abbas Ansari accepted the offer of the dialogue. However, the Geelani faction declined. The Government issued a formal invitation to Maulana Abbas Ansari, Chairman of the Hurriyat Conference, requesting him to meet the Deputy Prime Minister on 22nd January 2004 along with his colleagues.

First Round of Talks. The APHC delegation led by Maulana Abbas Ansari comprised Prof Abdul Ghani Bhat, Mirwaiz Umar Farooq, Bilal Ghani Lone and Fazal-ul-Haq Quereshi as members. They called on the Deputy Prime Minister on January 22, 2004. In a joint statement issued after the discussion the following major points emerged:

- It was agreed that the dialogue process was the first significant step initiated by the Government of India
- A step by step approach would lead to the resolution of all outstanding issues relating to Jammu & Kashmir.
- The APHC delegation stressed the need for an honourable and durable solution through dialogue and need for ending violence at all levels.
- The APHC delegation committed itself to the enlargement of dialogue process to cover all regions of the J&K and address the concerns of all communities.
- The Dy PM reiterated the Government's concern to safeguard the security of all people and ensure against the violation of their rights.
- A speedy review would be undertaken to examine the cases of those held in detention.
- It was agreed that the next round of discussions would take place in the latter part of March 2004.

Second Round of Talks. The Dy PM met the APHC delegation led by Maulana Abbas Ansari on 27 March 2004 for the second round of discussions and reviewed progress on issues raised in the first meeting. Fazal-ul-Haq Qureshi who was there in first round of discussions withdrew from this round of talks. Recognizing that, consequent to the Lok Sabha elections, a new central government was likely to be installed in the latter half of May 2004, it was agreed that discussion on substantive issues would commence at the next meeting to be held in June 2004.

Pursuant to the two rounds of discussions between the APHC and Dy PM, the Joint Screening Committee reviewed a number of cases of detenues held under J&K Public Safety Act, 1978 (PSA) and as on March 31, 2004 had recommended the release of about 43 detenues.

PM's Reconstruction Plan for Jammu and Kashmir

Following the installation of the new government at the centre, serious consideration was given to speedy action so as to seize the advantage of the goodwill earned consequent to the talks and not to lose out on credibility. The Prime Minister, announced a Reconstruction Plan for J&K involving an outlay of approximately Rs 24,000 crore.

The aim of the Reconstruction Plan was to cater to the need to strengthening the economic and social infrastructure and provide for the balanced development of the three regions of Jammu and Kashmir. The details of the plan are given in the section on economic and infrastructure development. The PMO, Planning Commission and the MHA were tasked to monitor the implementation of the Plan on a regular basis.

Second Round of PM-*Hurriyat* Talks

Prime Minister held another meeting with a six-member delegation of All Party Hurriyat Conference led by Mirwaiz Umar Farooq on 3 May 2006. The delegation was informed that the Union Home Minister would be establishing an institutional mechanism for a structured interaction in future.[7]

Second Round Table Conference

The Second Round Table Conference was held at Srinagar on May 24-25, 2006. In his concluding remarks, the Prime Minister said that the recurrent theme was to have a mechanism, which would provide opportunities for meeting more frequently in smaller groups and focus on specific issues, one at a time, for finding common ground and forging a consensus. The Prime Minister proposed the setting up of the following five Working Groups:[8]

Working Group I. Confidence-building measures (CBMs) across segments of society in the State.

Working Group II. Strengthening relations across the Line of Control.

Working Group III. Economic development.

Working Group IV. Ensuring good governance.

Working Group V. Strengthening relations between the State and the Centre.

Third Round Table Conference

The 3rd Round Table Conference was held on 24 April 2007 in New Delhi, under the Chairmanship of the Prime Minister. Members of the separatist groups were also invited to attend the Conference, but they stayed away. During the Conference, the recommendations of four Working Groups were presented and discussed: [9]

(i) **Working Group on CBMs across Segments of Society in the State.** The Conference gave in principle endorsement to the approach suggested, viz:
- Strengthening human rights protection.
- Rehabilitation of widows/orphans and other victims of militancy.
- Rehabilitation and return of Kashmiri migrants.
- Resolving outstanding issues relating to Refugees of 1947 and persons displaced in 1965 and 1971.
- Steps for preserving the rich and diverse cultural landscape of the State.

(ii) **Working Group on Strengthening Relations across the Line of Control.** The Conference endorsed the recommendations and applauded the ongoing efforts to strengthen people to-people contacts and promote trade and commerce across the LC.

(iii) **Working Group on Economic Development.** The Conference endorsed the recommendations and urged the Central and State Governments to take steps to carry them forward.

(iv) **Working Group on Ensuring Good Governance.** The Conference endorsed the recommendations and urged the State Government to implement them in earnest in order to bring greater efficiency, transparency and accountability into the systems and processes of governance and to bring the Government close to the people

The following actions resulted as a consequence of the talks:

- A time bound review of cases of detention under J&K PSA Act was completed.
- A high level meeting was held to reiterate the Government's commitment to the observance of human rights and finalise a proactive agenda in this context.

- It was decided to investigate all cases of human rights violations within a time frame of 90 days.
- A 3-member team was constitute to examine the forces for making them simpler and more people friendly.
- A handy card listing the do's and don'ts was distributed to security personnel as a constant reminder of the sanctity of human rights. This has been elaborated in the chapter on Human Rights.

Policy for Surrender of Militants and their Rehabilitation

Government of J&K adopted a new policy for the surrender of militants on January 31, 2004. 3676 militants availed of the surrender policy and laid down their arms by 31 December 2005. The salient features of this policy are as under:[10]

- A monthly stipend of Rs. 2,000 per month for a period of three years after surrender.
- An immediate grant of Rs. 1.50 lakhs to be kept in the shape of FDR in a bank in the name of the surrenderee for a period of three years which can be drawn by him on completion of three year period and subject to good behavior.
- Incentives for surrendered weapons to be given as per prescribed rates.
- Vocational training for self-employment to those who desire to undergo such training.

All Party Delegation (APD)

Following the unprecedented protests and violence of the summer of 2010, an All Party Delegation (APD) comprising 34 members of various political parties accompanied by the Union Home Minister and Parliamentary Affairs Minister visited the State of Jammu & Kashmir on 20-21 September 2010 and held discussions with representatives of political parties and various interest groups from the civil society at Srinagar and Jammu. [11]

On 25 September 2010, keeping in view the inputs received from the APD as well as inputs from State and the Central Government Agencies on the law and order situation in the State, Government of India approved an 8-point plan to be implemented to ease the situation. Provisions of the plan were as under:[12]

- Appointment of interlocutors for sustained dialogue.
- Release of students/youths detained for stone pelting.
- Review the cases of all PSA detenues.
- Review the deployment of security forces in the Kashmir valley.

- Ex-gratia relief to the families of the deceased persons at Rs 5 lakh per person killed in the civil disturbances since 11 June 2010.
- Appointment of special task forces to examine developmental needs of Jammu and Ladakh regions.
- Re-opening of all schools and colleges.
- Provision of additional central assistance of Rs 100 crore to the State Government to restore the damaged infrastructure of schools and colleges.

Appointment of Interlocutors.[13] The Central Government appointed three interlocutors for sustained dialogue with all shades of opinion and constituted special task forces to examine developmental needs of Jammu and Ladakh regions. Comments on the charter of the interlocutors and their report are given separately in this book. Main recommendations of the interlocutors are indicated at Annexure 5.

Initiatives by the PDP-BJP Government

With the installation of the PDP-BJP Government in early 2015, a fresh impetus was given to the resolution of the problem. While it is still early days, it is apparent that the government of Mufti Mohammed Sayeed believes in engaging with the separatists, at times even appearing to bend over backwards to placate them. The tactics have drawn a lot of criticism from the opposition parties and others of an alarmist bent of mind. Backed by the central assistance amounting to over Rs 70,000 cr, it is quite possible that the Chief Minister will be able to convince a significant segment of the population in the Valley that their future is better ensured by development and the creation of jobs rather than by a blind and senseless opposition to any government initiative.

Dileep Padgaonkar assessed the impact of the central assistance thus:[14] "Prime Minister Narendra Modi is expected to announce a financial package for Jammu and Kashmir. The total amount, anywhere between Rs 70,000 cr to Rs 100,000 cr, is almost double the figure that the previous regime had allotted for the state a little over a decade ago. The Centre's largesse is intended to give a powerful fillip to a gamut of development activities that are people-oriented.

".... the package could by and large change the narrative in Jammu and Kashmir. Successful implementation of the package will not vanquish separatist sentiment altogether. But it would go some way to arrest and perhaps even roll back its appeal especially amongst the youth.

"However, much would depend on how the development projects roll out in practice. From 2006-11 the UPA government commissioned several economists to prepare as many as seven research based and policy oriented reports on this very subject. Little information is available on the actions it took on the recommendations of the experts. However, an assessment of 16 schemes sponsored by the centre revealed that 15 to as much as 33% of grants allocated it to them were not spent, nor were targets achieved.

"If the government can execute the plan in a transparent and efficient manner, conditions will doubtless be created to facilitate discussions on the political issues plaguing this state. Their aim? To turn borders—between communities, regions and nations—into bridges."

NOTES

1. Official website of the Ministry of Home Affairs.
2. Official website of the Ministry of Home Affairs.
3. Official website of the Ministry of Water Resources.
4. Naseer Ahmed Kalis and Shaheen Showkat Dar, *Geo-political Significance of Kashmir: An Overview of Indo-Pak Relations* (IOSR Journal of Humanities and Social Science (IOSR-JHSS), Volume 9, Issue 2 (Mar.-Apr. 2013), pp. 115-123.
5. Annual Report 2003-04, Ministry of Home Affairs pp. 24-26.
6. Extracted fromvarious Annual Reports of the Ministry of Home Affairs.
7. Annual Report 2006-07, Ministry of Home Affairs p. 2.12.
8. Ibid, p. 2.13.
9. Ibid, 2007-08.
10. Ibid, 2005-06.
11. Ibid, 2010-11, p. 2.5.7.
12. Ibid 2010-11, p. 2.5.8.
13. Ibid 2010-11, p. 5.9.
14. Padgaonkar, Dileep, Times of India, 15 Jul 2015.

14

WHAM and CBMs

WHAM

"WHAM: Lessons from Jammu and Kashmir"[1], an article written by Rahul Bhosle was published by the Centre for Land Warfare Studies, New Delhi in 2009. Excerpts from the paper are included in the following paragraphs.

Understanding WHAM

WHAM can be described as a people-oriented process for establishing human, social and political linkages for the common good, contributing to building the concept of nationhood.

At the personal level, the hearts and minds campaign concerns security, honour and dignity of individual, family and society. At the societal level, a threat to culture, traditions, religion and identity would also lead to hostility in the masses. Once the personal and societal levels are combined, there is a general feeling of alienation of the people in areas affected by militancy.[2] Professor Ali A Jalali talks of structural legitimacy and rational legal authority as being central to winning hearts and minds.[3] WHAM, therefore, is the process of seeking the consent of the population for the presence of armed forces by accepting its necessity due to disturbed conditions in the area. It is seen as an action to strengthen friendly forces and win over uncommitted elements in society.

WHAM in a proxy war scenario has two dimensions, as it involves an external state as well as the indigenous people. This is, therefore, a tripartite relationship where more than one party is attempting to win over the people. Juxtaposing the love-hate triangle may be a pithy argument, but could appropriately explain why, despite deploying extensive resources, Pakistan has not succeeded in its endeavour and public opinion continues to tilt in favour of India. The Indian model of development and empowerment of the people of Kashmir has achieved better results. Thus, in an opinion poll by Peace Polls, from March to May 2008, 71 percent of Muslims in the State said they do not want to join Pakistan as opposed to 49 percent who do not want to join India.[4] However, this explains only one side of the argument. A proportion of the population continues to see separatism or *azadi* as a third option and not an either/or one between India and Pakistan. The main challenge for WHAM, therefore, is winning over this segment of the populace.

Strategy

The WHAM campaign is not an episodic response, but a long drawn-out, sustained strategy. It cannot effect change desired by external or internal elites, which is contrary to the sentiment of the people, in a short period of time. The flow of perception should thus attempt to gradually affect small changes, which will transform the mood in a sustained manner. If basic precepts are based on cardinal principles of human values and logical reasoning, and followed up by actions on the ground, people would eventually change their attitude and be willing to compromise with authority and even opt for sub-optimal solutions in the hope of better political choices in the days ahead. The challenge is to ensure that there is a steady positive trajectory of transformation.

Socio-religious fault lines are impermanent, and thus, can be effectively addressed to turn the clock back to moderation. In doing so, it should be appreciated that the sentiment of separatism is fairly deep-rooted and has to be addressed holistically. The strategy should thus be to reach out to the Kashmiri people as much as seeking their participation in activities of the Indian state. This should form one of the main themes of the continued WHAM campaign. These factors seem to be working in Kashmir and need to be taken to a positive conclusion.

The population will be more influenced if their internal grievances are addressed with alacrity and that should be the focus of the WHAM campaign. Given that the primary grievance of the people in Kashmir, at one time, was under-development, civic action rightly formed a key focus of transformation through development projects, which would improve the quality of life of the people and promote better understanding amongst the locals. Safeguarding human rights and minimising general inconvenience are the other arms of this strategy.[5] Conventional wisdom thus concludes that improved governance, delivery of services and development are the key areas of a hearts and minds campaign.

Civic actions have been further divided into active and passive facets to "help create a conducive environment, generate a healthy image for the army and resultantly a ground-swell for peace." Civic actions are designed to shift focus on "helping people to help themselves". While these are considered as active actions, passive actions to portray WHAM are indicated as "respect to elders and women, respect for local customs and traditions, good behavior of troops and minimum population control measures, in consultation with state administration."[6]

A three-pronged approach to winning hearts and minds comprises people-friendly operations, civic action and development and perception management, But WHAM goes far beyond people-friendly operations, civic actions or managing perceptions. It involves the entire process of governance—political, economic, and social, sports or trade. This would have to take into account the factor of alienation and degree to which it impacts society. Thus, each measure including operations will have to factor in possible responses based on emotions, sentiments, intellect, logic and temperament of the population. It would also have to consider how the action will be viewed by militant commanders managing the counter WHAM campaign and the spin that would be given to seemingly pro-public measures undertaken by the government. The Amarnath agitation is a classic case of how a win-win situation had been turned into a lose-lose one for both the people of the Valley and Jammu and the government due to lack of appreciation of this essential factor.

A FRESH APPROACH TO WHAM

Establishing the Strategic Context

At the highest level, the government has to demonstrate a genuine concern for dialogue, peace and harmony. Genuineness will be evident only if there is stated indication of accepting the result that emerges through such a process, whatever it may be. The government should be confident of a favourable outcome given that India's handling of problems in Kashmir has been extremely temperate and responsible. There are no accusations of genocide or ethnic cleansing, unique for one of the few incidents in global history of a conflict primarily based on identity.[7] That this may require acceptance of Kashmir as a disputed issue, which needs resolution through a tripartite dialogue is *sine qua non*, and thus, a larger debate for this position remains contested. However, such a dialogue will create a favourable impression on the Kashmiri psyche by attempting to reach out to the people, rather than continually questioning their loyalty. An innovative and flexible approach by the administration can defeat the tempo of dissension.

The aim of WHAM should be to merge identities without loss of distinctiveness, rather than maintaining exclusivity. A balance has to be evolved to build a collaborative regional and national identity by fostering ideas within Kashmir, by supporting leaders with a legacy for a holistic identity and by creating corresponding institutions and linkages. Moreover, nation-building through geographic and population coagulation is not unique to Kashmir, but applies across the board to other states.

People-Oriented Strategy and Operations

The WHAM campaign has to be the central feature around which the operational campaign should be based. This will not be a constraint on operational planning, but a basic consideration for implementation.[8] WHAM should be an operational strategy rather than a civic action addendum. The overall aim of a counter-militancy campaign will thus be to provide people with the right to live a normal existence without being subjected to the vagaries of militancy, population control measures, physical abuse such as body and vehicle searches and such like.

The tools of the insurgent and the counter-insurgent frequently appear to be the same. These are seen to be coercion, repression, intimidation and fear.[9] By constantly subjecting the people to controls, checks, frisking and midnight search and raids, the state authorities can generate a fear psychosis which replicates, in some measure, tactics employed by a terrorist. Many human rights activists term counter-terrorism as state terrorism. Human rights will thus have to be the focus of counter-insurgency strategy in the state.

Security is the primary focus of forces deployed for CI operations. The present model of security envisages that maximum operations are launched based on accurate intelligence. The army doctrine even envisages that operational gains could be sacrificed, in case the people are likely to be inconvenienced, which is a laudable approach. "Violation of Human Rights, therefore, must be avoided under all circumstances, even at the cost of operational success."[10]

Hearts and Minds at the Grassroots

A normal tactical operation can have major repercussions at the state and the national level. It is, therefore, important that counter-insurgents operating at the grass roots must be imbued with a sentiment of sympathy and empathy for the people of the Valley. Hearts and minds must start from the "hearts and minds" of the counter-insurgent who should imbibe the human approach.

To evoke this atmosphere, a humane approach towards the people, concomitant with the hard attitude towards the terrorist, in every commander and soldier or policeman, is a challenge. This will pose an eternal dilemma to the soldier, who frequently has to make a split-second judgment to return fire, which may lead to consequences which are unpredictable. Thus, proper education and training of soldiers assumes importance. While training will take care of the operational efficiency, education would build respect for human values.

Troops must be enthused to work towards the cause of merging Kashmiri identity with the national identity through a humane rather than a coercive approach. Psychological conditioning of troops operating in the Valley prior to induction is, therefore, important so that restrictive impositions are minimised.

Integrating Civil Society Institutions and Youth

The State and the Central governments need to actively work towards creating associations in all professional spheres to build effective linkages nationwide. This larger perspective will win sizeable gains in the days ahead.

Holistic education is a powerful means for expression of a collaborative regional and national identity. There are many mediums which need to be employed for this purpose. For instance, music shows as Indian Idol with participation of Kashmiri youth, will have a powerful impact on generating a balanced mix. Increased intellectual inter-action of Kashmiri teachers, scholars and students throughout the country is another facet. Such interaction should be held as much inside the state as outside it, to avoid the phenomenon of inversion, where holding such events inside the state by calling people from outside can be seen as another imposition from New Delhi.

Given the desire of the youth in J&K for higher education, and the limited number of seats in the colleges and universities there, quotas in colleges in states which have surplus capacity should be increased. This will go a long way in the integration of the youth, which is the future of the State, with the rest of the country.

WHAM International Campaign

The Kashmiri diaspora is divided into various segments, based on geographic divisions of the state. Diasporas generally tend to support secession, and the Kashmiri one is no different. Therefore, it is necessary to address Kashmiris living abroad through measures such as dialogue, seminars, talk shows etc to counter the negative propaganda and to impact a positive influence in the state. These, in turn, would shape international public opinion, including bodies which have been hostile from time to time such as the Organisation of the Islamic Conference (OIC). Here again, it needs to be underlined that winning every argument is not as important as building the perception that the state is willing to listen to different voices of reason.

Communication in WHAM

Translating goodwill generated through actions of the forces on the ground requires effective use of information tools available for the message to reach the masses. Targeting the strategic population is more important than the general population. This strategic population is generally very small but has a very large influence, even if it supports a limited cause.[11] This has to be the main focus of the strategic hearts and minds campaign planned at the highest level.

The interaction between the state and the people has to be based on core values, those of respect for human lives, rights and freedoms exercised without restraining the rights of others. The policy being conveyed or propagated has to be defensible and the message has to be conveyed through individuals who are non controversial and respectable.

A simpler strategy for WHAM would be to let actions speak in place of words. This is also the focus of "civic action as WHAM strategy" followed by the armed forces. The primary beneficiary of this strategy has been the Army as the people see it delivering the message.

Role of the Media in WHAM

The primary role of the media in counter-insurgency is to delegitimise the insurgent, particularly the philosophy of violence in the name of revolution.[12] Devising a media campaign for this purpose is important. Generally, it is assumed that good intent automatically gets translated into effective publicity; the reality is farther from the truth. When the rebels are out to subvert the message and the media is downright hostile, great thought has to be given not just to actions being taken but also the message that is to be conveyed to the people.

This has to be done by experts in the field, who understand the nuances of people's emotions, along with state authorities and security personnel, who operate in the area on a daily basis, to provide practical inputs. The campaign has to address the current concerns of the people and subtly link the same with the desired outcomes. A media campaign which goes against this dictum is unlikely to succeed, for the message will either fail to register with the audience or will be manipulated for subversive purposes.

The media is also bound to highlight unrestrained violence by the security forces, resulting in collateral damage. Since media is now a commercial enterprise rather than a profession, the influence of vested interests which are politically and commercially driven is considerable. In the Kashmir Valley, in particular, the media is known to be beholden to the militants, who seem to be dictating the agenda to a large number of media groups. The government, however, is not seen to be doing enough to reverse this trend. A detailed analysis of the media has to be carried out. While this may be considered by many, and the media in particular, as a restriction on their freedom, a survey done by an impartial NGO or media watch-dog classifying media sources as per its inclination, its known supporters, and its financiers would be in the professional interest of our national conscience. Such a detailed survey will add to standing of the media in Kashmir and prevent accusations of bias. Those operating outside the spirit of their compact with the state have to be dealt with as per the laws of the land, rather than allowing them a free run on the minds of the masses as is being done presently. It is frequently seen in the Valley that even newspapers running seditious propaganda are obtaining free and subsidised newsprint and government advertisements, not to talk of being financed by dubious sources.

It needs to be understood that the media is only the messenger. Thus, the dictum is restricted to "media is the most potent weapon for conducting psychological initiatives."[13] The media cannot help in covering up operational failures or human rights violations. The emphasis should be on positive people friendly actions, which will be "lapped up" by a news-hungry media, where competing mediums are leading to an eternal drought of content.

Countering Fundamentalist Ideologies

The roots of mutually supportive state and national identities have to be examined in detail. These could vary from legitimacy of accession, secular leanings of the people with the Indian Constitution, pan-cultural linkages and so on. Linking *Kashmiriyat* with the national identity could be one option. On the other hand, *Kashmiriyat* with its pan-secular appeal can be utilised to counter fundamentalist identities. A fine balance would thus have to be evolved between the two.

Counter-WHAM

Countering Indian efforts at WHAM is part of the overall strategy of the proxy war. The focus is on strategic communication with the masses by coercive manipulation of principal role players to its advantage. Generation of false statistics, creation of persecution, fictitious accounts of killing of Muslims or destruction of mosques by linking people's emotions with actions of security forces, which may or may not be true are standard tactics. For instance, by spreading false news of an attack by security forces on a mosque, a large crowd can be mustered to march towards government offices. Elements within the crowd earmarked previously indulge in slogan shouting, stone throwing and badgering the security forces, thereby provoking a reaction. In case, there is any loss of life or injury in this firing, the spiral of agitations is set into motion, thereby serving the purpose of the counter-WHAM operatives.

Pakistan and its cohorts have been waging a successful counter-WHAM campaign, which has an operational and media dimension. Control of vernacular media under duress is one approach. Coercion and intimidation is always a favourite weapon for countering WHAM and instigating the local leadership. This is instructive in the Amarnath case. On 21 August, in a wiretap operation, the police exposed *Tehreek-e-Hurriyat* leader Masarat Alam Bhat complaining to the *Hizbul Mujahideen* Chief Syed Salahuddin based in Pakistan of non-cooperation of the moderates led by Maulvi Mirwaiz Farooq referred to as *Baccha Maulvi* and the JKLF chief Yasin Malik referred to as "Gandhi" for spoiling the agitation.[14]

Sadbhavna as WHAM

Sadbhavana was a very good initiative of the army. It had two components; assistance in improving local infrastructure and WHAM. The former should be handed over to the local administration while the Army should concentrate on continuing with the latter. Initiatives like taking youngsters on a tour of the Indian mainland go a long way in bridging the gap between the State, in particular the Valley and other inaccessible areas, and the rest of the country. The Indian Army must continue to provide aid to civic programmes like 'Op Sadbhavna', but in a low profile manner. The initiative should appear to be that of the local politician and the civil administration and the publicity and credit should go to them. The Indian Army and the SF must gradually retreat into the background.

Conclusion

The core lessons for running a hearts and minds campaign would be evident from a survey of implementation of the strategy in all its facets, from the national to the operational to grassroots soldiering in Kashmir. Whatever be the context, winning hearts and minds is a human issue as much as a national security issue, which would be evident from the case of Kashmir. A two-pronged WHAM strategy is thus called for. The first would involve a dialectic process of reaching out to the Kashmiri people. The second involves countering efforts to negate a WHAM strategy by proxy operatives. Each part of the strategy is as important as the other, as the success of one will be dependent on that of the other.

It is also common wisdom that people will support the winning side, or at least, one which gives them hopes of winning. This could perhaps explain the frequent mood swings of the people in Kashmir, which frequently baffle analysts. As the separatists raise protestations to a high decibel, the mood of the people swings away from the government, and once this cloud of euphoria bursts, they come to reassess priorities and seek options which maximise their individual good. Fear is another factor which results in rapid change in temperament. Thus, people are liable to give one version in front of the security forces, and another, in front of the terrorist, frequently opting to overcome the immediate danger.

Sustained policies which establish the genuineness of the government and non-coercive measures employed are, thus, important. The Indian state and security forces have created a bank of goodwill in the Valley; translating this into integration of the people in the national mainstream is the main purpose and intent of the WHAM campaign of tomorrow. Given the complexity of issues involved, and interests of varied parties, the process is a long drawn one. Yet a human-centric approach will facilitate success. Commitment to reduction of human losses and equity of rights is necessary, for no amount of media and perception management can make up for collateral loss of lives in operations, either inadvertently or unintentionally. This, perhaps, would be the core lesson from Kashmir, adaptable to other environments as well.

CONFIDENCE BUILDING MEASURES (CBMs)

Indo-Pak relations have seen many positive developments since April 2003. The ceasefire continues to hold since November 2003. People-to-people contact has increased as a result of the continuing composite dialogue that was resumed following the commitment of the President of Pakistan in the Joint Press Statement on 06 Jan 2004, that the 'territory under Pakistan's control will not be permitted to be used to support terrorism in any manner'. High level political and official contacts between the two sides have continued with reference to the Composite Dialogue Process.[15]

Several infrastructural CBMs have since been initiated. Those applicable to Jammu and Kashmir include the inauguration of the Srinagar-Muzaffarabad bus service on 7 April 2006 and the resumption of the Poonch-Rawalakot bus service on 20 June 2006. These CBMs have enhanced contact between the people of both countries. There is popular enthusiasm on both sides for travelling across LoC. Action is now being taken to further streamline and expand such contacts.[16]

Other CBMs which having initiated by the Central and State Governments and the government of Jammu and Kashmir from time to time include the following: [17,18]

- The Government of India, in the wake of the devastating earthquake of 2005, provided immediate relief supplies and pledged assistance of US $25 million for reconstruction in quake hit areas in Pakistan/ POK.
- Commencement of train services between Banihal and Baramulla.
- Commencing the Haj pilgrimage directly from Srinagar.
- Modernization and declaration of the Srinagar Airport as an international airport.
- Simplification and further facilitation of cross LC travel on the Srinagar-Muzaffarabad and the Poonch-Rawalakote routes.
- Commencement of duty free trade across the LC in respect of identified commodities on 21 October 2008 after an agreement between India and Pakistan.

All these CBMs generally had a positive impact in terms of improvement in the overall situation in the State. Unfortunately, the composite dialogue process suffered a serious setback in the wake of the terrorist attacks in Mumbai on 26 November 2008. Nevertheless, the government seems determined not to allow incidents of such nature to derail of the process of normalization of the situation. After the tensions of 2008 and 2010, once the situation was brought under control, the Union Home Secretary

G.K. Pillai on 10 Jan 2011 said that as a credible CBM Union Government was planning to reduce the presence of para military forces in populated areas of Jammu and Kashmir by 25 percent over the next 12 months.[19]

NOTES

1. Rahul K Bhonsle, *Winning Hearts and Minds: Lessons from Jammu and Kashmir,*Manekshaw Paper, 14/2009, Centre for Land Warfare Studies New Delhi, KW Publishers Pvt Ltd, New Delhi
2. Lodhi Maleeha, *Winning Hearts and Minds of the People,* http://209.85.175.104/search?q=cache:Qd8EnCyKDlQJ:www.ispr.gov.pkaccessed by Ibid on 29 May 2009
3. Jalali, Professor Ali A, *Winning the Hearts and Minds of the People,* http://209.85.175.04/search?q=cache:HPVsUhm5wJMJ: www. ispr. gov.pk/LFS/LFS/Speeches/ accessed by Ibid on 31 May 2009
4. Irwin Colin, *Peace in Kashmir: Myth and Reality,* http://www.peacepolls.org/documents/peacepolls/000294.pdf, accessed by Ibid on 01 June 2009
5. Army Training Command, Indian Army, *Indian Army Doctrine,* www.indarmy.nic.in (quoted by Bhosle)
6. Ibid
7. Manoj Joshi, *The Lost Rebellion: Kashmir in the Nineties,* New Delhi: Penguin, 1999, pp. i-xi
8. Richard Halloran, *"Strategic Communication,"* Parameters, Autumn 2007, p. 4
9. Michael Fitzsimmons, *"Hard Hearts and Open Minds? Governance, Identity and Intellectual Foundations of Counter Insurgency Strategy,"* Journal of Strategic Studies, Vol. 31, No. 3, June 2008 p.. 339
10. Army Training Command, Indian Army, *Sub-Conventional Operations Doctrine,* www.indarmy.nic.in, accessed on 10 May 2009
11. Hoffman, Frank G, *Neo Classical Insurgency Parameters,* Summer 2007, p. 82
12. Hoffman, 55, p. 82
13. Army Training Command, n. 13
14. Praveen Swami, *"Tape Exposes Mirwaiz-Geelani Tension; Tehreek approached Hizb,"* The Hindu, 5 September 2008
15. Ministry of Home Affairs, Annual Report 2006-07, Sec 2.14
16. Ibid, 2006-07, Sec 2.15
17. Ibid, 2007-08, Sec 2.24
18. Ibid, 2008-09, Sec 2.18
19. Remarks of the Secretary, Government of India, Ministry of Home Affairs in response to a parliamentary question on 10 Jan 2011

15

The Way Ahead

"Governments that fail to meet the basic welfare and economic needs of their peoples and suppress their liberties, generate violent opposition to themselves."

—Samuel Huntington

The Jammu and Kashmir conflict is bleeding India both in terms of casualties and financially. The cost of conducting counter-insurgency operations over a protracted period is extremely high and a considerable drain on the national exchequer in the long run. The logistics of maintaining a large force for an inordinately long time can be crippling for any economy, no matter how strong.

History shows that order and stability are necessary pre-conditions for political, administrative, and economic reform; but without a realistic prospect of such reform, the population will always oppose the forces of order and stability. Hence, the priority for the government should be to complete all the on-going development and infrastructure projects at the earliest possible.

Stability and Normalization

The restoration of order and stability followed by the process of nation-building is extremely complex but the payoff will produce a complete transformation and greater regional reconciliation.

While order and stability are a necessary precursor of political, administrative, and economic reform, equally essential is the belief that political, administrative and economic reform will be delivered consequent to achieving order and stability. People who do not believe that they are going to get the political reform that they desire will resist, often with considerable vigour. It would take a major commitment in terms of the provision of human and other resources, and would take many years. There is no better proof of good intentions than improved infrastructure and sustained economic development.

The Pakistan Factor

The insurgency in Jammu and Kashmir could not have lasted this long but for the constant and steadfast support from Pakistan. The value of this support to the insurgents cannot be underestimated. However, India is a functional and vibrant democracy and has the resilience and inner strength to absorb the challenges posed by the proxy war in Jammu and Kashmir as part of the nation building process.

A safe sanctuary is vital to insurgencies and the insurgency in Jammu and Kashmir has had no dearth of sanctuaries across the LC in POK. With the overt and covert support from across the LC provided by Pakistan, there is always hope for the insurgents to retreat to their secure bases in POK after a setback to recover, re-group and reorganize for the next round of violence against the state machinery.

Luckily, the general public in Kashmir is not enamored with the radical brand of Islam espoused by the militant outfits because, thanks to the television coverage, they are aware of what is happening in Pakistan and Afghanistan after the radicalisation of society.

Despite any number of talks and assurances Pakistan has not been sincere in the withdrawal of its support and sponsorship of the armed struggle against the legitimately elected government of Jammu and Kashmir.

Actions by the State and Central Government

In the context of Jammu and Kashmir the vision, at all levels of government, is crystal clear ie the State is an inseparable part of India. That issue remains non-negotiable. Within this broad framework, the government is willing to discuss autonomy and other measures to arrive at a mutually acceptable solution.

Conventional wisdom suggests that unless the root cause of an insurgency is addressed, a satisfactory resolution of the conflict will not be forthcoming. The conflict is essentially a struggle for the hearts and minds of the population. The Government must provide the population security, a stable economy, and legitimate basic rights, such as:

- Freedom of the press to include the freedom to condemn government reforms as half-measures and criticize military tactics and leadership.
- Freedom of speech that allows supporters of the insurgency to stage mass rallies against the government.
- Freedom from random search.
- Speedy trials of detenues.

The grant of these rights should not appear to have been done in half-measures or under pressure. It should not appear as if the government is conceding to insurgent demands, but rather as a confident gesture from a position of strength. The effort should always be to push for dialogue and resolution whenever it is sensed that the insurgent groups are weakening in their resolve and maybe amenable for talks.

India, Pakistan and various insurgent groups with conflicting aims and interests are all claiming a stake in the outcome of the conflict. While not all parties must be satisfied to bring an end to the immediate conflict, the dissatisfaction of one or more parties will probably complicate the ending and may allow the insurgency to smolder and eventually reignite. While it is next to impossible to expect the insurgent groups to be satisfied with the ultimate resolution of the conflict, it is imperative that the people of Jammu and Kashmir, in particular the Kashmiri speaking people of the Valley, are reconciled with the resolution. Once that is achieved, everything else will automatically fall in place.

As mentioned earlier, the government cannot afford to go to the negotiating table with an absolutely rigid attitude. As per Paul Pillar, if the stakes are indivisible and neither side can get most of what it wants without depriving the other of most of what it wants, negotiations are less apt to be successful. Talks will break down precisely because the aspirations and expectations of the government and the separatists are so far apart, with nothing in between to contribute to the give and take of negotiation and bargaining.

Since the separatist groups need money to help sustain their operations, choking their supply of finances are sure to yield effective results. But there are challenges. These informal *hawala* networks remain largely outside government control and following the trail of money is extremely difficult. In a first of its kind, a charge sheet was filed by the ED in June 2015 against Firdous Ahmad Shah, Chairman of Democratic Political Movement, a constituent of Geelani's faction of Hurriyat Conference, Shah was charged for illegally obtaining money via Italy to fund terror in the State.

There should be a comprehensive approach to the resolution of the problem. Adhering to the following commandments would pay rich dividends:

- Ensure no further alienation of the population.
- Always ensure that the rule of law prevails.

Civilian and Administrative Reforms

Civilian and administrative reforms are crucial to the process of nation-building. Structurally, the systems for administering the state efficiently are all in place, but the performance is lacking in every sense of the word. What is required is for the administration to develop a spine and for the police force to develop the capability to maintain law and order and to conduct its routine operations. The request for additional central police forces should be made only in exceptional circumstances.

The conflict is far from over. This is a period of consolidation for both sides. The side that utilizes this time profitably is bound to reap richer dividends in the long run. The Government must utilize this time to implement reforms, improve administration and strengthen the social fabric of the State.

The security forces must utilize this time to improve the intelligence structure, train, refit and re-equip the forces. The police must utilize this time to improve its relationship with the population while at the same time keeping an ear constantly on the ground and a finger on the pulse of the people. Raising and training of specialist units must be expedited so that they are totally ready to meet the next round of violence as and when it erupts. Determining the end of the insurgency is not a simple matter, because there is no clear-cut end to the conflict. Intermittent waves of violence will keep disrupting the peace, so the security forces and the administration cannot afford to let their guard down.

Public support can be won only if reforms are both legitimate and effective. It is not enough for the government to mean well—or pretend to mean well—it must also follow through consistently over a period of time. The government must actually transform itself into a truly representative government. Civilians suffering through an insurgency will be slow to trust either side and will be very cautious in throwing their support behind the government. Support also may depend on the establishment of basic services, such as adequate food, clean water, electricity, access to medical facilities and employment. It is imperative that both basic services and basic rights should be addressed simultaneously.

Economic Development

Successful economic assistance often requires both aid and reform of economic policy and policy-making institutions. No one can accuse the central government of not providing enough finances in the budgetary allocations for the state of Jammu and Kashmir. The Prime Minister has sanctioned adequate funds for the economic development of the State. The focus should be on planned and balanced regional development for strengthening the physical, economic and social infrastructure, thereby improving the productive potential of J&K State. The state government should accord priority and emphasis on the development of good infrastructure, promotion of trade and industry especially tourism and the provision of adequate employment opportunities for the youth. What needs to be ensured is that the funds are actually expended for the purpose they were released and that no funds are siphoned off midway.

Politicians

The mainstream political parties in the State need to be reminded of their responsibilities in ensuring that they do not fish in troubled waters. As a whole, Indian politicians have been given too loose a rope and get away with mostly anything. The politician in Jammu and Kashmir is no exception. However, Jammu and Kashmir being a frontline state, the scope for flirting with terrorists and ANEs is limited. There should be no soft peddling in case it is proven that an individual has indulged in subversive activities. Politicians need to realize that there are some are boundaries which they can not transgress.

There is an allegation that some politicians are acting on behalf and for the benefit of some prominent families in the Valley for whom the conflict has become a cottage industry. They are interested keeping the conflict alive and maintaining status quo. It is not in their interest to see a speedy resolution of the problem. If that were to happen, their primary source of income, ie the central development funds, would dry up.

Elections

Free and fair elections are the hallmark of every democracy. The Indian state learned this lesson the hard way after the legitimacy of the 1987 elections was called into question. Since then, the elections have mostly been fair and free of government influence. This is the primary reason why the international community has accepted the legitimacy of Indian presence in Jammu and Kashmir. It has to be the constant endeavour of the Election Commission of India that no one is ever allowed to subvert the election process, no matter how unsavory the results might prove to be. Honesty in the conduct of elections is indeed the best policy.

Human Rights

Considering the situation, there are not too many human rights violations. However, since the situation is fluid there are new challenges every day, the security forces are on a constant learning curve and the code of conduct is under constant revision.

Media

The media in Jammu and Kashmir, particularly the vernacular media, has been accused of becoming an interested party in the conflict rather than the reflector of the truth; they do not check their facts and misreporting has more often than not been the norm.

While it is nobody's case to impose censorship on the media, it is definitely desirable that the media imposes self-discipline and self-censorship on itself. Freedom of media must go hand in hand with their duties and responsibilities.

The Indian Army and the Central Security Forces

Military operations alone cannot succeed if used as an alternative to the search for political solutions, or to impose a political solution on a hostile population. In Northern Ireland, successive British governments failed to end the violence until they presented a political solution that all parties, including those who had supported or sympathised with the violence, could accept as a credible basis for negotiation. Likewise, unless the proposed solution is fair and all-inclusive,the chances of lasting peace are slim.

Military force usually has the opposite effect from what is intended: It is often overused, alienates the local population by its heavy-handed nature, and provides a window of opportunity for terrorist-group recruitment. This terrorist strategy is often referred to as provocation: Terrorist groups seek to goad the target government into a military response that harms civilians within the terrorist organization's home territory. The aim is to convince the population that the military is so evil that the terrorists' radical goals are justified.

The security forces must be careful in their interaction with the public. They need to realize that arresting and mistreating innocents has an adverse effect, because once a person has been wrongly detained and brutalized, he becomes an automatic supporter of the separatist cause.

The military is part of the solution and not the problem. By and large people still have faith in the military.

There is a need to retrain our forces. Different types of threats require different types of response; and hence the need for differently trained troops.

Policing

In the context of Jammu and Kashmir, it has been an oft repeated criticism that the force ratio in the State is inordinately high. It must be appreciated that the police-to-population ratios mentioned earlier in the section on Police are only relevant to peaceful/violent societies. In a situation of insurgency the force levels are bound to increase manifold.

In armed conflicts all sides tend to behave badly and few abide by the Geneva conventions. As a safeguard against this tendency, ethical approach to policing has been included in the training curriculum of the central and state level police forces operating in the State.

The local police force has to replace the central police forces operating in the state. This force has to be specially trained in counter terrorist operations and modern methods of crowd control. This exercise is already underway. What is more important, however, is not the quantum of troops but the quality of manpower and training, which in the ultimate analysis will make all the difference. A proportion of the newly raised police battalions must be specially trained in counter terrorist operations. These battalions must not be used on routine police duties as by doing so they likely to lose their cutting edge effectiveness. Five such battalions should suffice. The composition of this elite force could be modeled on the Greyhound Commandos of the Andhra Pradesh Police. A short write-up on the Greyhounds is included at Annexure 5.

Working with local police and intelligence agencies is critical. They generally have better training and information to penetrate and disrupt terrorist organizations. They are the primary arm of the government focused on internal security matters. The military can strengthen the police forces by providing arms and other equipment and by training and mentoring the police forces. This strategy requires working "by, with, and through" local police forces.

Policing is likely to be the most effective strategy to destroy terrorist groups. Police generally have better training and intelligence to penetrate and disrupt terrorist organizations. This enables them to be best suited to understand and penetrate terrorist networks. Local police and intelligence know the language, people, culture, and terrain better than the central security forces drawn from all parts of the country.

Policing and intelligence should be the backbone of our efforts. Police and intelligence services are best placed to implement these activities. This strategy should make police and intelligence efforts the backbone of our counter-terrorism policy and move away from its mantra of fighting a war on terrorism. This requires a paradigmatic shift. It should also include rebalancing our resources and attention on police and intelligence work.

Police Reforms

Only an efficient, honest, professional and de-politicized police force is capable of providing a sense of security to the common man on the street. The police force needs to be diligent and fair in its dealings. Only then will the force be able to enjoy the trust and confidence of the citizens. Going by the figures reflected in the section on human rights elsewhere in this report, it is quite evident that such a force exists nowhere in the country. It is high time to initiate the police reforms which have been on the anvil for many years. Until the police force is freed from the clutches of the politician, it will never be able to enforce the rule of law in a fair and unbiased manner. Urgent police reforms are the need of the hour.

In the short term, what is required is for the police to be made more independent in its functioning so that they can be held accountable for their activities. In the context of the state, some recommendations are as under:

- Commence and complete the necessary restructuring of the force and work out the charter for the additional responsibility of counter-terrorism at an early date.
- Introduce a system for a fair review and redressal of public grievances.
- Introduce a community policing model.
- Strengthen the intelligence gathering mechanism. Make it totally computer based and engage analysts to develop the database on criminal and terrorist linked activities.
- Improve the inter-agency coordination for intelligence sharing and joint investigation.
- Complete the process of raising and equipping of the additional armed battalions and commence intensive training schedules without delay.
- Resist political appointments. Merit should be the sole criterion on which recruitment and promotions are decided.

- Any transgression by a police official should not be overlooked. Punishment should be meted out in accordance with the severity of the crime.

Intelligence

Intelligence is the principal source of information on terrorists. Police and intelligence agencies have a variety of ways to identify terrorists, including signal intelligence and human intelligence. The latter is preferable to signal intelligence as it can provide some of the most useful actionable intelligence. But it requires painstaking work and patience in recruiting informants who are already in terrorist organizations or placing informants in terrorist organizations. Intelligence collection and analysis can also be reinforced by countering the ideology and messages of terrorist groups through what is often referred to as information operations: the use of a variety of strategies and tools to counter, influence, or disrupt the message and operation of terrorist groups by using technological means to monitor the activities of the terrorist organizations.

With good intelligence, the police authorities should be able to identify terrorist communication hubs. This includes intercepting and monitoring terrorist communication through telephone, landline phone, email, facsimiles, and internet chat rooms, as well as tracking couriers. The mission should be to penetrate and seize terrorists and other criminals—their command structure, members, logistical support, and financial and political support—from the midst of the population.

A unified and coherent policy and a unified intelligence system, particularly between civil and military authorities, is an absolute necessity.

VDCs

VDCs provide excellent local intelligence which would not be available through normal methods. The VDCs have enabled the police to expand their human-intelligence network. They can be quite a force multiplier as they provide local advantage to the counter-insurgents over the insurgents.

Rashtriya Rifles

The Rashtriya Rifles was raised as a counter terrorist organization purely for the state of Jammu and Kashmir. They have achieved commendable results. Now that terrorism has been reduced to manageable levels, there is a thought in some circles that this force can be pulled out to be employed in other terrorist/Naxal affected areas of the country. Were this to happen, the State would lose out on a highly trained and effective force. Instead, the thinking should be as to how the role of this force can be expanded to include other spheres and to give it a kind of permanent Kashmiri character, much in the same way as has been given to the Assam Rifles in the Northeast.

The structure of the Rashtriya Rifles being such, it can easily be employed to replace the BSF as well as take over the tasks of the infantry battalions at the LC. The latter is beneficial to the Indian army also as it provides much needed relief to an already overstretched force.

By doing so, we do not lose out on a potent force. Insurgency may have diminished, but it definitely has not been eradicated. That will take many years and a proper resolution of the problem and acceptance of the ground situation by Pakistan, which does not seem likely in the near future. Hence it is imperative that the Rashtriya Rifles be retained within the state and employed accordingly.

The Demilitarisation Process

The increase in force levels has been as a direct consequence to an aggressive action by a belligerent neighbor. Except for brief periods in the early 1990s, other inductions have been the result of heightened threat. It is axiomatic, therefore, that total de-induction can only take place when the threat perception reduces. For that to happen, improvement in relations with Pakistan and China is a pre-condition.

Prolonged deployment of the central security forces and constant contact with the population coupled with the unfamiliarity with the language and local customs tends to breed distrust and contempt. The same operation conducted by a local force would probably meet with considerably less resentment, and the locals and the leaders would be more understanding and willing to consider it as part of duty by a uniformed force entrusted with the maintenance of law and order.

Before we consider demilitarisation, it has to be assessed whether the Jammu and Kashmir Police are capable of conducting limited counter-insurgency operations and maintaining law and order without the support of central security forces. If not, an alternate force capable of doing the job effectively has to be identified, recruited, trained and equipped. The composition of the new force has to be properly thought out. The composition of the force is suggested in the next chapter and is bound to be a time consuming process. It will take anything between 5 to 10 years before the new units are capable of functioning independently.

The armed conflict is almost over. It is entirely logical that there should be a discussion on re-deployment. It is being discussed at every forum. Steps have already been initiated. The Army is focused on the LC and counter-insurgency. Ultimate demilitarisation, in its true sense, can only take place once the Indo-Pakistan-China conflict is resolved.

16

Recommendations

Although the study pertains to demilitarisation, the recommendations are not restricted purely to the Security Services because the process of demilitarisation is intrinsically linked with the reversion of the situation to normal status and that can never happen unless sweeping reforms are undertaken to cover every aspect that affects normal life in Jammu and Kashmir.

Recommendations on the actions to be initiated by various departments of the government machinery are given in the succeeding paragraphs.

Central Government

Discussions and dialogue must continue. The Centre must be willing to talk with whoever is willing to talk with it. Eventually the solution will be found only at the discussion table. India is the big brother in the dialogue with the Kashmiri separatist leadership - magnanimity is expected. We may have to give concessions, forgive transgressions and overlook past pin-pricks if it can result in a durable peace. The nation is more important than the individual. If it helps to find a solution by dealing with known offenders, so be it. The attitude should always be positive and one that is open to new ideas and suggestions as long as these ideas are within the broad framework of what is acceptable to it. Rigidity of approach will not serve anybody's interests.

With Pakistan also, dialogue is the preferred option and must continue. But dialogue can never be in isolation; it has to be combined with diplomatic and other forms of pressure, to ensure that the Pakistani army ceases to use militant Islamic groups in their proxy war against India. Mercifully, the civilian leadership and large sections of civil society in Pakistan have now come to realize that confrontation with India is unlikely to produce any fruitful results.

Identify and empower the genuine pro-India Kashmiri Muslim element. Nurture the next generation of Kashmiri leadership being careful to make sure that they are not seen as stooges of the Government of India. We must learn from the mistakes of the past and not prop up local leaders merely because they speak the language we wish to hear. It is always best to adopt a neutral stance and let the popular leaders assume power, making sure that all activity takes place within the broad parameters of the Constitution of India. The Centre must not discourage dissent against the elected government. The people must always have a variety of leaders to choose from. Leaders who have grass root level support but are prevented from succeeding in the legitimate process will invariably try an alternate route.

The Interlocutors' Report must be submitted to a panel of experts to assess its implementability. Those recommendations, which can be implemented without much controversy or financial outlay, must be cleared on priority. The Government needs to be seen as serious in implementing reforms on ground rather than just sweeping matters under the carpet and indulging in endless rounds of talks.

Restructuring of the intelligence gathering mechanism and the coordination at national and state level is required to be undertaken on an urgent basis. Turf battles between different agencies have to be looked into and resolved.

Release of financial aid should be readily forthcoming for any project which is likely to improve the lot of the common man and result in a positive image of the country.

State Government

It is the responsibility of the State Government to provide good and fair governance to its people. The more governance becomes transparent and responsible, the lesser will be the tensions in the State.

The State Government faces many challenges, the biggest of which is to ensure as the speedy and successful implementation of economic and infrastructural activities in the State. The impact of this success would result in creating additional job opportunities and weaning away youth from terrorism.

There is a large segment of population which has been displaced by the unrest. Rehabilitation of this population needs to be undertaken more expeditiously.

Preventing violence is not the task of the security forces alone. It is mainly in the domain of the political leadership and the civil administration. In the conduct of counter-terrorism operations, there cannot and should not be any compartmentalization of effort. All the instruments of the government, civil and military must work together to achieve the common objective. Civil society must also be co-opted in this endeavor.

The state government must work in conjunction with the central government, the central security forces, the local administration and the local police force to arrive at a proper security doctrine which addresses all issues of security from the national to local level. They should not be any conscious attempt to undermine the relevance of the central forces. Egos and turf battles should not be allowed to set the agenda. National interest, efficiency and economy of effort should determine the outcome of the doctrine.

Political Leadership

The political leadership in the State has all the shortcomings of the political establishment in the Indian subcontinent. However, irresponsibility, cavalier disregard for the national interest in pursuit of narrow political goals and the siphoning off of public funds into private pockets have much greater damage potential in the frontline state of Jammu and Kashmir than the same shortcomings in the rest of the country.

The politician has the great responsibility of guiding Kashmiri society into the mainstream of national consciousness. Unfortunately, the Kashmiri version has not been able to elevate itself above the petty politicking, wheeling dealing and rug-pulling that is the hallmark of the average Indian politician. He is faced with the onerous task of soothing and repairing the damaged psyche of the young Kashmiri which is deeply scarred by two decades of violence. But he is constantly playing to the gallery, scoring brownie points and has been totally unable to endear himself to the public. It is these shortcomings that give a lever to the separatists to brand all politicians as stooges of the central government. The politician has to rise above selfish interests and do his bit towards improvement of governance and administration.

On issues of transparency and empowerment, there has been a marked level of nervousness in the politicians. This manifests itself in their vociferous objection to the introduction of the *Panchayati Raj* Act, which is expected to empower grassroots level leadership. A similar attitude and be seen as regards the Right to Information Act. At the political level there is a definite lack of enthusiasm to see the Acts operational.

Separatist Leadership

Inability of the separatist leadership to shed the baggage of the past is the biggest obstacle to the resolution of the problem. Despite the knowledge that continuing the struggle, especially the armed struggle, will only result in dragging the state further behind in all the parameters of the Human Development Index, they continue to pursue unrealistic goals. Some segments of the Kashmiri separatist leadership have finally understood that they cannot wrest their so called freedom by force of arms even with the support of Pakistan. But they are unable to express that sentiment publicly as it would render them irrelevant. Instead of welcoming concrete developmental measures which actually go a long way in improving the lot of the population, their attempt is to be an impediment at every step. They would be better served by attempting to negotiate a settlement with the government of India in which the Kashmiri finds pride of place within the secular Union of India.

The Process of Demilitarisation

The armed conflict is almost over. It is entirely logical that there should be a discussion on re-deployment. It is being discussed at every forum. Steps have already been initiated. Reduction of the paramilitary forces and re-deployment of the army is being considered. The army is more or less in the barracks and is focused on the LC and counter insurgency. Since reduction in insurgency is a fact, the security establishment is seriously considering reduction in forces. However, ultimate demilitarization in its true sense can only take place once the Indo-Pakistan conflict is resolved.

Demilitarisation necessarily is going to be a gradual, prolonged and long drawn-out process. Conditions have to be created for a gradual pull out so that there is no trauma or power vacuum once the forces pull out. The process entails an element of military risk and political courage and not political expedience. But unless we take the plunge, our claims of having restored normalcy will ring hollow.

The disengagement itself should be deliberate, planned and executed in a phased manner. The security situation has improved and the state police has demonstrated its confidence to progressively assume increased responsibilities. The army must now be prepared to reorient its operations, relocate and redeploy its forces. The experience gained by the army in combating terrorism must be passed on to the police force so that the transfer of control is as seamless as possible.

Adequate time has to be given for the police to raise, equip and train a counter insurgency/counter terrorism force. This would represent a logical and positive progression in the internal security campaign. It is a matter of continuous and review and joint decision-making by the army and the state police authorities. The state police must be careful not overestimate their own capabilities while the army needs to avoid skepticism and mistrust.

The measures to be adopted by each service are recommended in the succeeding paragraphs.

Indian Army

- Disengage but continue to remain in the Valley as a kind of threat-in-being to those terrorist elements which still intend to create trouble as and when the opportunity presents itself.
- Draw out a de-induction schedule so as to ensure that only that amount of force (with more than adequate reserves for unforeseen eventualities like Kargil) remains as is actually required.
- Enable the State Government set up a credible anti-terrorist organization and provide training to the J&K police in counter-insurgency operations. This is covered in greater detail in the paragraphs on the J&K Police.
- Strengthen the local police by providing arms and other equipment, and training and mentoring them.
- Intensify efforts and commit more resources on intelligence gathering.
- Continue to provide aid to civic programmes, but in a low profile manner. The initiative must be seen as that of the civil administration and the credit must go to the local politician.

BSF

The BSF should be de-inducted from the state of Jammu and Kashmir completely and their area of responsibility be handed over to the Rashtriya Rifles. If for some reason, this is not acceptable, their responsibility should terminate at the International Border and the LC onwards can be handed over to the Rashtriya Rifles.

Rashtriya Rifles

MHA had proposed deploying Rashtriya Rifles units in the Naxal-affected areas of the country. The Army, however, objected to the Home Ministry proposal as this would amount to disturbing the well-established counter-insurgency grid in J&K.

Instead of moving the Rashtriya Rifles out of the state, it is recommended that they should assume the mantle of the central force meant entirely for the border sealing and counter-terrorism duties in Jammu and Kashmir. Being a versatile entity, it can alternate between the functions of the BSF, army and the police. This potent force can thus be gainfully employed without having to prune its size or move it out of the state. An additional spin-off of this arrangement is that it will also enable additional regular army troops to be de-inducted out of the state. With this redeployment, it is unlikely that the state would ever require additional central forces to combat any challenge.

It is also recommended that the composition of the Rashtriya Rifles be changed to include a proportion of troops drawn from within the State. There are obvious advantages that will accrue, given the local knowledge of the terrain and language that these troops will bring with them. The existing system of limiting tenures in J&K to two years ensures that no one is able to grow roots or get cozy with undesirable elements. It should also be ensured that an individual does not get to serve in his own district. This is to safeguard against an individual getting embroiled in resolving his personal affairs in an extra-constitutional manner.

State Administration

- The state administration should make a determined effort to shake off its apathy and inertia and implement measures to enhance employment and job opportunities at the earliest. Efficiency should not be sacrificed at the altar of red tape.
- Reach out to the population by initiating reforms in administration and eradication of corruption at all levels.
- Address cases of police brutality, high-handedness and illegal detentions at the earliest.
- Institute a fair and responsive complaint redressal mechanism.

Police

- Implement police reforms. If this is not done, most of the other actions taken by the police force will amount to little.

- Commence the process of taking over the situation from the central police forces in less disturbed areas.
- Utilize this interim period to complete the process of modernizing the police force.
- Complete the process of raising, equipping and training the additional India Reserve Battalions.
- At least five of these battalions should be nominated as specialist commando battalions and trained intensively in counter-terrorist operations. They could be termed as the SOG or given any other nomenclature to distinguish them from the other battalions.
- Appoint a study group to lay down criteria for eligibility for selection of the commando battalions. It should be a volunteer force and given adequate compensation for the risks factor. It could be patterned on the model of the Greyhound Commando Force of the Andhra Pradesh police or any other model that the study group finds suitable in the context of Jammu and Kashmir.
- Provide training and weaponry to the JK Volunteer Force (an elite group of SPOs)
- Complete the process of improvement in the infrastructure as provided for in the Prime Minister's relief package for the J&K police such as upgrading police hospitals, accommodation for police personnel, establishment of a Rehabilitation Centre for Widows of Police personnel, schools for orphans of police personnel, etc.

Intelligence

Intelligence should form the backbone of the policing effort. The following measures are recommended to be undertaken immediately:

- This period of relative tranquility should be used to revamp the intelligence structure. Establish independent think tanks and committees of experts to provide inputs as to what needs to be done to fill up the existing voids in intelligence.
- The intelligence structure must be totally IT based and capable of functioning in a real time scenario.
- All incidents, no matter how trivial, must be recorded.
- Threads connecting seemingly unrelated incidents should be investigated thoroughly to arrive at a likely and credible threat scenario.
- Any assessed threat must be analysed in its entirety and taken forward to its logical conclusion. This requires a great deal

coordination and cooperation between the police forces and the intelligence agencies.

- Lay maximum stress on human intelligence. Human intelligence is preferable to signal intelligence, since there are limitations to using technological means to monitor the activities of the terrorist organizations. This requires according priority to recruiting informants and extensive penetration of terrorist networks.

VDCs

VDCs have proved to be of great value in providing specific intelligence to enable operations to be conducted against a focused target. The policy formulated by the state government on regularising the SPOs as constables should be implemented. There are about 25,000 SPOs presently operating throughout Jammu and Kashmir. Those that meet the criteria stipulated by the policy should be absorbed. The policy also stipulates an increase in honorarium. Periodic training, primarily drill and weapons training should be conducted by the nearest army/police unit.

AFSPA

The process of repealing the AFSPA or the dilution of its provisions, cannot take place over-night. It should be gradual and spaced in terms of time and area. The main criterion should be the confidence levels of the local police force in its ability to maintain law and order in its area of responsibility. The central forces can remain in location for some time to assist the local police should the need arise. The process would involve identifying districts which are considered relatively peaceful and capable of being self-administered in all the interpretations of the word. As a start, the AFSPA could be repealed across the Pir Panjal in the plains' districts of Jammu Province and then proceeding ahead with districts like Doda. It is imperative that the Indian Army be fully involved with this initiative because they are the most affected by the dilution/repeal of the AFSPA. This has to be a well thought-out decision and not an emotional one.

Development Programmes

Priority in the development schemes being implemented under the Prime Minister's Package should be accorded to the following:

- Enhancing the existing road network and increasing the number of alternate road links to the Kashmir Valley. This will reduce the sense of isolation in Kashmir and allow the people to integrate better with the mainstream.

- Complete the Udhampur-Srinagar-Baramulla rail line at the earliest. No slippages should be permitted at any cost.
- Convert all roads leading to Kashmir Valley to all weather status. Commission as many tunnels as possible to keep the roads below the winter snow line.
- Expand provision of basic services.
- Provide adequate thrust to employment and income generation.
- Implement the action plan for return of the Kashmiri migrants.
- Institute an effective monitoring and audit mechanism to ensure that the schemes are being implemented as per the priorities and that funds are being expended correctly and with no graft.

Afterword

The last 25 years in the history of Jammu and Kashmir have been momentous. The state has witnessed roller-coaster swings in mood from utterly despondent to periods of exhilaration; from the high of tens of thousands of defiant crowds shouting slogans in favour of *Azaadi* on the streets of Srinagar, to the low of the bitter grief of millions who were utterly devastated by the burning of the *Chrar-i-Sharif* shrine; from the frenzied and disorderly mobs indulging in stone pelting to the orderly lines of people waiting in long queues to cast their ballot.

The very existence of the state of Jammu and Kashmir as part of the Indian Union came into question as the state was converted into a battleground between hordes of terrorists and so-called freedom fighters on the one hand and the Indian security forces on the other. The former was whole heartedly aided and abetted morally, financially and with bases, arms and ammunition from across the line of control in Pakistan Occupied Kashmir and in the Pakistani mainland. *Jihadis* from practically across the Muslim world came in hordes to help the secessionist cause. As Manisha Gangahar says, "Militancy by 1995 outgrew its Kashmiri character and became Islamic in nature. Kashmiri nationalism was pushed back." For a while, it even looked as if they might actually succeed in weaning away Jammu and Kashmir from the Indian State. It took the combined might of the Indian Army and other paramilitary forces to halt the terrorists in their tracks and the reverse the situation. Today, we have reached the stage when the security forces have regained total control of the situation and the civil administration is able to function again. The situation on ground can be termed to be "normal" and finally the process of de-induction of central para military forces has commenced.

The Security Forces have performed commendably and have been singularly successful in containing the insurgency to such levels that it has been possible to conduct free and fair elections and to restore normal life. Despite sterling results, reduction in central security force levels has not been affected to the desired levels because there is a feeling in some quarters that the State, and in particular the Valley, will degenerate into chaos if central security forces are removed from the scene. The common perception is that the state police and administrative machinery will not be able to function normally and combat terrorism without being propped up by central support. This perception has to be corrected and cannot be allowed to dictate *status quo*.

The time is ripe for the state administration to commence building on the opportunity provided by the stable conditions and usher in the much needed, repeatedly promised and long awaited reforms. The emphasis now should be on the improvement of infrastructure, provision of fair and efficient governance and, most important, creation of additional employment opportunities. An all-out effort should be made to integrate the population into the mainstream. This is easier said than done, because ham-handed efforts at the same would only result in reinforcing the impression that the Indian (read Hindu) culture is being imposed upon the population and would alienate them further.

A serious effort has to be made to reduce the feeling of claustrophobia in the main towns and cities by reducing the visible presence of security personnel in the streets. This can be very easily achieved by laying extra emphasis on collection of intelligence and infiltration of anti-national networks. By doing so, the police will always remain one step ahead of the mischief makers and yet perform better and more efficiently without having to deploy too many troops on ground.

The time to act is now. It has to be understood that majority of the people are not anti-national but definitely anti-establishment for a reason. They have been deprived of justice and fair play for so long that they have ceased to expect any better of the administration. The administration needs to correct this misconception and address the grievances of the public in a fair and impartial manner. The results should be visible on ground at the earliest to have an impact on the minds of the population. The administration needs to develop a spine to stand up to political pressures and vested interests.

The planning process of demilitarisation should commence immediately. It could be some time before the physical de-induction of troops can actually commence. However, the detailed action plan can be prepared within six months. This plan would include exact details of units to be raised and it's time frame, the extent of training to be imparted and details of the same, exact number of units to be replaced and by whom and the disposition of the units being replaced and their ultimate destination. The whole process of de-induction would take anything between 5 to 10 years at the end of which the state of Jammu and Kashmir would be completely self sufficient in the maintenance of law and order and to a limited extent in the conduct of counter terrorist operations.

The Rashtriya Rifles will continue to remain a force raised and employed completely for the internal and external defence of Jammu and Kashmir. With this force available to the state administration, it is unlikely that there would ever be a need to requisition Indian Army troops for aid to civil authorities.

Insofar as world opinion on the legitimacy of the Indian position is concerned, no Indian need ever harbor the doubt that his presence in Jammu and Kashmir is questionable or immoral. We have an over 5500 year long cultural and physical connect with the State, Kashmir in particular, before which the barely 250 year ethnic Kashmiri Muslim rule pales into insignificance.

ANNEXURE 1

Questionnaires Circulated for the Purpose of Obtaining Feedback

QUESTIONNAIRE 1
(Demilitarisation)

1. Insurgency in the State of Jammu & Kashmir has entered the third decade this year. The Security Forces have been successful in containing the insurgency to such levels that it has been possible to conduct free and fair elections and to restore life to near-normalcy. Despite sterling results, it has not been possible to effect reduction in troop levels to the desired level because there is a widespread feeling that the State, in particular, the Valley will degenerate into chaos if the security forces are removed from the scene and that the State police forces will not be able to combat terrorism on its own. **Do you agree with this view?**

2. Demilitarisation is dependent on the assumption that conditions in Jammu & Kashmir will revert to normal one day. That assumption is not far-fetched since the average man in the streets is as interested in living a normal life as anyone else in the country. The realisation has also set in that the terrorists/separatists can never achieve their aim despite the full backing, covert or overt, of Pakistan. The message has been understood that there cannot be a military solution to the Jammu & Kashmir problem. The people of Jammu & Kashmir have to resolve their own problems but this cannot be achieved without the backing and consent of India. **Would you agree with this statement?**

3. The State of Jammu & Kashmir has one of the largest civilian to security personnel ratio prevalent anywhere in the world. There is a

constant refrain among sections of the political parties and secessionists asking for the withdrawal of the Indian Army from Jammu & Kashmir. It is also true that the situation can never be termed to be normal unless there is appreciable reduction in force levels especially of troops engaged in counter insurgency/counter terrorism operations. Therefore, it is essential that a serious thought be given to the demilitarisation of the State and an implementable time frame decided upon. **Would you consider a time frame of between 5 to 10 years for a complete transfer of power to the civil administration, which includes the Jammu and Kashmir police?**

4. The Jammu & Kashmir problem has two dimensions - external and internal. The Armed Forces have a major stake in both. Maintaining the territorial integrity of the nation is its primary *raison de etre*. As long as the borders need to be secured against Pakistan and China, there is no question of even considering its withdrawal from the borders. Therefore reduction of troops from the borders is directly linked to the threat perception from across. However, there are definite gains also for the security forces in Demilitarisation from the internal areas. Maintenance of law and order in the interiors is primarily the task of the civil administration. The longer the security forces remain bogged down in aid to civil authorities, the greater are the dangers of the forces getting embroiled in HR cases and losing their professionalism in the long run. **Do you agree that it is as much in the interests of the security forces to demilitarize?**

5. The subject assumes importance because the state of Jammu & Kashmir is viewed as an international hotspot and regarded as one of the potential flash points in South Asia. The issue of human rights violations is regularly raised within the country and internationally. India does not like to be reminded that the Kashmir issue needs to be resolved. It is in the interest of the nation that the situation reverts to normal as early as possible. Reduction in troop levels is the best indicator that the situation is normal. **Is it possible to effect a troop reduction to the pre-1989 levels and if not what measures must the State or Centre adopt before such reduction is considered feasible?**

6. **Impact of Demilitarisation**. The impact of Demilitarisation will need to be examined from various angles. Reduction in troop levels should be seen as the natural consequence of improvement in the ground situation and not as a sign of weakness of the security forces. Care has to be taken to ensure that there is no power vacuum created as a result of demilitarisation. We can ill-afford to have a state of anarchy

once the civil administration takes over. **Do you feel that there is a need to raise and train a force drawn from within the state which can augment the police force as and when the need arises?**

7. **AFSPA.** The Act has been the subject of many a bitter debate over the last year. It is felt that the Act is draconian. **Do you feel there is a case to repeal the act or to at least dilute its provisions?**

8. **Removal of the AFSPA.** Transfer of control to the civil administration is dependent on the attainment of a safe, secure and politically stable environment. The environment can be said to be stable and normal when the civil administration is able to enforce its writ. **Do you feel that the act can be removed from the whole State? Alternately, can it be repealed in a phased manner commencing with less disturbed districts.**

9. **Raising of a Local Counter Terrorism Force**. The Police Force needs to be trained to a level where they are capable of conducting counter terrorist operations on their own. Ultimately they should be trained to a level where the necessity to call in the Central Forces in aid of civil authority becomes the exception rather than the norm as prevalent today. If properly trained, equipped and motivated this force can be far more effective than the Army because their knowledge of local conditions and language put them on an equal footing with the insurgents. This has been achieved by the Greyhound Commandos of the Andhra Police. **Do you feel that a similar model can be adopted in our State?**

10. **Demilitarisation—a Long Drawn Process**. Demilitarisation necessarily is going to be a gradual, prolonged and long drawn-out process. Conditions have to be created for a gradual pull out so that there is no trauma or power vacuum once the forces pull out. Adequate time has to be given for the police to raise, equip and train a counter insurgency/counter terrorism force. The state of Tripura took almost 20 years to raise an effective police force to completely replace the Assam Rifles, with very positive results. Today the consensus is that Tripura ranks among the better policed states in the Indian Union. **What time frame do you feel is adequate to raise, equip and train a Special Task Force to make the State self-dependent in combating insurgency/ terrorism?**

11. **No Space for Political Pressures and Immaturity**. A smooth transfer of control to the civil administration should be the sole guiding principle in so far as demilitarisation is concerned.. Re-location and

re-deployment has to be worked out and this has to be linked to the attainment of a safe, secure and politically stable environment. There is no space for political pressures and political immaturity in a politically sensitive State like Jammu & Kashmir. There is bound to be tremendous pressure to speed up the process of Demilitarisation with politicians of various hues vying to claim credit for the process while at the same time pulling the rug under each other's feet in a game of one-up-man-ship. **Can any constitutional safeguards be factored into the process so that once it is set in motion, it cannot be derailed by anyone even if there is a change in government?**

QUESTIONNAIRE 2
(*Kashmiriyat*)

The reason for adding the second questionnaire, though not directly relevant to the subject of the study, was that it would be enabled the author to ascertain the true feelings of the respondents. Only the actual hardliners would be willing to go the full distance and sacrifice the concept of *Kashmiriyat* in their quest for total *Azadi* or merger with Pakistan.

1. Some definitions of ***Kashmiriyat*** by various scholars:
    - *Kashmiriyat* is the tradition of living together in one country with diverse cultures and religions
    - *Kashmiriyat* is not a religion but a culture influenced by three religions - Islam, Buddhism and Hinduism. There are many schools of thought in Islam but it was Sufi Islam which came to Kashmir.
    - "*Kashmiriyat*" is the principle of harmony; a principle that is the essence of the pluralistic culture of Jammu and Kashmir and one that should become the operating principle in the rest of the country.
    - It is a mix of two ideologies which makes it stand somewhere outside Islam.
    - Kashmir has had a rich and vibrant cultural history and a tradition of learning and scholarly pursuit since times immemorial. Through the ages, it has been a melting pot of ideas, which have been distilled into the finest traditions of learning, tolerance and cultural cohesion. Whether it be Islam, Hinduism, Sikhism or Buddhism, all these religions have for centuries been a part of the spiritual landscape of the State – the space termed as '*Kashmiriyat*'. **Would you please give your quote for the term?**
2. Khushwant Singh has written that the most serious consequences of *azadi* will be the exodus of non-Muslims—Kashmiri Pandits and Sikhs

—from the Valley. Don't accept their assurances that it will not happen. It happened when Kashmiri Pandits left the Valley in large numbers because they felt insecure. Mohammad Ali Jinnah and Jawaharlal Nehru gave us similar assurances preceding the Partition. **Presuming a scenario of total *azadi* do you feel that *Kashmiriyat* in the traditional form can survive?**

3. The reintegration of Muslims and Pandits appears difficult. An Islamic identity has taken shape, reportedly more so in the countryside. *Kashmiriyat*, a secular ethos, is beyond repair. The animosity among the three regions of Kashmir, Jammu and Ladakh may dilute, but will remain. It may still remain the state of Jammu and Kashmir. But its soul would be missing. **Your comments on this pessimistic view?**

4. *Kashmiyat* is now a dirty word for some hardliners who feel that it is being fostered upon them by Hindus to dilute the Muslim character of the Kashmiri people. **Your comments on this view?**

5. *Kashmiriyat* consists of two inevitable elements – secularism and nationalism and without these two constituent elements the "concept of *Kashmiriyat*" cannot be conceived. **Can this ideology be acceptable to a hardline Islamist?**

6. In an interview a girl from Srinagar, Irfana, said that the concept of *Kashmiriyat* was first propounded by Sheikh Noor-ud-din. "He taught us all to love our land-our Kashmir-and to live together as Kashmiris. That is *Kashmiriyat*. It's still there. It's hard to see it these days, because of the violence, but it is there-in the hearts of all Kashmiris." **Would you agree with this statement as being representative of the sentiment of the majority of common Muslim Kashmiri folk?**

7. The Muslim and Hindu people of Kashmir have lived in relative harmony and friendliness since the 13th century when Islam first became the majority religion in Kashmir. The Sufi-Islamic way of life that ordinary Muslims followed in Kashmir complemented the rishi tradition of Kashmiri Pandits (Hindus), leading to a syncretic culture where Hindus and Muslims revered the same local saints and prayed at the same shrines. **Can you visualize the future form of *Kashmiriyat* if it has to evolve without the contribution and presence, even if miniscule, of the Kashmiri Hindus?**

8. M J Akbar has written in 'Kashmir Behind the Vale' that the *rawaj* of Kashmir, its culture, enveloped the outsider instead of the reverse. The Kashmiri identity was always the dominant reality, making the

Emperor Jehangir remark that, while he could distinguish the Kashmiri from the Mughal, he could not distinguish a Kashmiri Muslim from a Hindu. **Is it true of today also that the difference between a Kashmiri Muslim and a Kashmiri Hindu, while apparent amongst themselves, is difficult for an outsider to fathom?**

9. **Does the term *Kashmiriyat* encompass the ethos prevalent in the entire state of Jammu and Kashmir or is it confined only to those who speak the Kashmiri language?**

Instrument of Accession

Instrument of Accession executed by Maharaja Hari Singh on October 26, 1947

Whereas the Indian Independence Act, 1947, provides that as from the fifteenth day of August, 1947, there shall be set up an independent Dominion known as INDIA, and that the Government of India Act 1935 shall with such omissions, additions, adaptations and modifications as the Governor General may by order specify, be applicable to the Dominion of India.

And whereas the Government of India Act, 1935, as so adapted by the Governor General, provides that an Indian State may accede to the Dominion of India by an Instrument of Accession executed by the Ruler thereof.

Now, therefore, I Shriman Inder Mahinder Rajrajeswar Maharajadhiraj Shri Hari Singhji, Jammu & Kashmir Naresh Tatha Tibbet adi Deshadhipati, Ruler of Jammu & Kashmir State, in the exercise of my Sovereignty in and over my said State do hereby execute this my Instrument of Accession and

1. I hereby declare that I accede to the Dominion of India with the intent that the Governor General of India, the Dominion Legislature, the Federal Court and any other Dominion authority established for the purposes of the Dominion shall by virtue of this my Instrument of Accession but subject always to the terms thereof, and for the purposes only of the Dominion, exercise in relation to the State of Jammu & Kashmir (hereinafter referred to as "this State") such functions as may be vested in them by or under the Government of India Act, 1935, as in force in the Dominion of India,

on the 15th day of August 1947, (which Act as so in force is hereafter referred to as "the Act').

2. I hereby assume the obligation of ensuring that due effect is given to provisions of the Act within this State so far as they are applicable therein by virtue of this my Instrument of Accession.
3. I accept the matters specified in the schedule hereto as the matters with respect to which the Dominion Legislature may make law for this State.
4. I hereby declare that I accede to the Dominion of India on the assurance that if an agreement is made between the Governor General and the Ruler of this State whereby any functions in relation to the administration in this State of any law of the Dominion Legislature shall be exercised by the Ruler of the State, then any such agreement shall be construed and have effect accordingly.
5. The terms of this my Instrument of Accession shall not be varied by any amendment of the Act or the Indian Independence Act, 1947, unless such amendment is accepted by me by Instrument supplementary to this Instrument.
6. Nothing in this Instrument shall empower the Dominion Legislature to make any law for this State authorizing the compulsory acquisition of land for any purpose, but I hereby undertake that should the Dominion for the purpose of a Dominion law which applies in this State deem it necessary to acquire any land, I will at their request acquire the land at their expense, or, if the land belongs to me transfer it to them on such terms as may be agreed or, in default of agreement, determined by an arbitrator to be appointed by the Chief Justice of India.
7. Nothing in this Instrument shall be deemed to commit in any way to acceptance of any future constitution of India or to fetter my discretion to enter into agreement with the Government of India under any such future constitution.
8. Nothing in this Instrument affects the continuance of my Sovereignty in and over this State, or, save as provided by or under this Instrument, the exercise of any powers, authority and rights now enjoyed by me as Ruler of this State or the validity of any law at present in force in this State.
9. I hereby declare that I execute this Instrument on behalf of this State and that any reference in this Instrument to me or to the Ruler of the State is to be construed as including a reference to my heirs and successors.

Given under my hand this 26th day of October, nineteen hundred and forty seven.

Hari Singh, Maharajadhiraj of Jammu and Kashmir State.

ACCEPTANCE OF ACCESSION BY THE GOVERNOR GENERAL OF INDIA

I do hereby accept this Instrument of Accession. Dated this twenty-seventh day of October, nineteen hundred and forty seven.

Mountbatten of Burma

Governor General of India.

SCHEDULE OF INSTRUMENT OF ACCESSION THE MATTERS WITH RESPECT TO WHICH THE DOMINION LEGISLATURE MAY MAKE LAWS FOR THIS STATE

A. Defence

1. The naval, military and air forces of the Dominion and any other armed forces raised or maintained by the Dominion; any armed forces, including forces raised or maintained by an acceding State, which are attached to, or operating with, any of the armed forces of the Dominion.
2. Naval, military and air force works, administration of cantonment areas.
3. Arms, fire-arms, ammunition.
4. Explosives.

B. External Affairs

1. External affairs; the implementing of treaties and agreements with other countries; extradition, including the surrender of criminals and accused persons to parts of His Majesty's Dominions outside India.
2. Admission into, and emigration and expulsion from, India, including in relation thereto the regulation of the movements in India of persons who are not British subjects domiciled in India or subjects of any acceding State; pilgrimages to places beyond India.
3. Naturalisation.

C. Communications

1. Posts and telegraphs, including telephones, wireless, broadcasting, and other like forms of communication.
2. Federal railways; the regulation of all railways other than minor railways in respect of safety, maximum and minimum rates and fares, station and services terminal charges, interchange of traffic and the responsibility of railway administrations as carriers of goods and passengers; the regulation of minor railways in respect of safety and the responsibility of the administrations of such railways as carriers of goods and passengers.
3. Maritime shipping and navigation, including shipping and navigation on tidal waters; Admiralty jurisdiction.
4. Port quarantine.
5. Major ports, that is to say, the declaration and delimitation of such ports, and the constitution and powers of Port Authorities therein.
6. Aircraft and air navigation; the provision of aerodromes; regulation and organisation of air traffic and of aerodromes.
7. Lighthouses, including lightships, beacons and other provisions for the safety of shipping and aircraft.
8. Carriage of passengers and goods by sea or by air.
9. Extension of the powers and jurisdiction of members of the police force belonging to any unit to railway area outside that unit.

D. Ancillary

1. Election to the Dominion Legislature, subject to the provisions of the Act and of any Order made thereunder.
2. Offences against laws with respect to any of the aforesaid matters.
3. Inquiries and statistics for the purposes of any of the aforesaid matters.
4. Jurisdiction and powers of all courts with respect to any of the aforesaid matters but, except with the consent of the Ruler of the acceding State, not so as to confer any jurisdiction or powers upon any courts other than courts ordinarily exercising jurisdiction in or in relation to that State.

Agreement Between Military Representatives of India and Pakistan Regarding the Establishment of a Cease-fire Line in the State of Jammu and Kashmir (Annex 26 of UNCIP Third Report - S/1430 ADD 1 to 3) 29 July, 1949

I. INTRODUCTION

A. The military representatives of India and Pakistan met together in Karachi from 18 July to 27 July 1949 under the auspices of the Truce Sub-Committee of the United Nations Commission for India and Pakistan.

B. The members of the Indian delegation were: Lieutenant- General S.M. Shrinagesh, Major-General K.S. Thimayya, Brigadier S.H.F.J. Manekshaw. As observers: Mr. H.M. Patel, Mr. V. Sahay.

C. The members of the Pakistan delegation were: Major-General W.J. Cawthorn, Major-General Nazir Ahmed, Brigadier M. Sher Khan. As observers: Mr. M. Ayub, Mr. A.A. Khan.

D. The members of the Truce Sub-Committee of the United Nations Commission for India and Pakistan were: Mr. Hernando Samper (Colombia), Chairman; Mr. William L.S. Williams (United States); Lieutenant-General Maurice Delvoie, Military Adviser, Mr. Miguel A. Marin, Legal Adviser.

II. AGREEMENT

A. Considering

1. That the United Nations Commission for India and Pakistan, in its letter dated 2 July, 1949, invited the Governments of India and

Pakistan to send fully authorised military representatives to meet jointly in Karachi under the auspices of the Commission's Truce Sub-Committee to establish a cease-fire line in the State of Jammu and Kashmir, mutually agreed upon by the governments of India and Pakistan;

2. That the United Nationals Commission for India and Pakistan in its letter stated that "The meeting will be for military purposes; political issues will not be considered," and that "They will be conducted without prejudice to negotiations concerning the truce agreement";
3. That in the same letter the United Nations Commission for India and Pakistan further stated that "The cease-fire line is a complement of the suspension of hostilities, which falls within the provisions of Part I of the resolution of 13 August, 1948 and can be considered separately from the questions relating to Part II of the same resolution";
4. That the governments of India and Pakistan, in their letters dated 7 July, 1949, to the Chairman of the Commission, accepted the Commission's invitation to the military conference in Karachi.

B. The delegations of India and Pakistan, duly authorised, have reached the following agreement:

1. Under the provision of Part I of the resolution of 13 August, 1948, and as a complement of the suspension of hostilities in the State of Jammu and Kashmir on 1 January, 1949, a cease-fire line is established.
2. The cease-fire line runs from Manawar in the south, north to Keran and from Keran east to the glacier area, as follows:

(a) The line from Manawar to the south bank of Jhelurn River at Urusa (inclusive to India) is the line now defined by the factual positions about which there is agreement between both parties. Where there has hitherto not been agreement, the line shall be as follows:

(i) in the Patrana area: Kohel (inclusive to Pakistan) north along the Khuwala Kas Nullah up to Point 2276 (inclusive to India), thence to Kirni (inclusive to India).

(ii) Khambha, Pir Satwan, Point 3150 and Point 3606 are inclusive to India, thence the line runs to the factual position at Bagla Gala, thence to the factual position at Point 3300.

(iii) In the area south of Uri the positions of Pir Kanthi and Ledi Gali are inclusive to Pakistan.

(b) From the north bank of the Jhelum River the line runs from a point opposite the village of Urusa (NL 972109), thence north following the Ballaseth Da Nar Nullah (inclusive to Pakistan), up to NL 973140, thence north-east to Chhota Qazinag (Point 10657 inclusive to India), thence to NM 010180, thence to NM 037210, thence to Point 11825 (NM 025354, inclusive to Pakistan), thence to Tutrnari Gali (to be shared by both sides, posts to be established 500 yards on either side of the Gali), thence to the north-west through the first "R" of Burji Nar to north of Gadori, thence straight west to just north of point 9870, thence along the black line north of Bijidhar to north of Batarasi, thence to just south of Sudhpura, thence due north to the Kathaqazinag Nullah, thence along the Nullah to its junction with the Grangnar Nullah, thence along the latter Nullah to Kajnwala Pathra (inclusive to India), thence across the Danna ridge (following the factual positions) to Richmar Gali (inclusive to India), thence north to Thanda Katha Nullah, thence north to the Kishansanga River. The line then follows the Kishanganga River up to a point situated between Fargi and Tarban, thence (all inclusive to Pakistan) to Bankoran. Thence north-east to Khori, thence to the hill feature 8930 (in Square 9053), thence straight north to Point 10164 (in Square 9057), thence to Point 10323 (in Square 9161), thence north east straight to Guthur, then to Bhutpathra, thence to NL 980707, thence following the Bugina Nullah to the junction with the Kishanganga River at Point 4739. Thereafter the line follows the Kishanganga River to Keran and onwards to Point 4996 (NL 975818).

(c) From Point 4996 the line follows (all inclusive to Pakistan) the Famgar Nullah eastward to Point 12124, to Katware, to Point 6678. Then to the north-east to Sarian (Point 11279), to Point 11837, to Point 13090 to Point 12641, thence east again to Point 11142, thence to Dhakki, thence to Poin: 11415, thence to Point 10301, thence to Point 7507, thence to Point 10685, thence to Point 8388, thence south-east to Point 11812. Thence the line runs (all inclusive to India), to Point 13220, thence across the river to the east to Point 13449 (Durmat), thence to Point 14586 (Anzbari), thence to Point 13554, thence to Milestone 45 on the Burzil Nullah, thence to the east to Ziankal (Point 12909), thence to the south-east to Point 11114, thence to Point 12216, thence to Point 12867, thence to the east to Point 11264, thence to Karo (Point 14985), thence to Point 14014, thence to Point 12089, thence following the track to Point 12879. From there the line runs to Point 13647 (Karobal

Gali, to be shared by both sides). The cease-fire line runs thence through Retagah Chhish (Point 15316), thence through Point 15889, thence through Point 17392, thence through Point 16458, thence to Marpo La (to be shared by both sides), thence through Point 17561, thence through Point 17352, thence through Point 18400, thence through Point 16760, thence to (inclusive to India) Dalunang.

(d) From Dalunang eastwards the cease-fire line will follow the general line point 15495, Ishman, Manus, Gangam, Gunderman, Point 13620, Funkar (Point 17628), Marmak, Natsara, Shangruti (Point 1,531), Chorbat La (Point 16700), Chalunka (on the Shyok River), Khor, thence north to the glaciers. This portion of the cease-fire line shall be demarcated in detail on the basis of the factual position as of 27 July, 1949, by the local commanders assisted by United Nations military observers.

C. The cease-fire line described above shall be drawn on a one- inch map (where available) and then be verified mutually on the ground by local commanders on each side with the assistance of the United Nations military observers, so as to eliminate any no-man's land. In the event that the local commanders are unable to reach agreement, the matter shall be referred to the Commission's Military Adviser, whose decision shall be final. After this verification,

Done in Karachi on 27 July, 1949

For the Government of India:

S. M. Shrinagesh

For the Government of Pakistan:

J. Cawthorn

Major-General

For the United Nations Commission for India and Pakistan:

Hernando Samper

M. Delvoie

ANNEXURE 4

International Cooperation—Indo-Pakistan Cooperation

BRIEF PROVISIONS OF INDUS WATERS TREATY, 1960

i. The Indus system of rivers comprises three Eastern Rivers (Ravi, Beas and Sutlej and their tributaries) and three Western Rivers (Indus, Jhelum and Chenab and their tributaries).

ii. The Indus Waters Treaty 1960 was signed on 19.09.1960 between India and Pakistan. It is however effective from 01.04.1960.

iii. Under the Treaty, the waters of Eastern Rivers are allocated to India. India is under obligation to let flow the waters of the Western Rivers except for the following uses:

   (a) Domestic Use,
   (b) Non-consumptive use,
   (c) Agricultural use as specified,
   (d) Generation of hydro-electric power as specified

iv. India has been permitted to construct storage of water on Western Rivers upto 3.6 MAF for various purposes. No storage has been developed so far.

v. India has been permitted Agricultural Use of 7,01,000 acres over and above the Irrigated Cropped Area (ICA) as on 1.4.60. Out of this additional ICA of 7,01,000 acres, only 2,70,000 can be developed (i.e. a total ICA of 9,12,477 acres including that on 1.4.1960) till storages are constructed and 0.5 MAF of water is released there from every year. ICA during 2008-09 was 7,92,496 Acres.

vi. Under the Treaty, India and Pakistan have each created a permanent post of Commissioner for Indus Waters. They together constitute the Permanent Indus Commission (PIC), which is entrusted with the implementation of the Treaty. The PIC is required to hold meetings and tours and submit report on its work to the two Governments every year. It has held 111 tours and 106 meetings so far.

vii. Both sides are required to exchange information related to river flows observed by them, not later than three months of their observation and to exchange specified information on Agricultural Use every year.

viii. India is under obligation to supply information of its storage and hydroelectric projects as specified.

viii. India communicates as a gesture of goodwill, flood data to Pakistan from 1st July to 10th October every year, to enable them to undertake advance flood relief measures. The arrangement is reviewed every year.

ix. The Commissioners may discuss the questions arising under the Treaty under Article IX of the Treaty related to Settlement of Differences and Disputes and in the case of non-resolution, take further action under this Article for resolution through a Neutral Expert, negotiators or Court of Arbitration.

[A neutral expert appointed by World Bank on Pakistan's request delivered Expert Determination on Baglihar Hydroelectric Project in Feb. 2007. Pakistan has initiated proceedings for setting up a Court of Arbitration, to resolve the issues of Kishenganga H.E. Project.]

ANNEXURE 5

Brief Report of the Group of Interlocutors for Jammu and Kashmir

The Central Government appointed the J&K Interlocutors Group on October 13, 2010. The Group submitted the Report to the Home Ministry. The Report was made public by the Home Ministry on 24 May 2012. Main provisions, in brief, are given in the succeeding paragraphs.

Political Recommendations

- The Group recommended that a Constitutional Committee (CC) should be set up to review all the central Acts that have been extended to the state of Jammu and Kashmir since 1952. The CC should come out with its findings within six months. According to the Group, the CC should review whether, and to what extent, the application of central acts to the state has led to an erosion of the state's special status.
- The word 'Temporary' in Article 370 should be replaced with 'Special' which has been used for certain states such as Assam, Nagaland, Andhra Pradesh.
- Central laws shall only be made applicable to the state if they relate to the country's security or a vital economic interest, especially in the areas of energy and water resources.
- Currently, the Governor is appointed by the President. The Group recommended that the state government shall give three names for consideration for the position to the President. However, the Governor shall finally be appointed by the President.
- Separate Regional Councils for Jammu, Kashmir and Ladakh should be created and certain legislative, executive and financial powers should be devolved to them. The subjects that could be transferred to the Regional Council include prison reforms, public health, roads and bridges and fisheries.

Cultural, Economic and Social Recommendations

- There are 16 centrally sponsored schemes which are mostly funded by the centre. However, most of the funds for these schemes have not been utilised properly. The Group recommended that an effective system to monitor these schemes should be put in place.
- An expert committee to review the state's financial needs should be constituted.
- The central government should tap the hydro-electricity potential of the state. Till date only 15 per cent of the potential has been harnessed. Additional hydro-electricity projects should be established for which the central government should meet the entire equity capital.
- Industrial establishments and other buildings occupied by the security officers should be vacated.
- Financial package of incentives on the pattern given to the North Eastern States should be given to the state.
- The hilly, remote areas should be declared as special development zones.
- The restrictions on the internet and mobile phones should be reviewed.

In order to fulfill these recommendations, the Interlocutor's Group proposed the following roadmap:

- The 'stone pelters' and political prisoners against whom no serious charges have been framed should be released.
- There should an amendment and review of the Armed Forces Special Powers Act, 1990 and the Jammu and Kashmir Public Safety Act, 1978.
- The state policy should provide for the return of Kashmiri Pandits.
- A judicial commission to supervise the identification of bodies buried in the unmarked graves should be established.

ANNEXURE 6

The Greyhounds of Andhra Pradesh Police (The Andhra Model)

General

If Andhra Pradesh has a relatively better track record than other states in tackling the Maoist insurgency, it is because of a holistic approach that has evolved during the last three decades. The State follows a carrot and stick policy to wean away potential supporters even as it has come down heavily on militant extremists.

The Greyhounds, an elite force drawn out of police personnel on deputation from the Andhra Pradesh police, was raised in 1989. Numbering approximately 3000 personnel, only the best make it to the squad. The unit is headed by an Inspector General of Police. All directly recruited officers in the State, from Assistant Sub-Inspectors (ASIs) to IPS probationers, undergo training at the Greyhound training centre. They serve a tenure of three years, and then are posted into the District Guard. This has resulted in the augmentation of the fighting capabilities of the entire police force.

Role and Responsibilities

- To deal effectively with left-wing extremist violence in the state.
- To provide security for VVIPs and VIPs.
- For deployment in grave law and order situations.
- To combat and control left wing extremism.
- To deal with emergencies arising out of natural disasters.

Training

The Greyhounds get training comparable to that of the NSG. The state's counter-insurgency response was crafted on a thorough understanding of the Maoist 'protracted war' model. Trainees are imparted specialized training with emphasis on:

- Field craft and handling of weapons.
- High standards of physical fitness and mental alertness.
- Operation in small groups of 15 to 25 commandos.
- Counter terrorist operations in urban, jungle and hilly terrain.
- Deep forest pursuit and combat.
- VIP protection.

Incentives

- **Extremists**. The State has devised comprehensive rehabilitation packages to help those quitting Maoist ranks, including their influential leaders, rebuild their lives by setting up small businesses like groceries or other income generating opportunities.
- **Police Personnel.** Apart from a 60 per cent over and above the normal monthly pay all police personnel have been insured by the State. The relief package for families of those killed on duty includes the following for the legal heir:
  - Paid the last pay drawn till the date of superannuation.
  - Allowed to retain government accommodation.
  - Given a government job.
  - Allotted a house site and a cash grant ranging from Rs. 9 lakhs to Rs.12 lakhs.

Miscellaneous

- The State has invested heavily in the modernisation of weapons, communications systems, transport and support technologies for each police station.
- Intelligence capabilities have been augmented at all levels.
- The unit has imparted commando training to police personnel from the states of Maharashtra, MP, Bihar, Chhattisgarh, Jharkhand, Orissa and West Bengal.
- Over the past two years, the rebel ranks have fallen from around 1,000 hardcore members to approximately 400.

Conclusion

In its short existence, the force has acquired credibility and dependability in the field of anti-terrorist operations. It has an excellent track record and is worthy of emulation by all states which face the challenge of insurgency and extremism.

Bibliography

Books

Akbar, MJ, "Behind the Vale", Roli Publishers, New Delhi 1991

Bammi, Lt Gen, "*War Against Insurgency and Terrorism in Kashmir*"

Bamzai, Prithivi Nath Kaul. "*A History of Kashmir: Political, Social, Cultural, from the Earliest Times to the Present Day*", Metropolitan Book Co, Delhi, 1962.

Bose, Sumantra, "*The Challenge in Kashmir*", New Delhi 1997

C. E. Callwell, "*Small Wars: Their Principles and Practices,*" 3rd ed: University of Nebraska Press, 1996

Chowdhary, Rekha, "*Identity Politics in Jammu and Kashmir*", Vitasta Publishing Pvt Ltd, New Delhi, 2010

Frederick Knight, "*Where 3 Empires Meet*" Nabu Press, 1895

Galula, David, "*Counterinsurgency Warfare Theory and Practice*", Published by Frederick A. Praeger, New York . London 1964

Grierson, Sir George A., "*Linguistic Survey of India*", Government of India Central Publication Branch, Calcutta, 1927

Sinha, Dr. PB and Athale, Colonel AA, *History of the Conflict with China, 1962* by History Division, Ministry of Defence, Government of India, New Delhi, 1992

Hussain, Majid, *Geography of Jammu & Kashmir*, Rajesh Publications, New Delhi

Khan, Nyla Ali, *Islam, Women and Violence in Kashmir: Between India and Pakistan*, Tulika Books, New Delhi, 2009

Kilcullen, David, "*Countering Global Insurgency: A Strategy for the War on Terrorism*", Canberra and Washington, D.C., 200410.

Kilcullen, David, "*The Accidental Guerrilla: Fighting Small Wars in the Midst of a Big One,*" Oxford, UK: Oxford University Press, 2009

Korbel, Joseph, "*Danger In Kashmir*", Princeton, 1954

Lamb, Alastair, "*Incomplete Partition: The Genesis of the Kashmir Dispute 1947-1948*", Published by Oxford University Press, 1997

Lawrence Wright, *"The Looming Tower: Al-Qaeda and the Road to 9/11,"* New York: Knopf, 2006

Lawrence, W.R. *"TheValley of Kashmir"*, London, 1895

Major General KS Bajwa, *"Jammu And Kashmir War (1947-48): Political And Military Perspective"*, 2003, Har-Anand Publications Private Limited, F -211, Chittaranjan Park, New Delhi 110019

Manoj Joshi, *"The Lost Rebellion: Kashmir in the Nineties"*, New Delhi: Penguin, 1999

McCuen, John J., *"The Art of Counter-Revolutionary War: The Strategy of Counter-Insurgency,"* London: Faber, 1966

Merom, Gil, *"How Democracies Lose Small Wars: State, Society, and the Failures of France in Algeria, Israel in Lebanon, and the United States in Vietnam,"* New York: Cambridge University Press, 2003

Nehru, JL, *"The Discovery of India"*, Oxford University Press, 2002 Edition

O'Neill, Bard E, *"Insurgency and Terrorism: Inside Modern Revolutionary Warfare,"* Washington, D.C.: Brassey's (US), 1990

Operations in Jammu & Kashmir, History Division, Ministry of Defence, Government of India, Nataraj Publishers, Reprinted edition 200521.

Pandit, RS, translation of Kalhana's *"Rajatarangini,"* Sahitya Akademi, New Delhi, 2010

Paul Pillar, *Terrorism and U.S. Foreign Policy*, Washington, D.C.: Brookings Institution Press, 2001

Ptolemy, *"Geographia"*, [Electronic resource] Books I & II

Raina. A.N, *"Geography of Jammu and Kashmir"*, National Book Trust, 1981

Sen, LP, Lt Gen, "Slender was the Thread" Sangam Books, India, 1973

Singh, Lt. General Harbaksh, *"War Dispatches"*, Lancers Publishers, New Delhi, 1991

Singh. R.L. *"India: A Regional Geography"*, The National Geographic Society of India, 1976

Ved Kumari, Dr, translation of *"Nilmat Purana* Vol I", J&K Academy of Art, Culture and Languages, Srinagar/Jammu, 1973

Wirsing, Robert G, *"India, Pakistan, and the Kashmir Dispute: On Regional Conflict and its Resolution"*, MacMillan, 1996

Published Articles

Barry Posen, *"The Struggle Against Terrorism: Grand Strategy, Strategy, and Tactics,"* International Security, Vol. 26, No. 3, Winter

Bhattacharya, B, *"The Rashtriya Rifles"*, Bharat Rakshak Monitor, Volume 3(2), Sep-Oct 2000

Bhonsle, Rahul K, *"Winning Hearts and Minds: Lessons from Jammu and*

*Kashmir, Manekshaw Paper, 14/2009,*Centre for Land Warfare Studies New Delhi, KW Publishers Pvt Ltd, New Delhi

Fitzsimmons, Michael, *"Hard Hearts and Open Minds? Governance, Identity and Intellectual Foundations of Counter Insurgency Strategy,"* Journal of Strategic Studies, Vol. 31, No. 3, June 2008

Frank G Hoffman, *"Neo Classical Insurgency,"* Parameters, Summer 2007

Gangahar, Manisha, *"Decoding Violence in Kashmir"*, Economic and Political Weekly, Vol – XLVIII, No. 04, 26 January 2013

GP Joshi, *"Police Accountability in India: Policing Contaminated by Politics"*, Insight, 29 April 2005

Halloran, Richard, *"Strategic Communication,"* Parameters, Autumn 2007

Hoodbhoy, Pervez, *"Rethinking Plebicite in Kashmir"*, Citizens Action & Ideas for Peace in South Asia, 22 December 2003

Huntington, Samuel P, *"The Age of Muslim Wars," Newsweek*, 17 December 2001

IDSA National Security Lecture Series, *Strategic Digest*, August 2008

Irwin, Colin, *"Peace in Kashmir: Myth and Reality,"* (http://www.peacepolls.org/ documents/peacepolls/000294.pdf)

Katoch, Maj Gen Dhruv C, *"War in the Western Theatre 1971"* Scholar Warrior Spring 2012, CLAWS, New Delhi

Khan, Nyla Ali, *"Islam, Women and Violence in Kashmir. Between India and Pakistan"*, Palgrave MacMillan, 2010

Llewellyn, Dr John, John Dew, *"Prospects For Iraq: Some Lessons From History,"* Unpublished Report, Lehman Brothers Global Economics 7 June 2004

Mathur, Anant, *"Secrets of COIN Success: Lessons from the Punjab Campaign"*, Faultlines: Volume 20, January 2011

Mousseau, Michael, *"Market Civilization and Its Clash with Terror,"* International Security, Vol. 27, No. 3, Winter 2002–2003, pp. 5–29. (2002–2003, pp. 24–26)

Nanda, Prakash, *"Kashmir Imbroglio: Whose Solution"?* Security Research Review, Vol12

Qureshi, Niloofar, *Three Congenital Ailments of Hurriyat*, Rising Kashmir, 08 Jun 2012

Ravi Rikhye and Dave Sandhu. *Indian XV Corps, Kashmir 1965*, v.1.0 April 7, 2002

Sabharwal, Lt Gen Mukesh , *"Operational Importance of AFSPA"*, IDR Issue Vol. 27.2 Apr-Jun 2012

Sapone, Montgomery, *"Ceasefire: The Impact of Republican Political Culture on the Ceasefire Process in Northern Ireland,"* Peace and Conflict Studies, Vol. 7, No. 1, May 2000

Sazawal, VK, *'The Boiling Frog'*, Naad,August 2010 issue

Shaheen Showkat Dar and Naseer Ahmed Kalis, *Geo-political Significance of Kashmir: An overview of Indo-Pak Relations.* IOSR Journal Of Humanities and Social Science, Volume 9, Issue 2 (Mar. - Apr. 2013)

Sumit Ganguly, *"Avoiding war in Kashmir"* Foreign Affairs 69: 5 (1990-91)

Study Group Rports

Ben Connable and Martin C. Libicki, *"How Insurgencies End,"* RAND Corporation 2010

Bradnock, Robert W, *"Kashmir: Paths to Peace"*, Chatham House , Royal Institute of International Affairs, London, 2010

Chalk, Peter, *"The Malay-Muslim Insurgency in Southern Thailand—Understanding the Conflict's Evolving Dynamic:* RAND Counterinsurgency Study—Paper 5, RAND Corporation, OP-198-OSD,

McCormick, Gordon H, Steven B. Horton, and Lauren A. Harrison, *"Things Fall Apart: The Endgame Dynamics of Internal Wars,"* paper presented to the RAND Corporation Insurgency Board, August 29, 2006

Pattison, Gordon, *"Analysis of Societal Conflict and Counter-Insurgency,"* The Cornwallis Group XIV: 2010

Seth G. Jones, Martin C. Libicki, *"How Terrorist Groups End,"* RAND Corporation 2008

Government Reports

Annual Report of the Bureau of Police Research and Development BPR&D

Annual Report, 1989-90, Ministry of Home Affairs, Government of India

Annual Report, 1993-94, Ministry of Home Affairs, Government of India

Annual Report, 1996-97, Ministry of Home Affairs, Government of India

Annual Report, 1998-99, Ministry of Home Affairs, Government of India

Annual Report, 2001-02, Ministry of Home Affairs, Government of India

Annual Report, 2003-04, Ministry of Defence, Government of India

Annual Report, 2003-04, Ministry of Home Affairs, Government of India

Annual Report, 2005-06, Ministry of Home Affairs, Government of India

Annual Report, 2006-07, Ministry of Home Affairs, Government of India

Annual Report, 2007-08, Ministry of Home Affairs, Government of India

Annual Report, 2008-09, Ministry of Home Affairs, Government of India

Annual Report, 2009-10, Ministry of Home Affairs, Government of India

Annual Report, 2010-11, Ministry of Home Affairs, Government of India

Annual Report, 2011-12, Ministry of Home Affairs, Government of India

Annual Reports, National Human Rights Commission

Directorate of Economics and Statistics, Planning and Development

Department, J&K, Srinagar *"Indicators of Economic Development, Jammu & Kashmir-1999-2000"*,

Home Office Online Report 23/03, *"Police Service Strength England and Wales"*,), taken from House of Commons Hansard Written Answers (http:// www. johnmann mp.co.uk/Commons/2003-03-28%2001.html)

J&K Government Plan for the return of Kashmiri migrants, 2006

NHRC Annual Report 1993-94 on Human Rights Violations in Jammu & Kashmir

Planning Commission Report on Jammu and Kashmir

Report of the Working Group on Human Rights Violations in Jammu & Kashmir – 2000

Report on Human Rights Violations In Jammu & Kashmir, 2010

Web Articles

BBC News Online article, *"Future of Kashmir"*, (http://news.bbc.co.uk/2/shared/spl/hi/south_asia/03/kashmir_future/html/7.stm)

Gokhale, Nitin, Defence Forum India.com the/forum/indian-army

Hameed, Syeda Saiyidain, *"On Regaining Kashmiriyat"*, The Tribune Online edition, Chandigarh, 2 Mar 2003

http://en.wikipedia.org/wiki/List_of_highest_mountains

http://en.wikipedia.org/wiki/Panun_Kashmir

http://www.ajk.gov.pk/

http://www.globalsecurity.org /military/world/india/rashtriya-rifles.html

https://www.cia.gov/library/publications/the-world-factbook /print/in. html

Indian embassy website (http: //www.indianembassy.org /policy/Kashmir/ Kashmir_ MEA/Indian_Position.html)

Kashmir Study Group website, (http://kashmirstudy group.com/awayforward)

Maleeha Lodhi, "Winning Hearts and Minds of the People," http://209.85.175.104/search?q=cache:Qd8EnCyKDlQJ:www.ispr.gov.pkaccessed by Ibid on 29 May 2009

Official website of the BSF

Official website of the CRPF

Official website of the ITBP

Official Website of the J&K Police

Official website of the Ministry of Home Affairs, Government of India

Official Website of the Ministry of Home Affairs, Govt of Sindh

Official website of the Ministry of Water Resources, Government of India

Official Website of the South Asia Terrorism Portal
Pak Embassy Website (http://www.mofa.gov.pk/pages/ Brief.htm)
Professor Ali A Jalali, "Winning the Hearts and Minds of the People," http://209.85.175.04/search?q=cache:HPVsUhm5wJMJ:www.ispr.gov.pk / LFS/LFS/Speeches
Text of Mr VK Menon's speech at the United Nations Security Council (*www.jammu**kashmir**now.com/.../VK-**Menon**-Speech-in-Security-Council)*
Website of the Jammu Kashmir Democratic Liberation Party (http://www.jkdlp.org)
Wikipedia article on Human Rights in Jammu and Kashmir
www.britannica.com/EBchecked/topic/588887/Tethys-Sea.

Media Reports

"Jailed Separatist urges U.N. Control for Kashmir", Reuters News service, 23 December 1993 and " *Kashmir leader disputes India Pakistan talks*", 31 December 1993
Dawn newspaper of Pakistan, 24th November 2008 issue
http://indiatoday.intoday.in/story/Andhra+model/1/91900.html. [India Today April 8, 2010]
http://zeenews.india.com/news/jammu-and-kashmir/indian-reserve-police-battalions-raised-in-jandk_611456.html 15 Mar 2010
Padgaonkar, Dileep, Times of India, 15 June 2015.
Shabir Ibn Yusuf, http://www.greaterkashmir.com/news/2012/Apr / 26/some-crpf-battalions-to-leave-srinagar-this-fall-71.asp
Sishir Gupta, Hindustan Times Dec 2, 2011
Swami, Praveen, "*Tape Exposes Mirwaiz-Geelani Tension; Tehreek approached Hizb*," The Hindu, 5 September 2008

Blogs

Shabir Choudhry, *www.drshabirchoudhry.blogspot.com*, 3 Dec. 10
horsesandswords blogspot.com/2006/03/op meghdoot.html, 26 Mar 2006

Index